Jeff Cox's 100 Greatest Garden Ideas

Jeff Cox's 100 Greatest Garden Ideas

Tips, Techniques, and Projects for a Bountiful Garden and a Beautiful Backyard

Rodale Press, Inc.
Emmaus, Pennsylvania

Library of Congress Cataloging-in-Publication Data

Cox, Jeff, 1940-
    [100 greatest garden ideas]
    Jeff Cox's 100 greatest garden ideas : tips, techniques,
and projects for a bountiful garden and a beautiful backyard / Jeff Cox.
        p.   cm.
    Includes bibliographical references (p.) and index.
    ISBN 0–87596–770–1 (cloth : acid-free paper).
    ISBN 0–87596–977–1 (pbk. : acid-free paper)
    1. Gardening.   2. Organic gardening.   I. Title.
II. Title: 100 greatest garden ideas.   III. Title: Jeff Cox's
one hundred greatest garden ideas.
    SB453.C773   1998
    635—dc21   97–45248
                                   CIP

Distributed in the book trade by St. Martin's Press

2 4 6 8 10 9 7 5 3 1   hardcover
2 4 6 8 10 9 7 5 3 1   paperback

Editor: Joan Benjamin
Senior Research Associate: Heidi A. Stonehill
Cover and Interior Designer: Karen Coughlin
Interior Illustrators: Ron Hildebrand, i, v, viii, ix, x, 1, 2, 3, 4,
    5, 6, 7, 8, 10, 11, 12, 14, 15, 16, 18, 19, 20, 22, 24, 25, 26,
    27, 28, 30, 32, 33, 34, 36, 37, 38, 40, 41, 42, 44, 46, 48, 50,
    52, 54, 55, 56, 57, 58, 60, 61, 66, 67, 68, 70, 72, 74, 76, 78,
    80, 81, 82, 84, 86, 88, 90, 96, 98, 99, 100, 102, 103, 104,
    106, 108, 110, 111, 114, 116, 118, 124, 126, 134, 135, 136,
    137, 140, 141, 142, 143, 144, 146, 148, 158, 160;
    John Kocon, 120, 122, 128, 150, 164; **Michael Maskarinec,**
    92, 94, 130, 132, 138, 152, 154, 156, 162, 166, 168, 170,
    172, 174, 176, 178, 180, 182, 184, 186, 188, 190, 192, 194,
    195, 196, 198, 200, 202, 204, 206, 208, 210, 212, 214, 216,
    218, 220, 222, 224, 226; **Randall Sauchuck,** 39, 93, 113
Cover Photographer: John Hamel
Photography Editor: James A. Gallucci
Layout Designers: Keith Biery, Jen Miller, Christopher Rhoads
Copy Editor: Ann Snyder
Manufacturing Coordinator: Patrick T. Smith
Indexer: Lina B. Burton
Editorial Assistance: Jodi Guiducci, Sarah Wolfgang Heffner,
    Lori Schaffer

Rodale Home and Garden Books

Vice President and Editorial Director: Margaret J. Lydic
Managing Editor: Ellen Phillips
Director of Design and Production: Michael Ward
Associate Art Director: Patricia Field
Production Manager: Robert V. Anderson
Studio Manager: Leslie M. Keefe
Copy Director: Dolores Plikaitis
Book Manufacturing Director: Helen Clogston
Office Manager: Karen Earl-Braymer

To Henry Napierala, who taught me
that good soil is more valuable than gold.

Contents

Great Garden Ideas for Fall

Great Garden Ideas for Winter

Introduction

I planted the first garden that I could call my own in 1969—darn near 30 years ago. Since then, I've planted a garden every single year, and I've learned something new with each garden. I tried out all kinds of ideas I encountered as a full-time editor for *Organic Gardening* magazine, and I came up with lots of my own discoveries by experimenting with all kinds of vegetables, flowers, fruits, trees, shrubs, and vines.

My vegetable gardens became more and more elaborate in the 1970s—until I learned that smaller, more intensely grown gardens were a lot less work. Then the gardens started getting smaller. But as my food gardens grew smaller, my ornamental gardens became larger, until I started looking at my whole property as a potential garden that I could plant.

In the midst of this learning curve, I moved from Pennsylvania to California. It was like waking up on a new planet! In the East, I knew many of the wild trees, shrubs, and weeds that grew in my region. And I knew the cultivated plants, too. My knowledge of the plants around me was intimate, from observing them and growing them over the years.

Suddenly, the world was full of unfamiliar, odd plants—both wild and cultivated. So, just as I had to learn East-Coast gardening years before, now I began the process of learning to garden on the West Coast.

Almost a dozen years have passed since my move west, and I'm still learning. But now I have a continent-wide

perspective of gardening (and a whole lot more gardening ideas to go with it!). These gardening ideas that I've learned through my nearly 30 years of hands-on gardening are so exciting that I've been spreading the news through books and magazines, and by gabbing about them on television and radio.

But there are lots of ideas and not a lot of time to present them all. As all kinds of gardening ideas were swirling around in my head, it occurred to me that I could save other gardeners a heck of a lot of trial and error by presenting them with the cream of the crop. I decided to distill thousands of tips and techniques into the 100 gardening ideas that have impressed me the most when I've seen them in action.

I racked my brain for the ideas that really help make gardening easier and harvests better and more abundant. After careful consideration, I came up with a list that I've turned into this book. What you'll find in *Jeff Cox's 100 Greatest Garden Ideas* is hard-won knowledge. Many of these

ideas were developed by other gardeners, but I've put all of them into practice in my own gardens and found wrinkles and refinements that make these good ideas even better.

It has been a privilege to identify these great gardening ideas and distill the

wisdom of thousands of gardeners into one book. These 100 ideas worked for me, and I'm sure they'll work for you. Give 'em a try and you'll see what I mean!

Jeff Cox

Great Garden Ideas

for Spring

1 This Handy Worm Bin Makes Great Kitchen Compost

The best solution I've found for dealing with daily kitchen wastes is to turn them into plant food. But it's not always convenient to take the scraps out to the compost pile—especially in foul weather. So I've built a bin that lets me compost *indoors*— with a little help from my friends. Build your own worm bin this spring for easy year-round composting.

You can compost year-round with a homemade worm bin. This lidded version works perfectly in a basement or heated outbuilding—the worms stay in and scrap-hunting critters stay out. Build your own worm bin from plywood and make a bottom out of a piece of hardware cloth that's cut to fit around the bin legs and tacked into place (A). Tack a sheet of creased sheet metal (B) to the bottom of the bin to direct "worm tea" to a collection bucket (C).

Feed the worms. I feed my leftovers to red worms (*Eisenia foetida*), special composting worms that eat their way through kitchen garbage. Red worms break down the kitchen wastes and turn them into worm castings, which are up to seven times more nutritious for plants than ordinary garden soil. The worms also produce a liquid waste that's similar to compost tea—I call it "worm tea"—that's one of the very best plant foods you can get. The process is odorless, and if you use a worm composting box like mine, it's also vermin-proof. Here's how to get started.

Do-it-yourself worm bin. Decide where you want your worm bin before you build it so you can make sure it fits. I put mine in the basement where I run my composting operation. But you can put it in any room or building where the temperature doesn't go below freezing or get above 85°F too often. (If you live in an area with a mild climate, you can set your worm bin up outdoors. Make sure you locate it in a shady area.) Follow these steps.

1 Build a 3 × 3-foot topless and bottomless box out of ½-inch exterior plywood and wood screws.

2 Set the box on 2 × 4 legs that are 36 inches long. Use 1½-inch flathead wood screws to attach the legs.

3 Add a hinged plywood top to the box that's secured with a hook and eye.

4 Use tacks to attach sturdy fine-mesh hardware cloth to the box bottom so the worms stay in and worm tea can drain out.

5 Using tacks, attach a piece of creased sheet metal or plastic sheeting to the bottom of the bin to carry the liquid to a collection bucket—I use a 2-gallon plastic bucket. (See the illustration on page 2.) Make sure that the sheet metal or plastic is set far enough below the wire mesh so the worm tea drains away quickly or your worms may drown.

(continued)

Materials List

4 pieces ½-inch exterior plywood 16 × 36 inches*

24 1½-inch flathead wood screws

4 2 × 4s 36 inches long*

1 piece ½-inch exterior plywood 36½ × 36½ inches*

2 hinges and screws

1 hook and eye

1 box large-headed tacks or small brads

1 piece fine-mesh hardware cloth 36½ × 36½ inches

1 piece galvanized sheet metal 36½ × 40 inches (have the hardware store cut the sheet metal to this size) or plastic sheeting

1 2-gallon plastic bucket

*Don't use pressure-treated wood or wood preservative on these materials because the chemicals used in these treatments can kill worms.

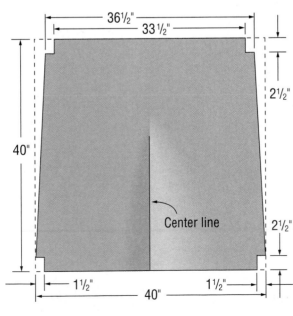

Cut a piece of sheet metal to the dimensions shown here and it will fit the bottom of your worm bin perfectly.

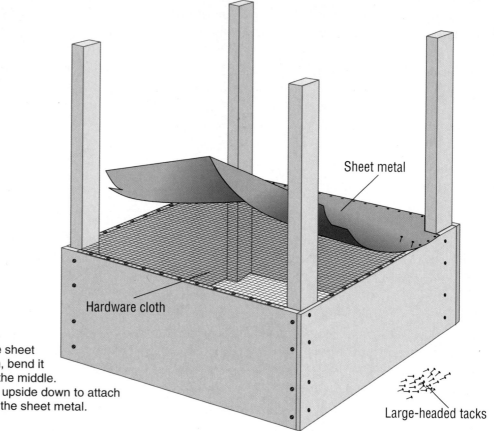

Sheet metal

Hardware cloth

Once you've cut out the sheet metal for your worm bin, bend it to form a crease down the middle. Then turn the worm bin upside down to attach the hardware cloth and the sheet metal.

Large-headed tacks

Getting your worms off to a good start. After you've built your bin, buy at least a pound—preferably two—of red worms from a bait shop. (Don't try this with garden worms; they won't survive.) Then make their home ready. Here's how.

Put about 2 inches of slightly moistened fallen leaves on the hardware cloth on the bottom of the box. Then tear newspapers—use only the black and white sections, no colored inks—into approximately 1-inch-wide strips. (Newspaper pages tear easily if you rip from the top of the sheet to the bottom.) Moisten these strips and place 2 inches of them on top of the leaves. Sprinkle the newspaper shreds with ¼ inch of good garden soil and you're ready to add worms.

Place the worms in the center of their bedding of leaves, newspaper, and soil, cover them with some more moist newspaper shreds, and give them a day's worth of kitchen scraps (at least a quart). Let them get settled for about a week, then start adding kitchen wastes on a daily basis.

There's usually plenty of moisture in kitchen wastes, but if things should begin to dry out, sprinkle a little water on the contents of the box to keep it moist. If you seem to be adding more scraps than the worms can handle at first, add more newspaper bedding and hold off on the kitchen wastes. Within a few weeks they'll reproduce enough to easily handle the wastes from your kitchen.

Collecting tea and castings. Four to six weeks after your worm bin is up and running, you'll have a steady supply of castings and tea to use. The tea is available at the tip of a

4

bucket. To get the castings, move the top layer of fresh and partially decomposing foodstuffs off to one side of the bin. Most of the worms are in the layer of food scraps, so move them aside at the same time. Wear gloves if you're squeamish, and gently pick up the worms and food with a child-size shovel or toy shovel. The castings will be underneath the food layer. You can harvest them with a plastic container or your shovel. When you remove the castings, add fresh bedding for your hard-working worms.

You can use worm castings and tea in your garden, in soil mixtures, or for fertilizer for both potted plants and seedlings. For a nutrient-rich soil mix, combine 1 part castings with 3 parts potting soil. When your plants need food, use the worm tea full strength as a monthly fertilizer, indoors or out. Or sprinkle ½ inch of castings on top of the soil of potted plants.

What to Put in Your Worm Bin

You can put all sorts of kitchen scraps in your bin— peels, rotten fruit and vegetables, eggshells, coffee grounds, used tea bags, and so on. What shouldn't you put in the bin? Don't add meat, bones, or meat by-products. Worms can digest these leftovers, but the meat stinks and attracts vermin. Don't add household pet wastes such as dog and cat feces either.

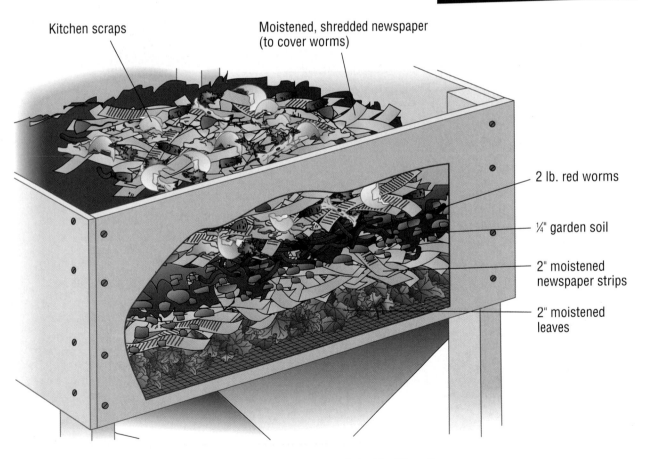

Kitchen scraps

Moistened, shredded newspaper (to cover worms)

2 lb. red worms

¼" garden soil

2" moistened newspaper strips

2" moistened leaves

Worms can turn your kitchen waste into compost and plant fertilizer, if you take good care of them. Layer bedding ingredients and scraps in the bin to get your worms started, then let the worms mix and process the stuff and turn it into black gold.

2 Train Spring Asparagus to Bear Summerlong Harvests

I used to think asparagus was strictly a spring crop. It's not! You can harvest big, thick, flavorful asparagus spears from spring until fall, if you know this harvest technique.

Section 3

Section 2

Summer Harvest

Section 1

Treat yourself to asparagus from spring until fall by harvesting your crop in thirds. Harvest spears from Section 1 for the eight weeks of May and June, allowing the spears in Sections 2 and 3 to go to fern. In week seven, cut down the fern on Section 2 so it will send up new spears—allow Sections 1 and 3 to grow undisturbed. Repeat the process on Section 3 for spears from the final eight weeks of the season.

Time your harvest. The asparagus plant, it turns out, doesn't care when you take spears from it, as long as you don't harvest for more than eight weeks each year. For asparagus in spring, summer, and even fall, all you have to do is plant double or triple what you would use for a spring crop and spread out your harvest.

Pick succulent spears in spring. Start by marking your asparagus bed into three sections. Take spears from the first section only for the first eight weeks of spring, and let the other two sections go—they'll produce ferny foliage and flowers.

Savor a summer crop. At seven weeks into the first harvest period, cut down the ferns on the second section, slicing them off cleanly just under the soil surface. In a week, this second asparagus section will begin to send up spears, which you can cut for eight weeks. After the harvest, you should let the plants rest and produce foliage again. Meanwhile, the plants in the first section will have put out ferny growth and started storing energy in their roots for next season.

Get your fill with a fall crop. Seven weeks into the second harvest period, cut down the ferns from the third section. When the third section starts sending up spears a week later, stop harvesting the second section and let it grow ferny leaves. The third and last section will provide you with spears right up to the end of the season. Spear production will taper off toward the end of the season, but what a treat to be eating garden-fresh young asparagus from May until October!

Tips for Growing Tender Asparagus

Contrary to popular belief, bigger is better when you're growing asparagus spears. Give them a taste test and you'll soon find that thicker spears are more tender and tasty than thin spears. That's because both thick and thin spears have a certain number of tough, fibrous strands in them. The smaller the diameter of a spear is, the closer the tough fibers are packed together, and the tougher the texture is. Larger spears have more succulent flesh between the fibers, so they're more tender. Here's what you can do to guarantee lots of fat, tender asparagus.

• Plant male plants (your seed catalog will tell you which is which). Male plants produce more spears than female plants since they don't spend energy producing berries. If you have an existing bed, pull out the female plants and replace them with males.

You can tell male and female asparagus plants apart in fall when the females produce berries.

Buy male plants from garden catalogs or garden centers, or start some extra plants in a nursery bed and move the males into your planting once you can identify them.

• Plant asparagus crowns on 2-inch ridges of soil in the bottom of 12-inch-deep trenches, so that there's a good 10 inches of soil over the top of the crowns. This deep planting encourages larger spears.

• Space the plants 2 feet apart in the trenches in rows 7 feet apart. Asparagus need lots of room to produce big spears, since one plant can fill a 6-foot-diameter circle with its roots.

• When you make new plantings, take only a light harvest the second year and wait until the third year after planting to take a full harvest. This gives the plants a chance to get established and make their biggest, healthiest growth.

3 Two Cabbage Heads Are Better Than One

You can get a double harvest of perfect cabbage heads from a single planting. All it takes is some good timing in spring and careful culture in summer. Coaxing a second harvest out of spring-planted cabbage is one of the most rewarding gardening techniques you can try. In addition to getting twice as much good eating, this system saves you the time and effort of planting a second crop in summer. You've got nothing to lose and lots of cabbage to gain!

Compost

Convince your spring-planted cabbage to give you two crops each year by leaving the plant's stalk, leaves, and roots intact after you harvest the first head (A). In a few weeks, a ring of four or five little tufts of leaves will appear on the stalk. Side-dress the plant (B), then let the tufts grow into small cabbages (C). Or cut off all but one of the new buds to harvest one good-size head of cabbage (D).

You've got options. You could get two harvests of cabbage a year by planting two sets of plants—one in spring that you'll harvest in summer, and one in summer that you'll harvest in fall. That's a good way to go if the weather or a pest problem turns on your spring crop. But most years, it's easier and faster to keep spring cabbage plants growing and producing all season long. Here's how.

Smart seed selection. Most cabbage seedlings take two to three months to form heads after they're transplanted to the garden. Check your seed catalog to see how long it takes specific cultivars to produce a crop, then select the plants with the shortest growing seasons. Early cultivars work best for spring-planted crops because they mature before the really hot days of July.

Timing is everything. The trick to getting spring cabbage off to a good start is to get small seedlings into the garden just as the hard freezes end. That perfect planting period is usually in early May in the very northerly regions, mid-April in most of the Mid-Atlantic states and Midwest, and late March farther south. (In California and the Sun Belt, set cabbage seedlings out in mid-winter for spring growth.)

Little seedlings with leaves just 1 inch across can stand long periods of cold. But seedlings with 2- to 3-inch-wide leaves will bolt (go to seed) if they're exposed to temperatures in the 40 to 50°F range for 30 days or more. If you want to ensure a good harvest, planting time is critical.

To time your plantings right, count back four weeks from the date of the last hard freeze in your area. (Call your local extension agent if you're not sure when your hard freezes end.) That's the time to start your seeds in flats or peat pots. When the seedling's true leaves reach 1 to 1½ inches wide, they're ready to harden-off. Move the seedlings outside to an area that gets partial shade and is protected from the wind. A cold frame is an ideal place for your seedlings since you can close the lid if a hard frost threatens. If you don't have a cold frame, keep the plants on a screened-in porch or close to the house. Move the plants inside if temperatures turn extremely cold. After a week outdoors, your cabbage seedlings will toughen up and be ready to set out in the garden.

Harvest very carefully. If you plant a relatively early cabbage cultivar in the garden in the middle of April, you'll have heads that are ready to harvest in late June. Temperatures will be heating up fast then, so watch the cabbages carefully—harvest the heads a little early if you see any of them starting to split.

Make your cut at the base of each head, leaving all the plant's big leaves and a bit of the stem. Before long, you'll notice small tufts of leaves appearing around the outside of the stem as the plant regroups and begins to grow again. That's the time to side-dress the plant with a shovelful of compost. Spread the compost around each plant, staying about 4 inches away from the stalk. Work the compost into the soil gently so you don't disturb the roots.

Are 2 (or more) heads better than 1? You choose. When you see the tufts developing into little heads, you have two options. You can let all the heads grow, which means you'll harvest many little cabbage heads in the fall, or you can cut off all the new sprouting heads except for one. If you choose the one-head option, you'll harvest one decent-size cabbage late in the season.

Whichever option you choose, make sure your plants have a steady supply of water as they grow. Keep the soil cool, and slow evaporation by placing 4 or more inches of mulch around the plants. When the first light frosts of fall arrive, it's harvesttime. And it's also time to think about coleslaw with a mustard dressing, or lightly cooked cabbage layered in a casserole dish with a medium white sauce and fried onions, or—well, you get the idea. Enjoy.

4 Grow Great Carrots, Even in Poor Soil

Hard, rocky soil means runty, woody carrots. If you'd rather have big, sweet, straight carrots (and who wouldn't), you need a loose growing medium without a lot of stones. Like me, you may have tried turning your hard, rocky soil into a carrot bed by adding soil amendments and picking out lots of rocks. But believe me—and my back—there's a better way: trench planting.

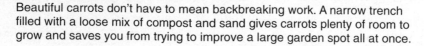

Beautiful carrots don't have to mean backbreaking work. A narrow trench filled with a loose mix of compost and sand gives carrots plenty of room to grow and saves you from trying to improve a large garden spot all at once.

Only improve the soil you use. There's no need to rework your entire garden when carrots only take up a little bit of space. Here's how I discovered the secret to great carrots without breaking my back. In early spring, in a particularly dense and shaley part of the garden, I watered the soil well so it was as loose as it could be. Then I took a flat-bladed shovel and dug a V-shaped trench just 3 inches wide and about 8 inches deep, or as deep as I could easily kick in the shovel blade. The work went fairly easily, and I quickly dug four 25-foot-long rows to give me a total of 100 feet of carrot row.

Then I filled the V-shaped trenches with a mix of 50 percent sand and 50 percent compost that I stirred up in my wheelbarrow. I planted a carrot called 'Nantes' (it's best for sweetness, and it's good in shallow soils such as my V-shaped trenches), and mulched between the rows. The sprouts emerged and looked fine. I made sure the seedlings didn't dry out by watering the rows one at a time with a soaker hose laid along the edge of the trenches.

The easiest thinning ever. When it came time to thin the carrots, I found that the loose sand and compost mix allowed me to easily prick out the extra plants with a dinner fork and move them to a spot in the compost mix where they had room to grow. The transplants fainted after I moved them, but with a little bracing with some extra compost and water from the soaker hose, they quickly revived and stood up straight again. Within two months, I was pulling big beautiful carrots out of the ground and, thanks to my loose soil mix, harvesting was extra easy.

Say Good-bye to the Carrot Rust Fly

In many parts of the country, carrot rust flies are a big problem for gardeners growing carrots. The flies lay their eggs in the soil where the leaf stems emerge from the carrot roots. Little white larvae hatch out and burrow down into the carrot, leaving rusty-looking trails that not only spoil the look of the carrot but the eating quality too.

A dusting of wood ashes over the carrot beds at planting time will help deter the carrot rust fly, but probably won't solve the problem completely. A better method is to cover the carrot rows with a floating row cover immediately after you plant the seeds. Floating row cover looks something like a large sheet of cheesecloth. It's porous enough to let rain in, thin enough to let the sun in, and lightweight enough to ride on the carrot foliage without crushing it. You can buy floating row cover in a variety of sizes at garden centers and through mail-order garden catalogs. Leave the cover on your plants all summer for the best results, then pick it up and store it out of the weather over the winter.

Another way to foil the flies is to skip the early sowing of carrots and put in spring peas. Plant a midsummer crop of carrots after the peas, and you'll break the life cycle of the carrot rust fly and get a good fall crop of carrots for fresh eating and storing in the ground. Carrots keep well if you leave them in the ground and cover their tops with 8 to 12 inches of mulch before the ground freezes. You can use grass clippings, hay, straw, or leaves to protect your carrots until you're ready to eat them. Just remember to mark the rows so you can find them again, even under a layer of snow.

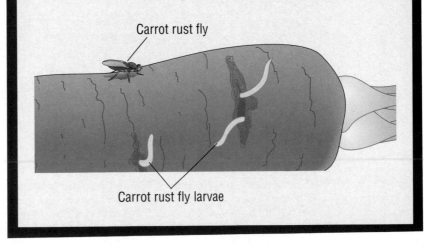

Carrot rust fly

Carrot rust fly larvae

5 Cauliflower (Almost) All Year-Round

If you think cauliflower is just a spring or fall crop, you're missing out! Thanks to cauliflower breeders, you can harvest this delicious staple from your garden just about all year-round, if you live in USDA Hardiness Zone 7 or warmer. In colder areas you can still get cauliflower from June through Thanksgiving. Here's how.

A

B

The leaves of overwintering cauliflower wrap themselves over the head to protect it from frost (A). But leaves aren't always enough protection. To protect a plant from temperatures of 10° to 0°F, wrap a tomato cage with plastic and place it over the plant, then fill the cage with fallen leaves (B).

It takes 3 types. You can stretch your cauliflower harvest to the limit by growing three different types of plants: early, autumn, and overwintering varieties. Each type is suited for a different season of growth, but they all produce tender, high-quality cauliflower heads. With a long harvest season, you'll get the freshest flavor and the most nutrition possible, and you're guaranteed a steady supply of snowy white heads without shelling out big bucks at the grocery store.

Plant early and often. Start by planting early cauliflower, like 'Early White'—they mature anywhere from 50 to 75 days, depending on the cultivar. These plants can take the heat of summer and still produce nice white curds, although in the very hottest days of summer, you may notice some discoloration.

You can set out transplants of one or more cultivars of early cauliflower successively, every few weeks from March to June, for harvests that start in mid-June and continue until the beginning of October. Or, you can make one planting in spring of several different early cultivars with varying days to maturity. Either way, you'll end up with a cauliflower harvest that lasts all summer into fall. If you live where spring weather is erratic, staggering your plantings is the safer option. A freak storm may wipe out one planting, but you can fill in with later plantings.

Start a crop in summer. When early cauliflower starts to mature, it's time to plant autumn cauliflower, like 'White Rock'. This type is bred to grow over summer and produce curds when the weather cools down in the fall. If you try to plant autumn cauliflower in spring, the plants will make small, misshapen, or off-color heads in summer's hot temperatures. Icy cold temperatures are just as bad—heavy frosts in fall will turn exposed curds yellow or brown. That's why autumn cauliflower is bred so the plants' leaves stay wrapped over the developing curds, protecting them from cold.

Direct-sow autumn cauliflower seed throughout the months of May and June, and they'll produce curds from August through November.

Winter-grown crops are tops. Overwintering cauliflower like 'Fleurly' thrives where winter temperatures don't go much below 10°F (the Pacific Northwest, coastal California, and parts of the Gulf Coast and Florida). With protection, you can grow overwintering cauliflower in Zone 7—if you're willing to take heroic measures to protect the plants, you can even grow them in Zone 6.

The overwintering cultivars do best when you sow them in the first half of July (August 1 at the latest). During the fall, overwintering cauliflower develops into sturdy plants that can winter over and produce heads from March to late May, depending on the cultivar.

Overwintering cauliflower needs a rich garden soil to get going, but the plants won't need additional fertilizer until they come out of their winter doldrums in late winter or early spring of the next year. When the plants begin to revive and grow in the spring, it's time to fertilize.

What Plants Want

The secret for getting the biggest cauliflower heads is to make sure the plants grow rapidly without any checks to their growth. They'll need plenty of water and soil nutrients, plus some cooperation from Mother Nature. All three types of cauliflower like a rich, well-drained soil, so amend your planting area with composted chicken manure or blood meal a few weeks before sowing or planting. Add rich compost to the planting holes when you set transplants out, too.

Water your transplants or transplant-size seedlings with compost tea for three weeks or side-dress them with compost or blood meal. Mulch the plants to keep moisture in the soil. That's all it takes to get a healthy crop of cauliflower that keeps going and going.

6 Three Crops That Are Tops Together

Growing corn, beans, and squash (or pumpkins) in the same patch of garden isn't a new idea—it was developed by the Native Americans, who call this super combination the "Three Sisters." Intermingling these crops is a fantastic way to get more production out of limited space. Combine this trio in the kitchen and you'll get outstanding taste and nutrition too. (Try a mix of corn, beans, and rice baked in squash halves!)

To create your own Three-Sisters garden, plant corn and beans in hills and add squash to every seventh hill. Plant at least 14 hills of corn to supply a family of four with enough ears for fresh eating, and add more if you want extra corn to dry.

What's the secret? The reason you can fit the Three Sisters into the same plot of ground is that these plants help each other grow. The corn acts as a support for the pole beans and the squash crowds out weeds and acts as a living mulch. In return, the beans improve the soil for future crops by converting nitrogen from the air into a form plants can use. What a partnership!

Get the soil ready. You need to do your part to make sure the Three Sisters get off to a good start. Corn and squash are heavy feeders that like lots of nitrogen in the soil. Prepare for their needs in early spring by covering the growing area with 1 inch of composted horse or cow manure, or ½ inch of composted poultry manure. Work the compost into the top 2 inches of soil.

Put each plant in its place. Start by planting the corn. You'll need a tall, sturdy cultivar that can support bean plants. Traditionally, Native Americans have planted flour, flint, and dent corns, but you can substitute sweet corn. Try a flour corn cultivar like 'Iroquois White' or sweet corn cultivars such as 'Black Aztec', 'Rainbow Inca', and 'Texas Honey June'. (See "Sources" on page 228 for ordering information.) Plant the corn in hills as the Iroquois do, setting out

five to seven evenly spaced seeds per hill. Make the hills 18 inches wide at the base, 10 inches wide at the top, and 4 inches high. Space the hills 4 feet apart.

When the corn is 6 inches tall, weed the hills and plant four or five bean seeds around the corn seedlings. The corn needs a head start before the beans start growing on them or they'll get smothered. Use pole beans such as 'Genuine Cornfield', 'Scarlet Runner', and 'Kentucky Wonder'.

Plant squash or pumpkins (as shown below) at the same time you plant the beans, placing the seeds around the corn seedlings in every seventh hill. Try 'Connecticut Field' pumpkins or any winter squash such as acorn or butternut.

Make sure the Three Sisters get plenty of water during the growing season. Because the plants are growing tightly in a

compact space, it's best to irrigate by flooding the ground or using a soaker hose. Stay away from overhead sprinkling—that only promotes mildew on the squash and bean leaves.

Handling the harvest. Once they mature, corn, beans, and squash are delicious fresh-picked and steamed. Winter squashes with tough rinds will keep just fine in a cool, dry place for many months and even over winter. Dried corn and beans will keep for six months or more if you dry them well. Hang corn ears in a warm, dry, well-ventilated place for a couple of months, then shell them after the weather turns freezing. Dry corn kernels until they feel hard when you press them with a thumbnail. Beans are just as easy to store as corn if you let them dry in their pods until they are hard, shell them, and keep them in a dry place.

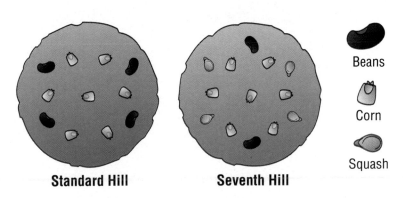

Standard Hill   **Seventh Hill**

Beans

Corn

Squash

Here's the Three-Sisters planting pattern. Plant six hills as shown at left, with a circle of corn kernels flanked by four bean seeds. For the seventh hill, use two bean seeds and four squash seeds as shown at right. Repeat this pattern until you have as many hills as you need.

7 Five Steps to Fabulous Cucumbers

Imagine biting into a crisp, sweet cucumber—ummm! Now imagine getting as many of those beauties as you want, all summer long. It's not a dream. These few simple steps in the spring will save you from runty, bitter cukes and guarantee harvests of prize-winning cucumbers from now on.

Stigma (female flower)

Stamens (male flower)

Pollinating Cucumber Flowers

Trellis your cucumber vines for healthier plants. You'll get better fruit set too since it's easier for bees to find the flowers on upright vines. If clouds rain on your parade and keep bees away, hand-pollinate blooms by dusting pollen from the male flower onto the female, as shown above.

Start with sex education. You've got to know the gender of your cukes. Most cucumbers, both hybrid and open-pollinated types, are monoecious, meaning that they produce both male and female flowers on the same vine. The vine's first five or six blossoms are usually male—their early appearance ensures that there's plenty of pollen available when the female blossoms open.

But there are also gynoecious cucumbers that produce only female blossoms. Since the female flowers are the ones that produce fruits, every gynoecious flower is a possible cucumber. These female-only vines will set fruit from their first four or five blossoms without a pollinator. Later blooms that appear farther out on the vine need male pollen to produce fruits. Seed companies usually include several seeds of monoecious cukes along with the gynoecious seeds to make sure the females have pollinators.

So, should you plant only female cukes to get the biggest harvest? Nope. The best way to ensure a long season from your cucumbers is to plant equal numbers of gynoecious and monoecious plants. The gynoecious types produce more fruit early on and then their production slowly tapers off. The monoecious types start out slower, but hit full production just as the all-female plants start to put on the brakes.

Pour on just enough water. Too much water will drown the plants' roots and stunt their growth. Too little water or irregular watering results in misshapen, bitter, or tasteless cukes. The best rule is to keep the soil evenly moist 3 inches down. Soaker hoses are ideal for watering since they don't wet the leaves. Damp cuke leaves are susceptible to mildews that choke off the vines' ability to function. If you must use overhead sprinklers, do it in the morning so the leaves have all day to dry in the sunlight.

Let there be light and heat. For top production, you've got to make sure your cukes get a full eight hours or more of sunlight each day. And don't plant them when the spring weather is still cool. They'll do much better if you wait until the soil and air are warm—at least a couple of weeks after your last frost date.

What if the weather won't cooperate with your plan? You can improve cuke production during rainy stretches by hand-pollinating gynoecious cucumber vines. Bees (the usual pollinators) aren't too active during cool, cloudy weather, so it's up to you to encourage fruit set. Start in the morning when the flowers are freshest, and use a fresh male flower for each female you pollinate. Simply dust pollen from the stamens of the male flower onto the stigma of the female flower.

Keep plants well fed. Cukes need plenty of grow-power, so prepare the spot where you'll plant the seeds by amending the soil with lots of rotted manure, well-made compost, or organic fertilizer mix. When fruits are setting, give the plants weekly doses of fish emulsion or kelp. Spray the soil with these liquid fertilizers. Keep leaves dry to prevent fungal diseases.

Trellis your cukes. Growing your vines up trellises instead of along the ground prevents disease, since the plants get better air circulation. Trellising also improves pollination since the flowers are held up in the air where bees can easily find them. (See Idea #11.)

Keep Picking Cukes to Keep 'Em Coming

Cucumbers will stop producing fruit if you let even one fruit stay on the vine too long. That maturing fruit will set seed, signaling the vine that it's time to stop producing fruits and start ripening seeds.

To keep your vines producing, inspect the vines daily, and remove fruits just before they reach full size, even if you don't intend to use them. You can always give extras to friends or add unwanted fruits to your compost heap.

8 Make Your Move in Spring for Fantastic Mums and Kale in Fall

I can't bring myself to quit gardening, even when that spoil-sport frost arrives to blacken the tomatoes and leave the squashes limp. So I've created an after-the-frost plan to keep my garden and me flourishing until weeks after the first cold snap.

In fall, when killing frosts destroy your tender garden plants, kale and chrysanthemums give you a combination of beauty and nutrition on into winter.

Divide mums on time. I get started on my plants in spring when the chrysanthemums begin to grow in my flower beds. That's when you should get started too, since mums need to be divided each year to produce a really spectacular show.

While the plants are still small, dig up the entire patch. Replant half of the plants in the flowerbed so each mum has plenty of elbowroom to grow. Take the rest of the divisions to the vegetable garden and plant them throughout the area where your warm-season (summer) crops will go. When planting time approaches for the summer crops, prepare the soil and plant your favorite vegetables between the mums—I like to grow eggplant, peppers, tomatoes, winter squash, and pumpkins.

As the chrysanthemums grow, pinch out the tips once or twice so they put out sideshoots and get nice and bushy. Pinch the plants back before July 15 in the North or before August 15 in the South—that will leave them enough time to produce flower buds for fall.

Get creative with kale. In mid-July, plant kale seeds in open spots in your garden. Or start seeds in pots and three weeks later transplant the young seedlings to the garden. Interplant your seeds or seedlings with the warm-season vegetables and chrysanthemums you've already planted, but don't let the established plants shade them or swamp them with foliage—choose spots where the kale gets plenty of sunshine.

When early frosts hit your garden, the warm-season crops will turn black and crash to the ground, but you won't be singing the blues. The bright green mounds of kale will emerge through the faded crops.

And then, in the cold days of November, the mums will open with a splash of rich autumn colors: golds, russets, reds, burgundies, and more! From the first frost and for many weeks to come, you'll have sweet, delicious kale, ready to use as a steamed vegetable, for juicing, and in soups and stews. And, thanks to the colorful mum flowers, your spirits will stay bright long after the rest of the garden dies away.

More Late-Season Crop Magic

Kale is one of the best crops for a late-season garden because once really severe cold hits, its flavor improves tremendously—right when you can really use some fresh vegetables. It's not the only great late-season crop, though: Brussels sprouts and parsnips also get tastier when cold weather hits. Direct-seed these crops in early- to midsummer so they'll mature after freezing weather arrives.

You may also find that a fall crop of spinach hunkers down nicely among the frost-blackened summer vegetables. Start fall spinach when temperatures stay below 75°F, and keep making new plantings until a month before the first frost date. You'll continue to get spinach for salads and juicing until the really severe weather hits, especially if you give your planting a protective mulch of straw.

Dig and divide chrysanthemums in the spring, replanting half of the rooted stems in your flowerbed and half in your vegetable garden.

9 Boost Pepper Production with Jungle Conditions

It's a jungle out there! At least it would be, if bell pepper plants had their way. Bell pepper plants like it consistently warm (not scorching hot) and humid. If they don't get what they want, the plants will sulk, drop their blossoms, and refuse to set fruit. Luckily, you can re-create jungle conditions no matter what your climate is like. Here's what to do.

Sunflowers

18" 14"

Grass clippings

For beautiful bell peppers, set your transplants deep and space them so their leaves just touch when the plants are full grown. Deep planting and the leafy canopy help keep roots cool. Mulch and the peppers' own leaves also keep moisture from escaping so your peppers get the extra humidity they love.

Choose the best cultivar for your climate. Many of the bell pepper starts you'll find at markets and nurseries are a cultivar called 'Yolo Wonder'. This plant was developed in Yolo County in northern California, and it thrives in that moderate climate. It does not thrive in the Midwest and Middle Atlantic states, where summer temperatures climb over 80°F for weeks at a time, and where hot drying winds cause moisture stress. In tough-climate areas, look for cultivars, such as 'New Ace' and 'Bell Boy', with smaller fruit and more temperature tolerance.

In the South, many peppers do well, but 'Miss Bell' and 'Park's Whopper' are standouts. In the cool maritime climate of coastal California and the Pacific Northwest, 'Early Prolific' usually wins comparison trials hands down. This is a pepper that does well in cool, cloudy weather, even in Alaska and England.

Plant peppers just right. Whether you grow your own plants or buy them, set the seedlings out in spring before they develop blossoms. You want the young plants to put their early energy into strong roots and a sturdy stem—not flowers. The soil should be loose, friable, well drained, and very nutritious.

Set your peppers deep—right up to their first set of true leaves. And give them plenty of space by planting the seedlings 14 inches apart in rows 18 inches apart. Mulch the peppers thickly with grass clippings, but keep the mulch pulled back from the stems for good air circulation. As the plants mature, they will be close enough to create a dense canopy over the clippings, which helps keep roots cool.

Pamper peppers for peak production. When the really hot weather arrives in late June, water the pepper plants deeply once a week, but soak the mulch every day. The water in the wet grass clippings will evaporate, keeping the leaves and fruits in a warm, humid environment—just like the one in moderate, tropical areas of South America where the ancestors of our bell peppers got their start.

When your daily watering program gets underway, side-dress each plant with nutritious compost or well-rotted cow manure, and give each plant a handful of limestone for added calcium. After this first dose of fertilizer, give the plants manure tea or fish emulsion every couple of weeks.

Finally, give the plants some shade in the heat of midsummer days. You can shade them by planting your peppers on the north side of a pea or cucumber trellis, or by planting a stand of tall sunflowers or sunchokes (Jerusalem artichokes) on the south side of the pepper rows. When the weather cools off later in the season, cut down the sunflowers or remove the trellis so the peppers get full sunlight.

And what will you get if you choose cultivars carefully and keep the plants well watered, well fed, and in a humid microclimate? Just the best pepper harvest you've ever had, all summer long!

A Gallery of Great Bell Peppers

Here are more peppers that are either suited to a particular climate or do well just about anywhere, if you give them the jungle conditions they like.

Name	Description
'Ace'	Great for northern and cool-season gardens.
'Ariane'	Dense leaf canopy holds in humidity.
'Bell Boy'	Dependable green bell pepper for most of the country.
'Cadice'	A fine pepper for northerly and cool-summer areas.
'Crispy Hybrid'	Developed to produce well in most parts of the country.
'Merlin'	Rated best hybrid bell pepper for Mid-Atlantic and northeastern states.
'Yankee Bell'	Developed especially for northern gardeners from Maine to Washington.

10 Use Tomato Cages All Year Long

Once I take the time and trouble to build long-lasting tomato cages, I want to use them, not store them. So I start out by using the cages as pea trellises in early spring. In summer I use them to support a bumper crop of tomatoes. And in fall, I convert them into plant protectors. Want to really get your money's worth out of your tomato cages? Here's how.

Summer

Spring

Fall

Get triple use from your tomato cages by using them all year long. Grow peas up the cages in spring, then support your tomato crop in summer. Finally, put your tomato cages around roses and other plants in fall to protect them from cold winter winds.

Bring your tomato cages out early. Choose the spot where your tomato patch will go and decide how many tomato cages you'll need. Two plants per person is plenty for fresh eating, and you'll need six paste tomato plants if you want enough for freezing and canning.

Make your tomato cages from concrete-reinforcing mesh—like the kind used for re-inforcing swimming pools (see Idea #15 for instructions). Then, in early spring, as soon as you can work the soil, prepare a spot where each cage will go. Loosen the earth in a circle slightly larger than each cage, then set the cages up in your future tomato patch. Space the cages 5 feet apart and weight the bottoms with stones or bricks so they don't topple over.

Put tomato cages to work as pea trellises. I use half the cages for trellises—I don't need that many peas—and leave the extra cages for an early planting of tomatoes (see Idea #14).

Choose early peas (those that take 60 days or less to mature) to grow up the cages. I use compact cultivars that don't grow over 4 or 5 feet tall—longer vines flop over on themselves and shade the stems underneath. There are lots of good cultivars to choose from, so pick your favorites. I particularly like 'Super Snappy', 'Super Sugar Mel', and 'Wando'.

Plant your peas every 2 inches in a circle around the outside of the cages, and mulch the area inside the cages heavily so that no weeds will grow. For a really luscious crop, dig a shallow trench about 4 inches wide and 6 inches deep in a V-shape around the outside of each cage and fill it with good, rich compost before you plant your peas.

Support tomatoes with versatile cages. Start your tomato seeds indoors and stagger the plantings. Time it so half of the seedlings are ready for planting after all danger of frost is past. The other half should be ready to go into the garden when the peas are finishing up. (If you plant your peas in early April, they'll usually be finished by the second week of June.) These tomatoes will start bearing a couple of weeks later than the first planting, which means you'll have some young, strong plants and primo tomatoes later in the season.

You don't have to wait until the last pea pod is set before taking down the vines. When you see the number of flowers and pods drop off dramatically, that's your cue to snip the vines off at ground level and pull them off the tomato cages. Remove the cages and the mulch and plant your tomato plants, then put the cages over the plants and weight the cages

down with bricks again. You want the soil to get as much sun as possible and warm up fast, so don't mulch your tomato plants—just leave the soil bare.

The pea vines and mulch will make great additions to your compost pile. Or you can use them as mulch somewhere else in the garden. The pea roots that are left in the ground after you cut the tops off will eventually decay and add nitrogen to the soil around the tomato plants.

Turn tomato cages into plant protectors. When the first light frost finishes off your tomato plants in fall, move the cages aside and pull out the plants and toss them in the compost heap. Then decide where you need plant protectors—in the vegetable garden where they'll warm late crops like cabbage, carrots, and parsnips, or in your flowerbeds where they'll hold a protective layer of insulating leaves around roses and other tender perennials.

Set the cages over the crops you want to protect, secure the cages with rocks or bricks, and fill the cages with fallen leaves. Your crops will stay toasty and ready to harvest well into winter, and tender flowers will come through the cold temperatures without a hitch. In early spring, take the cages off your plants and move the cages to your next tomato patch.

11 A Simple Garden Trellis for All Your Vines

Train peas, cucumbers, melons—even squashes—up a trellis and they'll thrive! "Growing up" means the plants get plenty of light and enough air circulation to discourage diseases like mildew. As an added bonus, you can get two crops in the space you normally grow one in. Give this nifty system a try by starting peas up the trellis in spring, then grow other vines up the same trellis once the peas are growing strong.

Metal fence post

6'

2'

Save space in your garden by growing vining plants such as melons and cukes vertically on a sturdy trellis. Your fruits will be healthier, and since they're held off the ground, you don't have to worry about them rotting. As the fruits form, fasten panty-hose slings under them to support their weight.

Set the stakes. In a sunny garden spot, space two 8-foot-tall metal fence posts 8 feet apart and drive them 2 feet into the ground. Add more posts on either side if you need a wider trellis.

Drive sturdy, notched wooden stakes into the ground outside the end posts. Then, fasten a strong but flexible wire to one of the end stakes and run it up to the first metal post, slipping it into the top notch that's knocked out of the metal. Run the wire to the other post, slipping it loosely into the top notch, then down to the other end stake.

Using Vise-Grips or pliers so you can grip the wire tightly, pull the wire as taut as you possibly can, then secure it to the end post. (If you don't have grips or pliers, wrap the remaining wire around a stout stick so you can grasp the ends of the stick.) Clip off the excess wire with wire cutters.

Attach the netting. Buy enough plastic garden netting to stretch the length of your trellis (it's available at garden centers and through garden supply catalogs). Get a box of S-hooks at the hardware store. Space the hooks at 18-inch intervals along the horizontal part of the wire. Unroll your plastic netting and hang it from the S-hooks—slip it into the notches of the posts when you

reach them. Keep the trellis fairly taut as you work your way along the row.

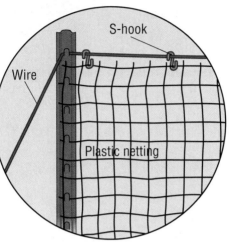

To set up your trellis, attach plastic netting to metal fence posts using wire and S-hooks.

Make perfectly spaced plantings. When the trellis netting is up, you're ready to plant peas. Leave open spots where the cucumbers or other vines will eventually go by placing 6- to 8-inch-wide rocks where you want the plants to grow. The cukes, melons, and squashes can go into the garden when all frost danger is past—the peas will be growing nicely by then. Just find the stones, remove them, and set your cucumber, melon, or squash plants in the open spots.

Grow the new vines right up the trellis with the peas—they won't bother each other. You can remove all of the dead vines at once at the end of the growing season.

End the season with a quick cleanup. Allow the vine tops to dry on the trellis until they're brittle, then pull off as many as you easily can. Some tendrils and pieces of vine will cling but that's okay. (When you fold the netting, most of these will crack and fall off anyway.)

When the trellis is fairly clean, simply remove the S-hooks and lift the netting off the fence posts. Lay it flat on the ground and either fold or roll it up. Unwrap the wire from an end stake and roll it up like a skein of yarn as you lift it off the posts so you can use it next year. Wiggle the fence posts until you can pull them free and pull up the end stakes, too. Store the posts, stakes, trellis, and wire together in the garage or shed, and you'll have the perfect trellis for all of your vines for years to come.

Support Big Fruits

Ripe cantaloupes, watermelons, and winter squashes weigh a lot, so they need support when they're growing on a trellis. You can make them slings from a variety of porous materials such as panty hose, mesh onion bags, or loose-weave cheesecloth.

Run the material under each fruit when it's small, and adjust the support sling as necessary as the fruit grows. Tie the sling ends directly to the netting, or if a fruit is particularly heavy, attach the sling to the trellis post.

12 Grow Vegetables in Your Lawn

If you don't have room for a garden, or if you've used up all of your garden space, don't despair—plant vegetables in your lawn! I've planted tomatoes in holes dug in the lawn and gotten better yields than from plants grown in garden soil amended with manure or compost!

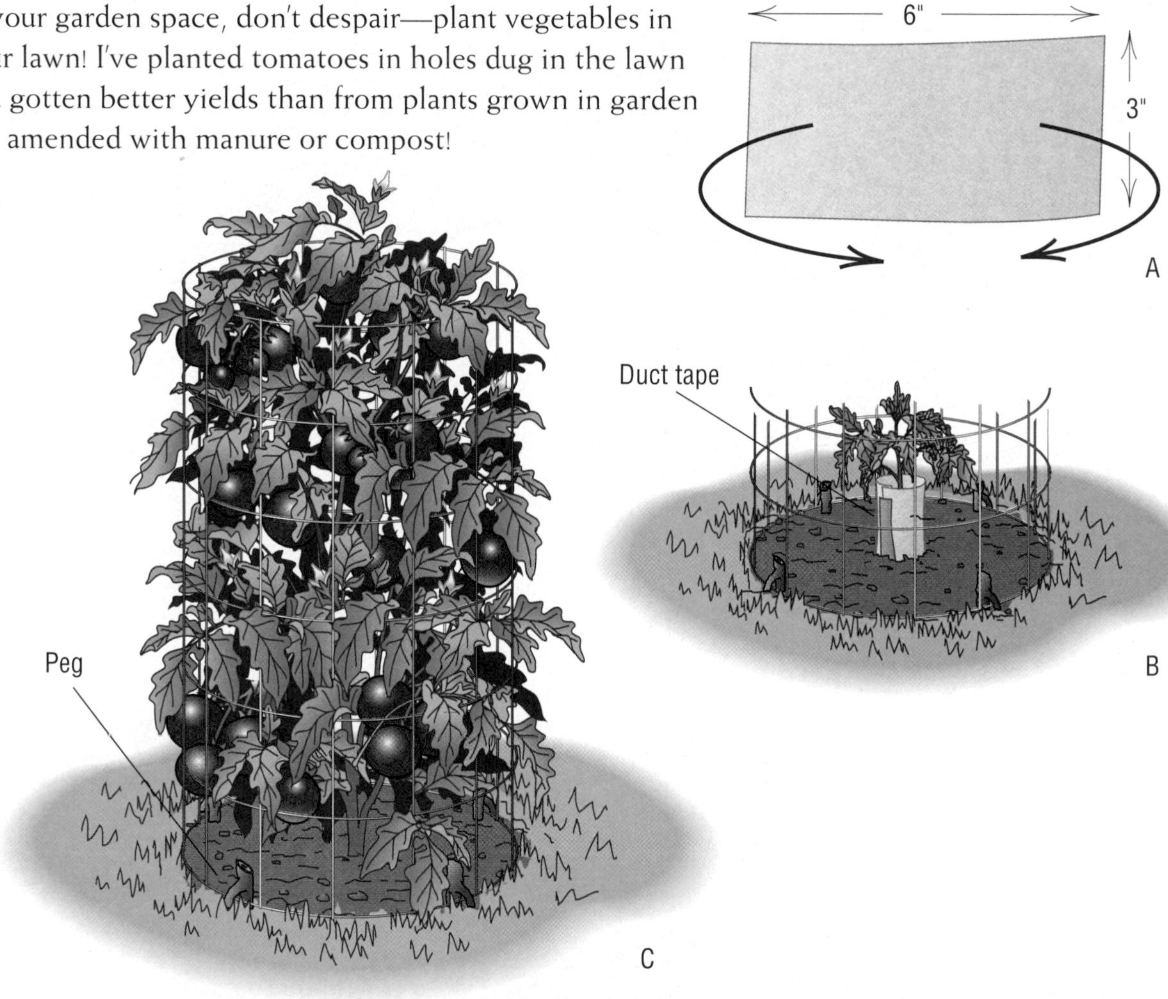

6"

3"

A

Duct tape

B

Peg

C

Don't let cutworms keep you from growing luscious vegetables in your lawn—stop these pests with collars made out of cardboard (A). Curl a collar around each seedling's stem, tape the collar closed, then push it 1 inch deep into the soil (B). By the time the collar falls apart, the plant will be large (C) and the danger from cutworms—which attack young seedlings—will be over.

Pick a pretty spot. You don't have to limit your crop choices just because you're short on space. It's just as easy to grow eggplant, peppers, and other vegetables in your lawn as it is to grow tomatoes. To try this your-self, start in spring. Choose a piece of your property that's been a lawn for years, one that hasn't been fertilized or sprayed with chemical lawn care prod-ucts, especially broadleaf herbi-cides. Pick a spot that's in full sun and where the lawn looks healthy. Avoid planting in areas that are rank with weeds or where the grass is thin or spotty. If you let grass clippings stay on your lawn after mowing, that's perfect—they break down and add organic matter and fertilizer to the soil.

Roll 'em up and set 'em out. Next, make tomato cages by rolling 9-foot lengths of 5-foot-wide concrete-reinforcing mesh into tubes. (You can find the mesh at building supply stores.) Fasten the edges to-gether with plastic-coated wire or plastic ties. Now take a sharp-edged shovel to the spot in the lawn you've chosen for your vegetable patch, and cut a circle in the sod that's the same diameter as your tomato cage.

Dig under the sod, loos-ening it and prying it up until it comes free in one piece. With a trowel, poke the bottom of the sod so the soil that's clinging to

the roots falls back into the bare spot. The sod piece makes a great addition to your compost pile—place it upside down in the pile so it will break down faster—or use it to fix a hole in another part of your lawn.

Where you removed the sod, dig a hole to the depth of your shovel blade and loosen the soil. Plant a tomato or other vegetable transplant in the hole and put a cardboard cutworm

collar around it. Cutworms live in the soil under sod, and you don't want them chopping down your seedling at night with their raspy mandibles.

Finally, set your tomato cage over the seedling. It should fit snugly up against the grass. Pin the bottom of the cage to the soil with rocks, bricks, or pegs so the cage won't topple over when it's top-heavy with a fruit-laden plant.

Anchor Tomato Cages with Branch Trimmings

It's a good idea to anchor your tomato cages to the ground so they don't tip over in storms or when plants get top-heavy. You don't have to buy fancy stakes to do the job, though. You can make your own pegs out of branches you've pruned off trees or shrubs.

Select a branch with a side branch emerging at an angle (A). Cut off the excess so you're left with a 4- to 6-inch-long peg with a stub coming off of it (B). Sharpen the bottom of the peg so it's easy to push into the soil (C), then use the stub to hook the bottom wire of the tomato cage to the ground (D).

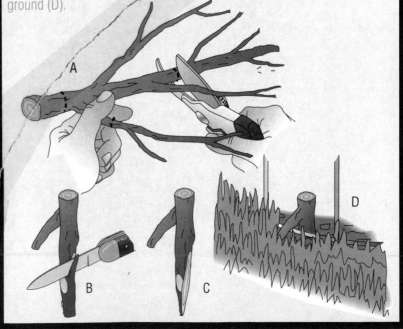

13

Solarize Your Soil for Earlier Harvests

Warm-season vegetables like tomatoes, eggplant, beans, squash, and peppers won't really get growing until the soil temperature's hot—around 70°F. So if you want your earliest harvest ever, pre-warm the soil before you put your plants in the ground. Early tomatoes are my weakness, so I mostly use this technique in my tomato patch, but you can use it for all warm-season crops. Here's how:

Mulch

Clear plastic

You can harvest crops like peppers and tomatoes up to two weeks earlier if you prewarm the soil before planting! Cover the entire planting area with clear plastic sheeting, seal the edges with soil, and let the ground bake for four weeks before setting out your transplants. Cut holes in the plastic so you can set your plants in the ground, then completely cover the plastic with 4 inches of mulch.

Cover the soil. Four weeks before you normally set out tomato plants (or other warm-season vegetables), shallowly dig or till your planting area. You just need to get weeds and leftover fall plantings out of the way so the bare soil is exposed.

If the soil is dry, water it thoroughly. Then cover the area completely with a single sheet of clear plastic sheeting. You can buy big sheets of plastic at most hardware stores. It comes in various widths up to 16 feet, so you can cover almost any tomato patch with a single sheet.

Weight the corners with stones so winds don't blow the plastic away as you work, then shovel soil onto the edges of the sheeting. Make sure the edges of the plastic are completely covered to keep cold air from seeping in. Then stand back and watch the soil heat up.

Uncover the benefits. Even on cloudy days, the sun will warm the air under the clear plastic—on clear days, it will positively roast it. If the sun is strong enough, temperatures under the plastic can reach 140°F and more, which is enough to kill weed seeds and the roots of stubborn perennial weeds like bindweed, at least in the upper couple of inches of soil. The benefit you're after, though, is the daily dose of heat that will warm the top layer of soil under the plastic to a depth of 6 to 8

inches—just deep enough to warm the root zone for young plants.

When it comes time to plant, you can either remove the plastic sheet or, better still, cut holes in it for your tomato plants. Once your plants are in the ground, cover the whole patch, plastic and all, with a thick layer of mulch to shield it from the sun. If you don't, the plastic will overheat the soil, harming or even killing your seedlings.

The plastic and mulch will not only keep weeds from growing over the summer but will hold that hard-won heat in the soil longer than if you had removed the plastic and exposed the bare soil to the weather. The plastic helps hold moisture in the ground too, since it can't evaporate through the sheeting. When your plants do need a drink, set a hose beside them one by one, and let the water dribble into the soil slowly, through the slits in the plastic.

Discover another way to warm the soil. A hot bed is also a tried-and-true way to keep plants warm. Make one by digging out a trench 18 inches wide and 24 inches deep. Put 10 to 12 inches of fresh horse, cow, or pig manure in the bottom of the trench, then fill the trench with soil. You can plant tomatoes in this hot bed a week or two earlier than you normally would because the decaying

manure generates a gentle heat that filters to the surface, warming the soil as it goes. (You'll still need to protect plants if night frosts threaten.) At planting time, the plants' roots are high enough above the fresh manure that they won't get burned by the nitrogen and ammonia it gives off. By the time roots grow enough to penetrate the manure, it's decayed enough so it won't harm them.

Pick Your Plastic

There are lots of choices when it comes to plastic for covering your garden, including clear, white, black, and even bright colors like red. Each is good for different uses. For simple heating, clear plastic is "clearly" the best. It allows solar radiation in, but doesn't let it back out again. It's the famous greenhouse effect applied to your tomato patch.

White and red plastics encourage plants to grow because they reflect light back at their leaves. (Tomatoes are particularly fond of red plastic, while potatoes grow best under white plastic!) These colored plastics don't warm the soil much, but they're good to use as mulch. Black plastic is better at heating the soil than white plastic, but its best use is for weed control. Weeds can't get any light through the black barrier so they wither and die. For great growth, use white, red, or black plastic on top of the clear plastic instead of mulch.

14 Frost-Proof Your Tomatoes for an Early Harvest

It seems to take forever for those first tomatoes to ripen up! And they're so frost-sensitive, putting them out before the last frost date is more silly than smart, unless you know how to protect your plants from the cold. I'm not willing to wait until late July or August for my first vine-ripe tomato, so here's how I plant extra-early and keep Jack Frost away.

Protect early tomato plants from cold by surrounding them with 1-gallon plastic milk jugs filled with warm water and you can harvest tomatoes a month earlier than usual. If a really hard freeze threatens, throw a cloth over the top of the plastic-covered cage for extra protection.

Cage out the cold. Start with a tomato cage—either your own homemade model or a store-bought version. At the hardware store, buy a roll of clear plastic that's at least 3 mils thick. It should be as wide as your cage is tall and long enough to wrap all the way around the cage with about 6 inches left over. (It takes nearly 10 feet of plastic to wrap a 3-foot-diameter cage.) Place the plastic around the wire mesh cage, bringing the loose edge around until it overlaps the plastic underneath. Use duct tape or packing tape to fasten the plastic to itself, making sure it's pulled tight so it doesn't sag and slip off the cage.

Pour on the heat. Now, put your tomato plant into the ground three weeks earlier than usual. Next, fill four 1-gallon plastic milk jugs with warm water and put the tops on. Surround the young plant with the jugs, set as close to the plant as you can without crushing it. Now slip the plastic-wrapped tomato cage over the jugs and the plant, and weight it to the ground with bricks or stones so it won't blow over in the wind.

During the day, heat from the sun will collect inside the plastic-wrapped cage and warm the water in the milk jugs. In the evening and at night as temperatures drop, the jugs will gradually give up their heat to the air inside the tomato cage.

Your plant protector will ward off frost and will keep your tomato comfy even during cold nights that would fatally nip unprotected plants.

After the frost danger is over, you can take the plastic wrap off your tomato cage. And once the nights turn nice and warm, you can dispense with the milk jugs too. It's important to unwrap the cage when hot summery weather arrives, because too much heat can build up inside the closed cage and bake your tomato.

How hot is it? I've used a thermometer to measure the heat inside the wrapped tomato cage. On one warm late April day with plenty of sunshine, the outside air temperature was about 78°F, while it reached almost 90°F inside the cylinder at ground level.

While warm temperatures will stimulate the tomato plant's growth, temperatures over 90°F can bring growth to a screeching halt. So on those occasional hot, sunny days early in the season, lift off the cages during the warm afternoons and replace them after dinner when things cool off. The jugs of sun-warmed water will keep the plants warm all night.

Speed the Season with Early Tomatoes

Another way to speed up your tomato harvest is to plant early tomatoes—plants that produce fruits 50 to 70 days after they're transplanted into the garden. Midseason tomatoes take 70 to 80 days to mature, and late-season love apples need 80 to 90 days to produce a crop. Here are six tomatoes you can try that are not only early, they're cold-tolerant too!

Choose indeterminate cultivars if you want a steady stream of tomatoes all season long and you have space for large plants that need caging. Determinate plants are smaller and better behaved, but they tend to produce all their fruits in a short time period.

Name	Days to Maturity	Description
'Siberia'	48 to 55	Determinate. Clusters of bright red 3- to 5-ounce fruits on a small, bushy plant.
'Early Girl'	52	Indeterminate. Bright red, meaty, 4- to 6-ounce slicing tomato.
'Stupice'	52 to 65	Indeterminate. Produces plenty of sweet, 1- to 2-ounce fruits.
'Siletz'	52 to 70	Determinate. Deep red, tasty 10- to 12-ounce fruits.
'Oregon Spring'	58 to 60	Determinate. Meaty fruits weigh 4 to 6 ounces and have very few seeds.
'Scotia'	60	Determinate. Damp weather won't stop this plant from producing 4-ounce fruits.

15 A Year's Worth of Tomatoes for an Hour's Work

Start your tomatoes off right and you won't have to spend hours weeding, watering, and fertilizing during the heat of the summer. All it takes is one hour in the spring to get the soil and mulch just right and you'll get all the tomatoes you need—guaranteed!

Spring

Indeterminate tomatoes

Determinate tomatoes

Summer

Prepare for the growing season at planting time with newspaper mulch and compost and you won't have to worry about weeding, fertilizing, or watering your tomatoes. Support rangy indeterminate plants and well-behaved determinate types with wire cages for the best results.

What's in a name? Before you start seeds or buy seedlings of tomato cultivars, make sure you're getting plants that ripen when you need them. If you want tomatoes to make sauce or juice, or to can or freeze, choose determinate tomatoes such as 'LaRoma' and 'Viva Italia Hybrid'—they produce all of their fruit at once for a single harvest. Indeterminate tomatoes, such as 'Early Girl', 'Better Boy', and 'Sweet 100 Hybrid', are great for slicing and salads since they keep growing and producing tomatoes all season until frost.

Dig each plant a hole. When your tomatoes are big enough to plant, select a rectangular area about 24 feet long and 12 feet wide that gets full sun all day long. This site can be in an existing garden or even in your lawn. Don't worry if there are weeds or grass growing there.

Dig out eight holes 18 inches across and a good foot deep, then loosen the soil in the bottom of the hole for another 6 inches. (Eight plants will provide a family of four with a summer's worth of fresh tomatoes, plus plenty for putting up.) Space the holes two abreast, 6 feet apart across the width of the bed, and about 5 feet apart down the length of the planting area.

If the soil is good garden soil to begin with, all you need to do is add a shovelful of fin-ished compost to each hole. If the soil is poor, mix finished compost 50/50 with the soil in each hole. Add a shovelful of sand to the mix too, if you're dealing with thick, clunky clay.

Put down the paper. Spread the entire area, except the holes, with an 8- to 12-page-thick pad of newspaper. You can use black and white and color sections— just avoid advertising inserts since the colored inks may contain toxic heavy metals. Weight the edges of the newspapers down with stones to keep them from blowing away, then put in the plants.

Water the transplants thoroughly by placing the hose on a trickle at the base of each plant. Use this same watering method whenever your tomatoes need a drink. (It won't be too often, because the newspapers will hold moisture in the soil.)

Do fence them in. Next, make tomato cages by rolling 9-foot lengths of 5-foot-wide concrete-reinforcing mesh into tubes. You can get the mesh at building supply stores. This tough wire mesh won't rust out or crumple under the weight of a full-grown tomato plant, so you can use the cages year after year. Twist the end wires together, or use pieces of wire or plastic ties to hold the cages shut.

Place a cage over each plant and weight the bottom in three places with heavy stones or bricks to keep the cages from toppling over. Then, cover the entire rectangular area with shredded bark mulch, straw, or some similar good-looking mulch. This top layer of mulch not only looks nice, it holds in moisture and keeps weeds out. And that means you can spend your time in the hammock instead of the tomato patch until it's time to harvest!

To Sucker or Not to Sucker?

The shoots that arise in the leaf axils of the tomato plant are called suckers. Legend has it that for top tomato production, you should remove the suckers. True or false?

Sucker

The answer depends on what you mean by top tomato production. If you want the plant to put more energy and grow-power into fewer fruits, thereby creating larger fruits, remove the suckers. For more sheer poundage, but somewhat smaller tomatoes, let those suckers grow.

So if you're going for big slicers for your burgers or for the blue ribbon at the county fair, remove the suckers. But if you want big yields for tomato sauce, let them grow.

16 Simple Steps to Bigger, Better Vegetables

It's a thrill to grow giant vegetables that make your neighbor's jaw drop with astonishment or win prizes at the local fair. There are a few tricks to growing huge pumpkins, mammoth cabbages, and gigantic peppers, but they're simple ones, so you don't have to be an expert to make them work. For BIG results, just pick the right plants this spring, then water, weed, feed, and thin the fruits.

For monster crops of pumpkins (or other vegetables), plant seeds of a large-fruited variety. Then keep the plants stress-free by watering with a soaker hose whenever the soil dries out. Remove all but one fruit from the plant (A) so the vine puts all its effort into the pumpkin. Then, as your prize-winning fruit grows, set it on a piece of tile or linoleum to keep it away from pests and moisture damage (B).

Choose vegetables that can reach giant size. A tomato that's genetically programmed to produce cherry-size fruit will not grow beefsteak tomatoes no matter how you treat it. So start by selecting seeds of plants with large fruits. Seed catalogs and packets will steer you in the right direction. Look for cultivars with the words "big," "giant," or "mammoth" in their names, like 'Big Max' pumpkins.

Baby your plants. Make sure there are no checks to your vegetables' strong, steady growth. Cultivate carefully and mulch the soil so your plants aren't stressed in any way. A plant that's injured as a seedling isn't likely to reach its full genetic potential. Neither will one that's damaged by frost or extreme cold, wind, hail, water-logged soil, or a lack of water.

Even a day or two of water stress can throw a plant into a state of suspended growth while it waits for rain—or you—to provide relief. Keep your soil evenly moist by covering the ground surface with a layer of mulch. And take care to give plants plenty of water in midsummer, when they're growing strong.

Provide plenty of nutrition. Start with a soil test so you'll know exactly which nutrients your soil's got and which it needs to maximize plant growth. Call your local Cooperative Extension agent to find out how to take a soil sample and where to send it for testing. Make sure you mention that you'd like organic recommendations.

The soil test will show you the amount of each major nutrient in your soil and will include a pH rating. Remember pH from science class? It's the scale from 1 to 14 that tells you how acidic or alkaline your soil is. A nearly neutral pH of 6.0 to 6.5 is just right, because that's the range where most nutrients are available to most garden plants. It just so happens that 6.0 to 6.5 is also the pH of well-made, finished compost.

So the easiest way to ensure rich soil with the right pH is to add compost to your garden before planting. You'll need to add 4 to 20 pounds of compost per 10 square feet of planting area, depending on whether your soil is high or low in nutrients. Keep the soil fertile throughout the growing season by watering your plants weekly with fish emulsion solutions or with compost or manure teas.

Make more from less. You'll need to thin the fruits on each plant so just two or three are left—or just one, if you're after the biggest fruit of all. Whether you're growing eggplants, peppers, cantaloupes, watermelons, tomatoes, winter squashes, or pumpkins, the fewer fruits on the plant, the more energy the plant can put into the remaining fruit. Want a jumbo tomato? Take off all the tomatoes on the vine except one and watch what happens. There's no yield advantage to doing this, as total yields in pounds will be way down. But in this case, it's the visual impact of big vegetables that you're after. And boy, will you get plenty of visual impact!

Big Veggies Need Frequent Feeding

When plants put on a growth spurt, start giving them weekly fertilizer feedings. Fish emulsion, compost tea, or manure tea will do your plants a world of good, but you have other options to maximize plant growth. Use what's easiest and most available for you.

You can side-dress plants by working a couple of shovelfuls of compost or aged manure into the top inch of soil. The roots will get a steady supply of soluble nutrients each time it rains.

Foliar feeding is another way to encourage plants to grow bigger and better. You can use compost tea (avoid manure-based teas on edible fruits), kelp, or seaweed extract to feed plants through their leaf pores. Plants are most responsive to these nutrient boosters during stressful times. They'll welcome a foliar feeding after transplanting, during fruit set, and during stretches of extremely hot weather or drought.

17 Sow Small Seeds Evenly and Easily

I don't broadcast small seeds by hand anymore. I tried sifting tiny carrot seeds through my fingers and using a shaker to spread little lettuce seeds evenly, but it never worked. The seeds always seemed to fall in clumps that had to be thinned later. Thinning is a tedious job I'd rather avoid, so I devised a system to spread small seeds evenly…with a rake.

Space little seeds like carrots (A) and lettuce (B) evenly from the get-go and you won't have to come back and thin them later. For easy spacing, mix tiny seeds with enough soil or compost to cover them ¼ to ½ inch deep. Then spread the mix out evenly over the planting area using a board or rake (C).

Know how much you want to grow. The first step is to look at the list of small-seeded crops listed in the chart on page 39 and choose the ones you want to grow. Decide how much of each crop to plant by multiplying the number of people in your family by the number listed in the "Plants per Person" column in the chart. Then find the spacing and planting depth for each vegetable—they're listed in the chart, too.

If you're growing a crop that isn't listed in the chart, look up the "Plants per Person" information in vegetable gardening books, like *Growing Fruits and Vegetables Organically*. (See "Recommended Reading" on page 233 for more vegetable gardening book recommendations.) If you need spacing and planting depth information, check books, seed catalogs, or seed packets. Once you've gathered the planting information, you're ready to use my system.

Let's use carrots as an example. For fresh eating, you'll want to plant 30 plants per person. For a family of four, that's 120 carrots ($4 \times 30 = 120$). See how many seeds are in your seed packet (for this example we'll say there are 1,500 seeds in the package). Divide 1,500 by 120 to see how much of the package you'll need

($1,500 \div 120 = 12.5$). You'll discover that you need just over 12 percent of the package—I always round up to the nearest whole number, which in this case comes to 13 percent of the package. Hang onto that figure and go onto the next step.

Work out the spacing. Planting in beds instead of rows saves lots of space, so figure out how much room a bed of 120 carrots needs. It's easy to come up with the dimensions if you use square feet. Start by looking at the chart. You'll see that carrots should be spaced 3 inches apart in all directions. Now determine how many carrots you can plant in a square foot.

Using a piece of graph paper, draw a square-foot area letting each square equal 1 inch. The object is to fit as many carrots into the square-foot area as possible, keeping them 3 inches apart. In the illustration on this

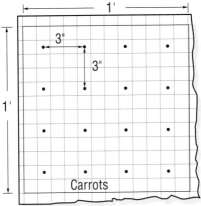

Whether you're planting carrots or some other small-seeded crop, it's easy to figure out how many plants will fit in a square foot if you count it out on a piece of graph paper.

page, you'll see that you can fit 16 carrots in a square-foot space. The carrots aren't 3 inches from the edges of the square foot, but that's okay. You just need them to be 3 inches apart from each other. (For crops that need more room than carrots, allow the full amount of space between plants and the edge of the planting area.)

Divide 120 carrots by 16 to find out how many square feet of bed space you'll need for the planting ($120 \div 16 = 7.5$). Round up to the nearest foot, and you'll see that for this example, you'll need 8 square feet of planting space.

Carrot seeds should be planted ½ inch deep, so pour the seeds from your packet onto a small flat dish and scoop up about 13 percent of the seeds (13 percent of 1,500 seeds = one-eighth of the package). Pour the rest of the seeds back into the packet for later sowings.

Bring the soil to the seeds. Instead of adding the seeds to the soil at planting time, you'll add the right amount of soil to the seeds. In this case, you need enough fine screened soil or compost to cover the carrot seeds to a depth of ½ inch. It takes 2½ pints of soil to cover a 1-square-foot area to a depth of ½ inch if you spread it evenly. You'll need 8 times that amount for your 8-square-foot planting area ($8 \times 2.5 = 20$ pints). There are 8 pints in a gallon, so 2½ gallons of soil will do the trick.

Pour the seeds into a 5-gallon bucket along with the soil or compost and use a trowel to thoroughly mix them together. Prepare the 8-square-foot area of your planting bed by working the surface to form a fine seedbed. Don't add high-nitrogen fertilizer to the soil, since too much nitrogen tends to make carrots split and get hairy.

Planting oh so evenly. Dump the bucket of compost and seeds into the middle of the planting area. Use your rake to smooth the compost/seed mix from the center to the edges of the bed in all directions. Try to get ½ inch of it evenly spread over the whole surface. When the compost is spread as evenly as you can get it, press the surface down lightly with your hand or a piece of wood. This helps seeds pick up soil moisture more easily. Water gently until the soil is thoroughly wet. (It's important to use light fluffy compost or soil to plant your seeds because you want the seeds to settle down to the bottom of the ½ inch of soil.)

After planting, keep the soil moist until the carrots sprout. If you've spread the compost evenly, there'll only be a few extra carrots to pull instead of what usually seems like hundreds of them. You'll be done with thinning in the blink of an eye.

Step-by-Step Soil Mixing

Suppose the little seeds you want to plant aren't listed in the chart on the opposite page. Don't fret; just use this handy guide. It takes you through the process of figuring out how much soil you need to spread seeds evenly and at the right planting depth.

Start by selecting the crop you want. Then answer these questions. You'll find the answers in seed catalogs or on seed packets.

How far apart in each direction should the mature plants be?_____

How many plants do I want at this sowing? _____

Calculate the square footage of the planting_____
(see Example A below)

How deep should the seeds be planted?_____

Calculate the amount of soil needed for the seed/soil mix_____
(see Example B below)

Example A: Leaf lettuce should be spaced 6 inches apart in all directions in the bed. Decide on how many plants you want for the season—assume 15 plants per person for a family of four or 60 lettuce plants. You don't want all of your lettuce to mature at once, so divide the 60 plants into five or six separate plantings, setting out just 10 or 12 plants every 20 days. To prepare for the first planting, determine how many plants will fit in a square foot of space. To do this, draw a square foot on a sheet of graph paper, letting each square equal 1 inch. You'll see that you can fit 4 lettuce plants in a square foot, so you'll need 3 square feet for the planting of 12 plants.

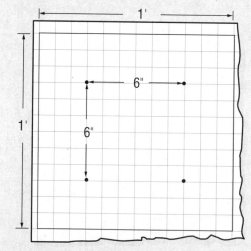

Example B: To plant lettuce seeds ¼ inch deep, you'll need to know how much soil will cover 3 square feet of planting area ¼ inch deep. It takes 1¼ pints of soil to cover a square foot ¼ inch deep. So you'll need 3 times that amount, or 4 pints (1.25 × 3 = 3.75). Remember that there are 2 pints in a quart and 4 quarts in a gallon. You'll need 2 quarts, or ½ gallon, of soil.

Small-Seeded Vegetables

Mix the following vegetables with fine compost or screened soil before seeding—you'll save yourself lots of thinning.

Vegetable	Spacing in All Directions (in inches)	Planting Depth (in inches)	Plants per Person
Broccoli	18	½	5 to 10
Brussels sprouts	24	½	5 to 10
Cabbage	15 to 24	½	5 to 10
Carrots	3	¼ to ½	30
Cauliflower	15 to 18	½	5
Celery	6 to 12	¼	6
Chinese cabbage	15 to 24	½	5 to 10
Collards	6 to 12	½	3 to 5
Corn salad	2	¼	3 to 5
Endive	8	¼	3 to 5
Kale	15 to 18	½	2 to 5
Kohlrabi	4 to 8	½	10 to 20
Leeks	4	¼	10
Lettuce, head	9	¼	7
Mustard	3 to 6 for young greens, 12 for mature plants	¼	3 to 5
Onions	4 to 6	¼	25 to 50
Parsley	8 to 10	¼	2 to 5
Parsnips	4 to 6	½	20
Rutabagas	4	¼	8 to 10 for fresh eating, 30 for storing
Sorrel	8	¼	3 to 5
Tomatoes	18 to 24	½	2 to 4 slicing types, 6 paste types
Turnips	4	¼	8 to 10

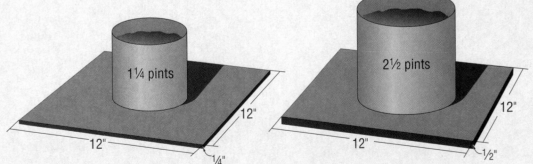

To sow fine seeds evenly, it's easier to mix them in good soil or screened compost and spread it on the garden bed than to try to scatter seeds on the bed. You'll get best results by using the simple calculations on pages 37 and 38 to find out how much soil or compost you'll need for each type of seed. For lettuce seeds, you need 1¼ pints to cover a square foot of bed ¼ inch deep (the correct planting depth for lettuce). For carrots, you'll need 2½ pints of soil to cover a square foot of bed to their correct planting depth, ½ inch.

18 Meet Crops' Needs with the Right Amount of Feed

Vegetables are like people—some are heavy feeders, while others get by on just a little food. I don't have time to individually feed each vegetable in my garden, so I came up with a two-year feeding schedule to meet my plants' needs. The beauty of this system is that it's easy to combine with a crop-rotation schedule. Try it and you'll not only get bigger harvests but fewer pest problems too.

Combine your fertilizer and crop-rotation schedules by making a series of three or more beds, then giving only the odd beds a heavy dose of compost. Plant heavy feeders in the rich beds and light feeders in the lean beds. The following year, feed only the lean beds with compost. Rotate heavy feeders into the new rich beds and light feeders into the new lean beds.

Divide the tasks. Crop and feeding rotations are a lot easier to organize if you have more than one bed. Start by dividing your garden into three beds or multiples of three—nine is ideal for a wide variety of crops. Separate the beds with mulched paths, or use raised beds if you prefer. The beds can be different sizes depending on how much of each crop you want to grow.

Make a simple drawing of your beds and label it year one. You'll use this drawing to map your feeding and crop-rotation schedules. I grow a lot of vegetables so I use a nine-bed rotation plan. Don't worry if you don't have that much space—three beds will work just as well.

Notice in the sample map that in year one, beds 1, 3, 5, 7, and 9 (the rich beds) get early-spring applications of composted manure—2 inches of composted cow, pig, or horse manure, or 1 inch of composted poultry manure. If you don't have access to animal manure compost, add any well-made compost to your beds. Just add a little extra of the stuff to your beds—2½ inches should do it. Turn the compost into the beds as soon as you can work the soil in spring so they're ready and waiting at planting time. In the second year, these beds will get no compost at all and will be considered lean beds.

Beds 2, 4, 6, and 8 (the lean beds) get no compost the first year. In their second year, these beds get 2 inches of composted manure and become rich beds. Rotate the fertilizer applications each year as shown on the sample map. Remember that after a few rotations, the beds will be very fertile—it's just their levels of available, soluble soil nitrogen that change as plants use it up.

Feed according to need. Now take a look at the vegetables listed in the chart on page 43. They're listed according to how rich a diet they need. Choose which plants you want to grow, then plant heavy feeders in the rich beds and light feeders in the lean beds. When you make succession plantings during the growing season, follow heavy feeders with heavy feeders or with legumes and grasses to improve the soil. For example, if you harvest a heavy feeder like spinach in summer, follow it with more spinach or a legume like beans. Follow light feeders with more light feeders or with soil-building legumes and grasses. For example, if you harvest a light feeder like peas in spring, follow it with another light feeder like carrots or with a legume like clover to improve the soil.

Keep 'em moving. Each year, as you rotate the rich and lean beds, your crops will rotate too. The heavy feeders will move to rich beds and the less hungry plants will move to lean beds. That's the easiest crop-rotation system I know! If you've got plenty of time and would like to figure out crop rotations that will give you the most insect and disease protection, here's what you need to know.

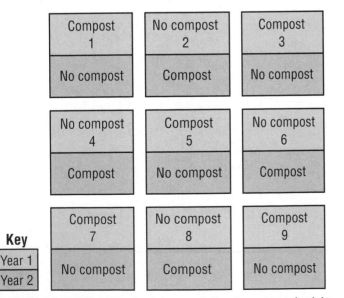

Here's how to fertilize nine beds on a rotating two-year schedule. In the third year, revert to the first-year fertilization schedule.

Related plants (like broccoli and cabbage) are likely to have the same insect and disease problems, and moving them from place to place makes it harder for pests or diseases to build up. Whenever possible, let two or three years go by before you plant a particular crop family in the same bed again. The easiest way to do this is set up a crop rotation and fertilization schedule like the one shown on this page. It's a great way to guarantee healthy, happy plants.

Rules for crop rotations. Here are some general rules for rotating crops. Follow them as best you can in the space you have. Whenever you aren't sure what to plant after a particular crop, plant a legume such as beans or peas. These members of the pea family can convert nitrogen from the air into a form plants can use. They are a particularly good choice after plantings of heavy feeders like corn or tomatoes since they help build up the soil.

Beet family. Plant amaranth and beets—the light feeders of this family—after heavy feeders and before pea-family members, which will put nitrogen back in the soil. Plant the leafy heavy feeders of this family after light feeders.

Cabbage family. Plant legumes the year before you plant heavy feeders from the cabbage family. The legumes will add nitrogen to the soil to give hungry crops an extra boost.

Carrot or parsley family. This family includes coriander, dill, fennel, and parsley. These herbs are light feeders so you can plant any crop you choose the year before they go in the ground. Follow carrot-family members with legumes.

Grass family. Plant wheat, oats, or rye before tomato- or squash-family crops. These grasses help control weeds and improve soil drainage by breaking up the earth with their roots.

Morning-glory family. Like other root crops, plant sweet potatoes after heavy feeders and before pea-family members.

Onion family. Follow this family with legumes. Asparagus is a perennial that comes back year after year. Set aside a permanent place for this crop and amend the soil as you would for a rich bed before planting.

Pea family. Rotate the members of this family with all other crops. They help improve the soil by adding nitrogen and have few pest problems.

Squash family. Plant winter rye or oats the year before you plant cucumbers and their kin (melons, squash, and pumpkins). These grass-family members will help choke out weeds. Follow squash-family plantings with legumes to rebuild the soil.

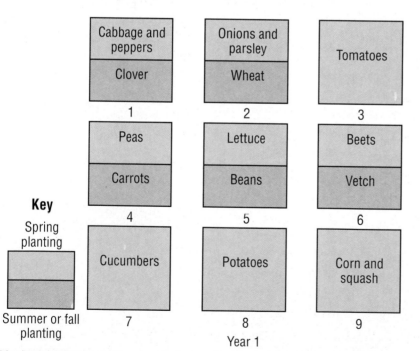

Key

Spring planting

Summer or fall planting

Cabbage and peppers / Clover — 1

Onions and parsley / Wheat — 2

Tomatoes — 3

Peas / Carrots — 4

Lettuce / Beans — 5

Beets / Vetch — 6

Cucumbers — 7

Potatoes — 8

Corn and squash — 9

Year 1

Moving plants around in your garden confuses insects and keeps diseases from building up in the soil. Here's a rotation plan that matches the fertilizer schedule on page 41 and also separates members of the same plant family. In year two, move the plants in Bed 1 to Bed 2, Bed 2 to Bed 3, and so on. Continue moving each planting one bed over in succeeding years.

Feed Needs of Common Vegetables

Choose heavy feeders to plant in your rich beds and light feeders to plant in your lean beds. Separate members of the same botanical family whenever possible to discourage insect and disease problems.

Heavy Feeders			Light Feeders			
Beet family (Chenopodiaceae)						
Orach	Spinach	Swiss chard	Amaranth	Beets		
Cabbage family (Cruciferae)						
Arugula	Cabbage	Cress	Mustard greens	Rutabaga		
Broccoli	Cauliflower	Kale	Radishes	Turnips		
Brussels sprouts	Collards	Kohlrabi				
Carrot or parsley family (Umbelliferae)						
Celery			Carrots	Dill	Parsley	
			Coriander	Fennel	Parsnips	
Grass family (Gramineae)						
Corn			Oats	Rye	Wheat	
Morning-glory family (Convolvulaceae)						
			Sweet potatoes			
Onion family (Liliaceae)						
Asparagus			Garlic	Leeks	Onions	Shallots
Pea family (Leguminosae)						
			Alfalfa	Clovers	Peanuts	Soybeans
			Beans	Lentils	Peas	Vetches
Squash family (Cucurbitaceae)						
Cucumbers	Pumpkins					
Melons	Squash					
Sunflower family (Compositae)						
Artichoke	Endive		Jerusalem artichoke			
Chicory	Lettuce		Sunflower			
Tomato family (Solanaceae)						
Eggplants	Peppers	Tomatoes	Potatoes			

Sunflower family. Follow the heavy feeders in this family with a legume crop to restore the soil.

Tomato family. Plant wheat, oats, or rye before the heavy feeders in this family. They'll help control insects and weeds.

Plant legumes after tomato-family members to help restore the soil. Plant potatoes after heavy feeders.

19 Beautiful, Bountiful Bush Fruits for (Almost) Free

Plant your yard with bush fruits and you'll beautify your landscape, increase your property value, and get something good to eat. Not a bad return on your investment! For an even better return, you can propagate bush fruits yourself. That way, your only costs will be the purchase price of parent plants and a little bit of time.

Grow your own currants (and other bush fruits) from cuttings. First, trim crowded branches back to a main stem or to 2 inches above the ground (A). Then trim these cuttings to 12 inches long and nick out all but the four top buds. Plant the cuttings in a nursery bed until they're ready to transplant to your garden (B). Soon you'll be picking red-ripe currant clusters to turn into jelly or jam.

Make your bush fruit bed.
Once you grow (and eat) bush fruits such as blueberries, black currants, red currants, gooseberries, or huckleberries, you'll want more. One parent plant doesn't cost too much, but planting stock for a whole row of bush fruits can be expensive. Here's how to get plenty of plants and fruit without spending lots of money.

(Before you plant black currants, check with your local Cooperative Extension agent. Some states have a ban against these plants because they are alternate hosts of white pine blister rust.)

Get started in early spring by digging out a nursery bed 6 inches deep, 3 feet across, and as long as you like. Site the bed where it gets morning sun, but is somewhat protected from the hot afternoon sun. If you don't have a site with afternoon shade, make your own shade by setting a piece of lattice on the west side of the bed or by planting a row of sunflowers.

Refill the dug-out bed with a growing mix made of finished compost or a 50/50 mix of compost and perlite. The idea is to create a loose, friable, nutritious, and water-retentive growing medium. If you don't like the idea of digging a bed, make a raised nursery bed by placing 4 to 6 inches of compost on top of soil that's been loosened with a spading fork.

Easy-does-it propagating.
In spring, just before the buds start to swell, selectively prune branches from your bush fruit parent plants. Cut off good-size healthy stems that cross or are too close to other branches. That way you'll get good cuttings and improve the look of your existing shrubs at the same time.

Trim the cut ends of the stems so you're left with cuttings that are 12 inches long, then nick out all but the top four buds. Sink the cuttings into the prepared nursery bed until the lowest of the four remaining buds is 2 inches above the soil surface. Place the cuttings a foot apart in all directions, firm the soil around the stems, and water them in well. Water the cuttings every day for the next week. The following week, water every other day, and after that, water the cuttings deeply once a week until you're sure they're sprouting leaves and holding their own.

Keep the cuttings in the nursery bed the entire growing season and through the winter. The next spring, before the buds break, dig up each rooted cutting, making sure there's a generous rootball, and transplant it to its permanent location. Then prepare for fantastic, fruitful harvests!

Fill your yard and table with bush fruits. Once you decide to adorn your yard with fruit-bearing shrubs, you'll find they offer as many landscaping possibilities as flavors. Set bush fruits out as a hedge along the back or side of your vegetable garden or yard. Or use them like ornamentals along paths, beside your house or outbuildings, or in mixed borders with perennials.

Gooseberries make useful hedge plants—once you've experienced the pain of a gooseberry thorn, you'll think twice about pushing through that hedge again. But oh my, gooseberry pie! And blueberry and huckleberry pie, too. Red currants make gorgeous, uniquely flavored jams and jellies. And black currants cook into a delicious purple-black syrup that makes an outstanding topping on ice cream.

Pruning Basics

Treat red and black currants and gooseberries the same way. Prune only to thin the bushes and remove older unproductive canes. Keep one-, two-, and three-year-old stems, but remove any stems that are entering their fourth growing season. You can cut the younger branches back a little if they are very long and drooping. Just don't shear the bushes, or you'll cut off most of the fruit buds.

Blueberries and huckleberries usually don't need any pruning at all. Occasionally you may need to remove a branch or two to help them maintain a nice, open, uncrowded shape.

20 Get Two Red Raspberry Harvests from the Same Plants

You can get two crops of luscious red raspberries a year if you know how these plants respond to pruning. If you whack down all the canes once a year, you'll get a harvest once a year. If you prune the canes selectively twice a year, you'll get two harvests each year. It's simple! Here's what I do.

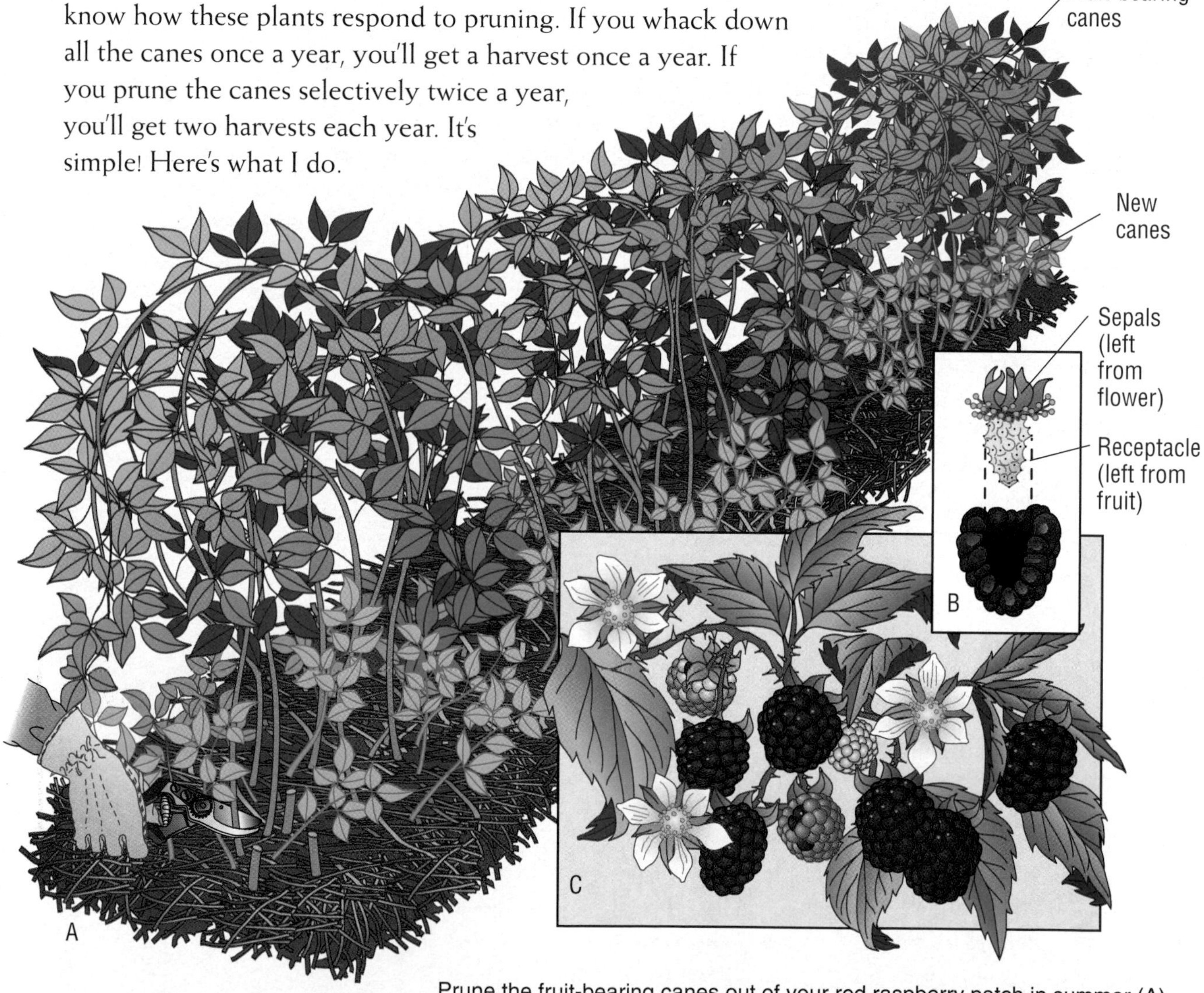

Fruit-bearing canes

New canes

Sepals (left from flower)

Receptacle (left from fruit)

Prune the fruit-bearing canes out of your red raspberry patch in summer (A) when they're easy to identify by the remnants of flowers and fruit (B). You'll be rewarded with a bountiful crop of berries (C) in summer and fall.

Plant fallbearers in spring. There are two types of red raspberries: summerbearing types and fallbearing types. To get an extra harvest, you need to buy fallbearing raspberries (they're also called everbearing—which is what they'll be if you prune selectively). I like fallbearers best anyway because they produce a crop the first year you set the plants out. Summerbearing red raspberries don't produce any fruit until their second growing season.

Choose virus-free fallbearing plants to avoid disease problems and set them out in your garden in early spring. Choose a site in full sun with well-drained soil. Center the raspberries in beds that are 3 feet wide and 8 feet apart. Space the plants 3 feet apart, water them well, then mulch the entire bed with 6 to 8 inches of straw. The mulch will keep weeds out of the patch and hold moisture in the soil, which helps ensure a good harvest.

Pick and choose. Red raspberries need regular pruning to stay healthy and productive. That's because their canes only live for two growing seasons, then they die and are replaced by new canes. You need to keep the old, nonfruiting canes pruned away so there's room for new canes. Pruning also prevents disease problems.

People who grow fallbearing red raspberries usually fall into one of two camps, each with a different method of pruning. The first camp uses what I call the "mow and go" method. They harvest their berries in fall, then mow all of the canes down each winter. This is certainly an easy way to handle pruning—all you need is a heavy-duty lawn mower or a sturdy pair of pruning shears. The plants will put up all new shoots in spring, and they'll produce a good crop of fall berries. It's a good method if you're short on time, but you'll sacrifice the summer harvest.

I'm a member of the second camp, which uses the "pick and choose" method. By removing canes selectively, I get a summer harvest in addition to the regular fall crop. Here's how it works.

Let your plants stand after the fall harvest instead of cutting them down. The following spring, the plants will put up new canes, which will fruit in fall. The older canes from the previous year will give you a small but tasty crop of berries in summer. As soon as the summer harvest is over, cut the fruit-bearing canes level with the ground. The fruit-bearing canes are easy to identify right after the harvest, which makes summer pruning simple.

Prune and feed in winter. In late winter, prune your plants a second time to keep the patch in bounds and space the canes properly. Narrow rows, just 1 foot wide, are easy to work on and provide the air circulation plants need to stay healthy. Cut canes outside the narrow rows first. Then remove canes within the rows, so you're left with three to five healthy, evenly spaced canes per foot of row. Take out skinny canes and leave the sturdy ones. After pruning, side-dress the plants with compost so they'll have plenty of energy for next year's crop.

When spring rolls around again, you'll have a bed with last season's canes and a set of new canes. And the process will begin all over again. You'll always get two crops of berries per year—a summer crop from the old canes and a fall crop from the new canes.

Buyer Beware

Buy virus-free plants to start your red raspberry patch. Plants that you get from friends or neighbors may carry viruses, which will doom your chances for a productive bed. Wild brambles carry viruses too, so keep them 1,000 feet away from your planting. If you end up with infected plants, the only option is to destroy them—there is no cure.

Purchase virus-free plants from reputable nurseries that specialize in raspberries. (See "Sources" on page 228 for mail-order nursery recommendations.)

21 Mow Better Strawberries

You've got to renovate strawberry plants and direct their runner growth yearly, or they'll get overcrowded and yields will plummet. Typically, renovating and training are big jobs that involve pruning leaves, stems, and runners, and lots of raking, digging, and replanting. I'm always on the lookout for an easier way, so when I discovered this lawn mower method for renovating strawberries and controlling runners, I knew I had it made!

Runner

Baby strawberry plant

You can prune off excess strawberry runners by hand, but a mower will do just as good a job in much less time. If you've got a mower bag, you can forget about raking the prunings and move on to more pleasant tasks. A mower comes in handy in fall too when it's time to renovate the plants by cutting off old leaves and stems.

Make the beds with your mower in mind. A lawn mower is a great tool for working with strawberries, but it needs space to operate. Dig strawberry beds that are 3 feet wide and as long as you like. Be sure to leave a mower's width of space between beds. Then, work the soil about 6 inches deep with a spading fork or tiller, adding compost as you go.

If you live in Zones 3 through 6, set out your plants in early spring, as soon as you can work the soil. In Zones 7 through 10, plant in fall or late winter. Use what's known as the "matted row" growing system. Plant a line of strawberries down the center foot of the bed, spacing the plants 18 inches apart in the row. Mulch the entire bed with 4 to 6 inches of straw to keep weeds out.

Hold them back until they're ready. As spring turns into summer, your new strawberry plants will grow and develop. Remove any flowers that appear during the first three months after planting so the plants put their energy into making strong root systems. If the strawberries put out runners—long stems that form new strawberry plants at their nodes—trim them off too. Just run the mower between the rows! In the fall after the ground freezes, mulch the plants with more straw to protect them from winter cold and winds.

Let strawberries plant themselves. In spring, pull the mulch away from the strawberry crowns. The plants will be ready to grow and give you a full crop of berries. They'll produce a generous supply of runners too—let them fill in the space between the mother plants with babies.

Keep the runners within 18 inches of the mother plants by cutting off runners that wander farther away. You'll only need to prune the extra runners off every three weeks or so, and you can make quick work of that job with…the lawn mower.

Renovate the easy way. When the strawberry plants go dormant in fall, but before hard winter sets in, it's time to renovate the bed. Get out your lawn mower and set it as high as necessary so you don't chop off the plants' crowns. Mow off the leaves and stems and collect them in your lawn mower bag or rake them out of the bed. Toss the leaves and stems in the compost bin unless you see signs of disease—in that case, put them in the trash.

Now, dig up any strawberries that have wandered out of your 18-inch-wide rows and pull up any weeds. Thin the baby strawberry plants so they are at least 6 inches apart. Then put an inch of compost over the entire bed to keep the soil productive. When the ground freezes, mulch the plants with straw for winter.

That's it. Just keep mowing and spacing plants as needed over the years. After three years, you should start over in a new bed with fresh, disease-resistant, virus-free plants. That way you can avoid trouble with deadly fungal diseases such as fusarium or verticillium wilt.

Stretch the Strawberry Season

For lots of fruit over a long season, I plant two different types of strawberries—Junebearers and everbearers. Junebearers are daylength-sensitive. That means that they need long days to produce flowers, set fruit, and ripen their big crops of berries. These summer strawberries are great for freezing and for pies, because they produce most of their fruit over a couple of weeks in June or July (they may produce as early as April in California and Florida). You can buy Junebearers that ripen in early-, mid-, or late-season. Choose some cultivars that ripen at each time and you can stretch the season. But what about the rest of the summer and fall?

That's where everbearing strawberries come in. Day-neutral everbearers provide a regular supply of berries to snack on all summer until frost. You can also plant standard everbearers, which produce a big spring crop and a smaller fall crop. Either way, you'll have tasty strawberries to eat for a good long time!

22 Double Your Harvest—Grow Vines on Fruit Trees

It doesn't seem to matter how much garden space you have—it's never enough. The apple tree is right where you want to put a grapevine. Well, don't let a lack of "floor" space stop you. Grow fruiting vines up into the fruit trees in your yard. You'll get a double harvest of fruit from the same space, and you won't have to build any vine trellises!

Grapevine — Semidwarf apple tree — Mini-pumpkin vine — Semidwarf cherry tree

You stack things on top of each other in the house when you need more space, why not in the garden? Semidwarf fruit trees make outstanding living trellises for grapes and vegetables such as cucumbers and small-fruited pumpkins. You can even grow large-fruited plants such as winter squash, watermelons, and gourds if you tie cloth or panty-hose slings from branch to branch to support the fruits.

Get your vines off the ground. Trees and vines are more compatible than you think. After all, vines grow on trees in nature—that's the way they're designed. Take a look at the woods in the East and Midwest. You'll see lots of wild grapes dangling from trees, and neither the tree nor the vine is any the worse for the arrangement.

Grapes aren't the only vines that thrive in trees. You can train beans, cucumbers, gourds, small melons, peas, and even squash vines to reach for the sky too. These mild-mannered vines won't cause your trees any problems. You may get a little less tree fruit each year where the vine leaves shade out developing fruit buds. But the vine crop will more than make up for what you lose from the host tree. And fruits like apples often overproduce anyway and need a bit of thinning.

Semidwarf fruit trees, which grow 12 to 15 feet tall, make great living trellises for all kinds of vines. Of course you can use any kind of tree (even non-fruiting ones) to support a vine. But fruit trees make a great addition to your landscape, and I recommend planting a few.

Start vines off right. Choose which kind of vine you want to grow and plant it several feet away from the tree trunk in spring. Work a shovelful of compost into the soil as you plant. Lean a bamboo or wooden pole from the young vine into a lower branch of the tree. Most climbing vines will easily find their way into the tree if you get them started up the pole, but grapes need a bit more help.

Tie 'em up. Use plant ties to direct the longest grape shoot up the pole during its first growing season. In the second growing season, remove all shoots but that longest one and use your fingernail to nick out all but the five end buds. This longest shoot will become the grapevine's trunk. Once the new growth reaches the limbs of the tree, gently tie them in place. You can remove the ties once the vine gets a good grip on the branches. Keep all new growth pruned off the lower part of the grapevine to encourage more topgrowth.

Haul in the harvest. Vines will head for the light once they get into the tree. That means the flowers and fruit will tend to form along the outside of the tree where it's easiest to harvest. Just image getting grapes and apples from the same tree in fall! It's kind of like growing a living fruit bowl.

Don't Judge a Garden by Looks Alone

In summer, your tree and vine combinations may look jumbled, even a bit messy. You'll get used to that look in a hurry. After all, you're getting twice the food from a single space.

I got hooked on the jumbled look on my first visit to France. I traveled to the beautiful region of the Dordogne, where I ran into Rene Maquet. This fellow lived alone in a small two-room house without windows, with a rough fireplace, and with hundreds of potted plants in various stages of growth everywhere.

We took a ride to one of his farm fields, neatly laid out and carefully cultivated with a small tractor he owned. On the way back to his place, he asked me if I wanted to see his garden. I said sure. We drove a few miles on a two-lane blacktop road, and then a half mile down a dirt road.

He stopped the car by an overgrown weed patch being taken over by young trees. He smiled. "Where's your garden?" I asked. "Right there," he said, pointing at the weed patch. "Go in. Look around."

I did and discovered to my astonishment that this overgrown jungle was no weed patch at all. Grapes, melons, cucumbers, and more grew into the small trees, which were not trash trees, but apples, cherries, peaches, plums, and pomegranates. The "weeds" were herbs like dill and big plants of clary sage. Nearer the ground grew thyme and oregano, and everywhere were individual lettuces, strawberry plants, beets, chard, and riots of vines bearing watermelons—all of it tumbled together into as productive a quarter acre as I've ever seen anywhere.

23

Drape Vines over Shrubs for Showers of Flowers

Look around your yard—I bet you've already got several of the simplest, showiest, and least expensive vine supports around: shrubs. Those unassuming mounds of green can turn your yard into a display garden in a single season, with a little help from a vine. You won't need to buy or build arbors, fences, pergolas, trellises, or walls to create a fabulous display of flowering vines.

Clematis 'Niobe' and a 'Gruss an Aachen' floribunda rose make a beautiful summer-blooming combination. The rose gives the clematis vine support and shades its roots, while the clematis blooms turn the rose into a garden centerpiece.

Choose vines carefully. Make sure you pick light, airy vines to grow over shrubs, since the idea is to decorate the plant, not smother it. Probably the most useful vine of this sort is the large-flowered Jackman clematis (*Clematis × jackmanii*). This vine has a natural talent for displaying itself with other plants. It twines its stems around shrub and tree branches so it's barely visible until its starry flowers open wide in summer. Jackman clematis has a wide growing range (Zones 5 to 9), but will die back to the ground each winter in the coldest areas. These vines bloom on new growth that emerges in spring, so you'll always have plenty of flowers.

Clematis vines are great for adding color and glamour to shrubs with small or inconspicuous blooms like euonymus (*Euonymus* spp.) and privets (*Ligustrum* spp.), or for accenting shrubs with showy foliage like smokebush (*Cotinus coggygria*). They really put on a show scrambling over evergreen shrubs like junipers, too.

Give your vines a boost. It doesn't take much effort to get a flowering vine like clematis to grow into a shrub or small tree. Plant the vine in spring, about a foot away from the shrub you want to decorate. Amend the planting area with a shovelful of compost before planting.

The vine will take care of the training itself by arranging its stems throughout the shrub so they get enough light. If the shrub is pruned into a tree form, or if you want to train vines into small trees, run a piece of rope or twine from the tree to the ground to direct the vines.

Plan on roses for grand combinations. One of the most useful and beautiful shrubs to combine with clematis is the shrub rose. This is a pairing made in heaven. Clematis is leggy and bare at its base, and likes to have its roots and lower stems shaded. Its top, on the other hand, makes a lovely spray of pretty leaves and gorgeous, wide-open flowers in shades of white, blue, pink, purple, and red. Shrub roses are, not surprisingly, shrubby plants that hide and shade the base of the clematis vines. The rounded rose flowers create a nice contrast to the wide, flat clematis blooms. You can't go wrong when it comes to color combinations for these two plants either—the possibilities are endless, and watching your choices bloom is a thrill.

If you'd like to grow roses like vines and send them up into shrubs and small trees, choose one of the many climbing roses available. The most vigorous climbers will need a hard yearly pruning to keep them manageable.

Favorite Pairings

Notice when your favorite shrubs and vines bloom and pretty soon you'll start thinking of great combinations. Here are a few of my favorites.

Blue mist shrub and nasturtiums. Blue-fringed flowers cover the blue mist shrub (*Caryopteris x clandonensis* 'Heavenly Blue') from August to frost. It's hardy in Zones 5 to 9. In late summer, let vining nasturtium twine through the shrub, splashing it with intense orange, red, and yellow color.

Summersweet and scarlet clematis. Look for the pink flower spires of summersweet (*Clethra alnifolia* 'Pinkspire') in July and August. That's when scarlet clematis (*Clematis texensis*) opens its little urn-shaped, scarlet blooms too. This combo works in Zones 4 through 8.

Rose-of-Sharon and a climbing rose. When the blue flowers of this rose-of-Sharon (*Hibiscus syriacus* 'Blue Bird') open in August, the pink blooms of 'Climbing Cécile Brunner' will be there to greet them. Grow this twosome in Zones 5 through 9.

Bridalwreath spirea and perennial sweet pea. In early spring the dainty white flowers of bridalwreath spirea (*Spiraea prunifolia*) open. When they finish blooming, the perennial sweet pea vine (*Lathyrus latifolius*) opens its rose-pink, red, or white flowers for a summer show in Zones 5 through 8.

24 Willow Water Works Wonders on Woody Cuttings

Have you ever made a fence of willow branches, then watched in amazement as your "fence" sprouted and grew into trees? Willow branches contain a natural rooting hormone so they're easy to grow, but cuttings from other trees and shrubs are much harder to root. Should you give up rooting difficult plants? No way! Give your woody cuttings the same advantage willows have by soaking them in willow water before planting.

12"

Willow water is an all-natural rooting hormone that's a cinch to make. Crush 12-inch-long willow cuttings to loosen the wood fibers, then cut the mashed branches into 2-inch-long pieces. Fill a jar with the willow pieces, then cover them with water and let the mix stand for a couple of days before using it.

Take a swing at making willow water. In the spring, willows have lots of rooting hormone concentrated in their branch tips—it's a good time to make willow water and a good time to take cuttings of most woody plants.

When you see weeping willow branches showing their yellow-green new leaves, take your pruners and cut off the tips of the slender branches, making your cuttings about a foot long. Gather several dozen willow branch tips.

Lay the cut branches on the floor or sidewalk and crush them with a baseball bat, hammer, or similar tool. You don't have to beat them to a pulp; just crush them lightly so the wood fibers are loosened a little. Then cut the branch tips into 2-inch pieces and stuff a quart jar full of them. Fit as many willow pieces into the jar as you can and fill it with water. The rooting hormone in willow branch tips is soluble in water, so soaking the branch tips trans-fers the hormone to the water. Let the pieces soak for a couple of days, then pour some of the liquid into a short container like a plastic freezer container or small jar.

Take fresh cuttings of the plants you want to root and stand them up in the container of willow water. Cover the stems with liquid to just below the leaves. Allow the cuttings to soak in the willow water for a day before transplanting them into pots.

Getting Started with Softwood Cuttings

Lots of woody plants are easy to propagate if you take cuttings from the succulent new soft growth they put out in spring or summer. You'll have good luck with azaleas, cotoneasters, forsythias, lilacs, magnolias, photinias, pyracanthas, spireas, summersweet, weigelas, and many other woody plants if you follow these steps.

1. Using a sharp knife or pruning shears, cut 3- to 6-inch-long cuttings off the branch tips, then snip the leaves off the bottom half of each cutting. Trim extra-large leaves in half by cutting each one across its middle. This reduces the leaf surface so the cuttings lose less water and have a better chance of surviving.

2. Soak the cuttings in willow water, then pot them up in a sterile potting mixture—a mix of half sand and half peat will do the trick.

3. Place the potted cuttings in a spot that gets afternoon shade so they don't bake on warm days, and set them in a cold frame or inside a plastic bag to keep them from drying out.

When you water the cuttings, use the leftover willow water. Water frequently to keep their rooting ends moist. Keep the soil moist but not soggy. In two to four weeks your cuttings will have roots, and you can move them to individual pots or a nursery bed to finish growing.

You can take softwood cuttings of woody plants like azaleas from early spring to late summer after the branches leaf out. The stems should be flexible but mature enough to break when you bend them (A). Soak the cuttings in willow water to encourage quick rooting (B).

Mountains of Mums and Masses of Asters

When it comes to mums and asters, I like blooms—masses and fountains and cascades of colorful flowers! Sure you can thin out the buds so you'll only have a few big spectacular flowers, but I prefer plants covered, even smothered, with blooms. And I get them! Here's how I do it.

Single

Spider

Decorative

Pompon

Mums are a must if you're looking for fall color. Choose hardy decorative, pompon, and single types for your flowerbeds, and leave the less hardy fancy types like spider mums for greenhouse growers. Once your plants are in place, divide and pinch them in spring to guarantee spectacular results.

56

Don't leave them alone. Lots of gardeners buy mums and asters, plant them, and let them be. They'll bloom all right, but by leaving these plants alone, you're missing out on the big show. A little care will guarantee you fountains of fall blooms, right when you need a splash of color most.

Mums and asters are perennials. They die back to the ground each winter, then return each spring when their winter-hardy roots send up new shoots. These tough plants grow so vigorously in good, rich, loose soil that they need to be divided often. If you don't divide and replant them, the plants get overcrowded and the centers of the plants get woody and die out. Asters need dividing every other year, and chrysanthemums will thrive if you divide them every year or two. I like to make things easy, so I divide my mums one year and my asters the next. That way I have a smaller job each spring and my plants stay in good shape.

The great divide. Each spring, you'll notice that mums and asters put out growth around the outer edge of last year's clump. This new growth is what you want to keep, since the old center growth won't bloom. Here's how to rejuvenate these clumps of new and old growth.

In early spring, when the plant's new growth is just a couple of inches tall, dig up the entire clump with a shovel. Slice the new growth free of the old woody center of the plant, then replant the new growth and discard the old part. See the illustration on page 19.

Pinch those plants back twice. Starting new clumps of mums or asters regularly ensures that your plants have plenty of room to grow and bloom their best. But there's one more step to getting more flowers. Both mums and asters tend to produce blooms at the tips of their stems. So, the more stems plants have, the more flowers they'll produce.

There's a simple technique for making mums and asters bushy so they'll make more blooms, and it's called pinching. Here's how to do it. When the emerging plant stems are 6 inches tall in the spring, use your fingers or pruning shears to pinch out the top ½ inch of growth, back to the first leaf. This stops the stem from putting all its grow power into the tip and forces it to produce sideshoots from leaf axils all over the plant. When these sideshoots are 6 inches long, pinch back their tips by ½ inch or so. Depending on the length of your growing season and when the flowers bloom, you may have time for a third pinch.

The time it takes your plants to go from forming flower buds to blooming is what horticultur-

Mums don't mind getting pinched. Removing the top ½ inch of growth makes plants bushier and sturdier.

ists call the "response time." If you pinch too late in the season, your plants may not have time to develop new buds and bloom. Most mums have response times of 7 to 12 weeks, so to be on the safe side, make your last pinch when there are still 12 weeks before your mums or asters bloom.

In Zones 5 to 7, which includes most of the middle part of the country, asters bloom from late August through September, and chrysanthemums bloom from September through November. Their exact bloom times will vary depending on which zone you're in and by the kind of chrysanthemum you're growing. For example, different types of mums (known as "classes") will start flowering anywhere from September 15 to November 15 in Zone 7. Check with your garden club to find out what blooms when in your area.

26 Delightful Delphiniums All Season Long

Beauty doesn't have to be fleeting—at least when it comes to delphiniums. Typically these plants put on a beautiful, though short, show from late June to early July. But, with some planning and know-how, you can have blooming delphiniums in your garden through most of the growing season! Here's a trick that will make your neighbors scratch their heads in wonder.

Stretch the delphinium season all the way into fall with potted plants and strategic pruning. Potted plants (left) will flower in summer, and again in fall, if you cut them back after blooming. And garden-grown delphiniums will bloom straight through summer and fall if you cut off some flower spikes (right) before they open to stagger the bloom times.

Go shopping. Get started by purchasing some small, thrifty seedlings the year before your year-long season of display. (Two or three dozen plants will put on a beautiful show.) Usually these seedlings come in 4-inch pots. Plant half of the seedlings in your garden and leave half potted, moving them to larger-size pots as needed. Start by transferring the potted plants to 6-inch pots, then 8-inch pots, and finally, by the end of the season, 10-inch pots. Their potting medium should be compost mixed with one-quarter sand.

During the spring, keep the potted plants where they get lots of sunlight, but by early June, move them to a spot where they get afternoon shade. Feed all of your delphinium plants two or three times during this first year with compost or manure tea. Whenever flower buds appear, pinch them out, but never remove any leafy growth. You're building big roots for the next season, so you need all the leaves you can get.

Late to bed and early to rise. Your potted delphiniums will go dormant in late October or November. That's the time to move the pots to a spot where they won't get trampled. Hill soil up around the pots and cover them with mulch. Put a light covering of straw or chopped leaf mulch over the garden-grown plants too.

The following spring, when the potted plants show signs of growth, pull the pots out of their winter beds and place them by a south wall, preferably one made of stone or brick for the warmth. Feed the delphiniums with a side-dressing of rich compost, and keep feeding them with manure tea every time you water until they flower. The combination of the wall's warmth and the fertilizer will stimulate them to bloom quickly, usually a full month earlier than plants grown in the ground.

Thin, stake, and snip. When the potted plants send up flower spikes, thin out all that are slimmer than a pencil. Leave just one to three spikes per pot (the more vigorous the plants are, the more spikes you can leave). By now you'll see new growth emerging on the delphiniums that overwintered in the ground. Move the potted flowers to your delphinium bed and plant them, pot and all, in the soil to start your season-long show. Next, set out stakes to support the flower spikes of all the delphiniums.

Now start looking for the first flower buds on the garden-grown plants. When you see buds, snip the flower spikes on one-third of the plants back to 8 inches tall. Let the remaining flowerstalks grow until you see that their flower buds are fully formed and ready to open.

Then cut one-third of the developed spikes back to about a foot tall. (The cut spikes will open if you put them in vases and bring them in the house.) Make sure that you thin the spikes on all the plants you allow to flower, whether they're garden- or pot-grown. Leave only the most vigorous spikes for the most spectacular blooms.

When the potted delphiniums finish blooming, the uncut flower spikes in your garden will open their florets and continue the bloom season. Remove the potted plants from the garden as soon as the flowers fade, and cut back the spikes nearly to the ground. Keep these plants well watered and fed, and they'll grow and put up bloom stalks again in fall. When the potted plants get ready to bloom again, put them back in the delphinium bed for the final show.

Fall-flowering delphiniums. Meanwhile, what's happening to the delphiniums that are in the ground? After the uncut plants have finished blooming, the plants that were cut back to 8 inches will come into bloom. They'll be followed by the plants you cut back to 1 foot. This last group will flower in September, perhaps even into October. And they'll overlap with the second flowering of your potted plants for a really big show.

27 Create a Low-Maintenance Lawn with Flowers and Herbs

Green grass lawns are great if you've got heavy foot traffic, but chances are a lot of your lawn doesn't get that much wear and tear. Those low-use areas are where I plant spreading flowers, herbs, and ground covers. They're a lot more interesting—and a lot less work—than grass.

Roman chamomile

Woolly yarrow

Ajuga

Lawn grass

With a good start, plants such as ajuga, Roman chamomile, and yarrow will grow until they touch and make a seamless ground cover. Remember that large areas of just a few grass substitutes interwoven in a free-form planting look better than many different grass substitutes planted in a hodgepodge of small areas.

Choose plants that match your site. There are grass substitutes that will fit any conditions you've got, including shade (pachysandra and periwinkle), partial shade (ajuga and barren strawberry), and sun (mother-of-thyme and Roman chamomile), as well as dry and wet soils. Just make sure you choose plants that can take some foot traffic so you don't lose the use of your lawn. (Add footpaths if you want an herbal lawn in a high-traffic area.) Most grass substitutes like good, moist topsoil to get started in. But some, including yarrow and the thymes, will tolerate poor soil—a handy trait when you're trying to plant areas where your grass struggles.

Get rid of the grass. Start with a small area in an out-of-the-way part of your lawn. Use a spade or sod cutter to cut and lift the sod off in strips in spring. You can use the sod pieces to patch a worn spot of grass or sod a new area. Or, turn the pieces of sod upside down and stack them to create a quick compost pile that will break down into rich soil.

Plant replacements. Spread good topsoil or a few inches of compost (make sure it's free of weed seeds) over the bare earth. Then plant seedlings or direct-seed your grass substitutes. You'll need lots of plants to cover a lawn area, so use seeds when you can find them. Many lawn sub-

stitutes are only available as plants, so buy them in flats at a nursery or through mail-order

catalogs that offer quantity discounts. See "Sources" on page 228 for recommendations.

Plot Before You Plant

You'll save lots of money and planting time if you find out how many plants you need before you buy. Start by measuring the area you want to plant. Then draw the shape of the planting area on a sheet of graph paper, letting each square represent 3, 6, 12, or more inches—whatever it takes to fit your plan on one sheet of paper. Count how many plants you'll need using the spacing listed on pages 62–63 or the recommendations from the nursery or mail-order company where you bought your plants.

Many grass substitutes have a spreading or even invasive habit—that's how they can stand up to abuse like foot traffic. These plants get established quickly, but they'll also run into your flowerbeds and borders. Like grass, most ground covers need edging strips or edge maintenance to keep them in bounds. (Lucky for you, most lawn substitutes aren't as hard to control as lawn grass. Grass is persistently invasive, with its underground stolons always reaching for new territory.) If invasive plants make you nervous, choose the less-aggressive herbs, such as chamomile and thyme, for your lawn.

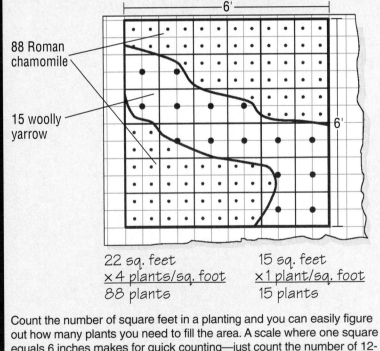

88 Roman chamomile

15 woolly yarrow

22 sq. feet
×4 plants/sq. foot
88 plants

15 sq. feet
×1 plant/sq. foot
15 plants

Count the number of square feet in a planting and you can easily figure out how many plants you need to fill the area. A scale where one square equals 6 inches makes for quick counting—just count the number of 12-inch squares in each planting. In this example, the yarrow takes up 15 square feet and is spaced 12 inches apart. It will take 15 plants to fill the area. The Roman chamomile takes up 22 square feet, but since the plants are spaced 6 inches apart, you'll need four times that many.

(continued)

Super Lawn Substitutes

Unless specified as toughies that can take a lot of traffic, the following plants tolerate some foot traffic, but not heavy use. Use them in a part of the yard where you don't walk or play frequently. Plant a mix of flowering and edible herb ground covers and you'll not only have a low-maintenance lawn, but one that smells good, looks good, and is tasty too!

Name	Description	Growing Hints
Woolly yarrow (*Achillea tomentosa*)	A covering of grayish hairs makes this plant's aromatic leaves look woolly. Let woolly yarrow grow and it will produce pale yellow flowers and reach 8 to 12 inches tall.	These plants do not like high heat and humidity and are best for northern yards. They like full sun and will thrive even in poor soil. Mow plants in areas where you walk to keep them low. Set plants 1 foot apart. Zones 3 to 7.
Ajuga or bugleweed (*Ajuga reptans*)	These 4- to 10-inch-tall plants come in a variety of leaf colors, including green; bronze purple; a mix of white, pink, and green; and gray green. The leaves look leathery and are topped by spikes of blue or white flowers in spring or early summer.	You can grow this ground cover in sun or shade in well-drained soil. It tolerates dry shade, which makes it a particularly useful lawn-substitute for tree-filled lawns. Set plants 12 to 15 inches apart. Zones 3 to 9.
Mountain sandwort (*Arenaria montana*)	These 2- to 4-inch-tall creeping plants spread to form a carpet of narrow grasslike green leaves. White flowers appear in late spring or early summer.	Plant in full sun in the North, and partial shade in the South. Mountain sandwort grows best in well-drained soil and only needs water during dry spells. Set plants 1 foot apart. Zones 3 to 8.
Roman chamomile (*Chamaemelum nobile*)	This herb forms a thick sweet-smelling mat of bright green lacy leaves if you keep it mowed. The leaves grow only 2 inches tall but the flowerstalks reach 12 inches tall.	Sow Roman chamomile seed in full sun in well-drained soil. If you're setting out plants, space them 6 inches apart. Zones 3 to 8.
Crown vetch (*Coronilla varia*)	This plant spreads by rhizomes (underground stems) and makes an 18-inch-tall, thick, sprawling mat. It's covered with pink and white cloverlike flowers during the summer.	Here's a good choice for dry, well-drained sites in full sun. Use crown vetch on slopes and in places where you can't mow. Keep it away from flowerbeds or it may take over. Set plants 1 to 2 feet apart. Zones 3 to 9.
Mock strawberry (*Duchesnea indica*)	Strawberry-like leaves form an attractive mat just 2 to 3 inches tall. Fruits look like little strawberries, but they aren't good to eat.	Grow plants in full sun or partial shade in any type of soil. Keep this spreader away from flowerbeds— it's invasive. Set plants 1 foot apart. Zones 4 to 10.
Winter creeper (*Euonymus fortunei*)	This mat-forming evergreen ground cover grows 1 to 2 feet tall. Its long vining stems root and spread like crazy. For small spaces, try the 3- to 4-inch-tall cultivar 'Kewensis'.	Winter creeper thrives in sun or partial shade which makes it a good choice for difficult areas like banks. Set plants in well-drained soil. Space seedlings 1 to 2 feet apart. Zones 5 to 9.
English ivy (*Hedera helix*)	Lustrous evergreen leaves grow on vines that just keep spreading. Plants stay 6 to 8 inches tall when grown as a ground cover. The vines will climb 90 feet tall on trees and walls.	Plant English ivy in full sun or dense shade. This vine can be invasive so grow it far from lawns and gardens. Mow or prune English ivy to keep it under control and to direct it where you want. Set plants 2 feet apart. Zones 5 to 9.

Name	Description	Growing Hints
Rupturewort (*Herniaria glabra*)	This 1- to 3-inch-tall herb forms a dainty mat. It's covered with tiny succulent leaves that are evergreen in Zones 8 and 9 and deciduous in cooler zones.	Rupturewort grows very slowly. Use it in small areas like between paving stones, or mix it with other slow-growing ground covers to fill in larger areas. Set plants 6 inches apart. Zones 4 to 9.
Creeping Jenny (*Lysimachia nummularia*)	Rounded leaves and yellow flowers look nice all summer long. Trailing stems root where they touch the ground. Plant golden creeping Jenny (*L. nummularia* 'Aurea') near flowerbeds—it's less invasive. 'Aurea' is named for its yellow leaves that turn lime green in summer.	This is one of the best ground covers for moist areas. It prefers full sun in cool climates and partial or full shade in warm climates. Keep creeping Jenny away from lawn areas or it may invade. Set plants 8 inches apart. Zones 3 to 8.
Mazus (*Mazus reptans*)	This creeper grows only an inch or two tall. It has bronzy green leaves that are evergreen in warm climates. Tubular purple flowers bloom just above the mat of foliage in spring and early summer.	Give mazus a site in full sun or partial shade with rich, well-drained soil. Set plants 1 foot apart. Zones 5 to 8.
Japanese pachysandra (*Pachysandra terminalis*)	Shiny, toothed, evergreen leaves make this ground cover look attractive year-round. The plants grow 8 to 10 inches tall. Look for creamy white flower clusters in spring.	Plant this ground cover in partial or full shade. It prefers fertile, moist soil. Pachysandra's spreading rhizomes will cover bare areas fast but aren't hard to control. Set plants 10 inches apart. Zones 4 to 8.
Moss pink (*Phlox subulata*)	Small needlelike leaves are evergreen and give this 6-inch-tall plant a mossy look. Masses of showy pink, purple, blue, or white flowers appear in spring.	Mow plants after flowering to keep them tidy, or just let them grow. Moss pinks need full sun and well-drained soil. They'll grow on slopes and they make good border plants since they aren't invasive. Set plants 1 foot apart. Zones 2 to 9.
Three-toothed cinquefoil (*Potentilla tridentata*)	This plant's three-leaflet leaves turn wine red in fall. Clusters of little white flowers appear in early summer. This mat-forming, semi-woody plant grows 1 foot tall.	Here's a ground cover that likes well-drained soil in full sun. It's a good choice for covering dry, rocky slopes. Set plants 1 to 2 feet apart. Zones 3 to 7.
Mother-of-thyme (*Thymus serpyllum*)	This herb grows 2 inches tall and spreads out to form dense mats of fragrant foliage. Clusters of purplish flowers bloom on 4-inch-tall stems during the summer.	Give plants full sun and a well-drained site where the soil isn't too rich and they'll thrive. Space thyme 8 inches apart. Zones 4 to 7.
Common periwinkle (*Vinca minor*)	Plant this evergreen vine in a spot where it can grow rampantly into 6- to 8-inch-tall mounds. Its tangled trailing stems root where they touch the ground. Lavender blue flowers set off the glossy leaves in spring.	This ground cover is a winner in shady areas near the house or under trees. It will grow in average or rich soil. You can shear the plants back in early summer for thicker growth. Set plants 2 feet apart. Zones 3 to 9.
Barren strawberry (*Waldsteinia fragarioides*)	This evergreen strawberry-look-alike makes a thick 6-inch-tall carpet. It produces small yellow flowers in spring, followed by hairy, inedible fruits.	This is a ground cover for partial shade or moist sunny areas. It likes humus-rich soil but will tolerate poorer sites. Space plants 2 feet apart. Zones 5 to 8.

Great Garden Ideas

for Summer

28 Grow Your Own Organic Mulches and Compost Boosters

There's no such thing as plant waste in my garden—every leaf and stalk has a use. Get double duty out of your garden plantings by growing herbs, foliage plants, and vegetables that you can also use as mulches and compost boosters.

Sunflower

Ornamental kale

Mint

Chopped-mint mulch

Sunflower-leaf mulch

Grass-clippings mulch

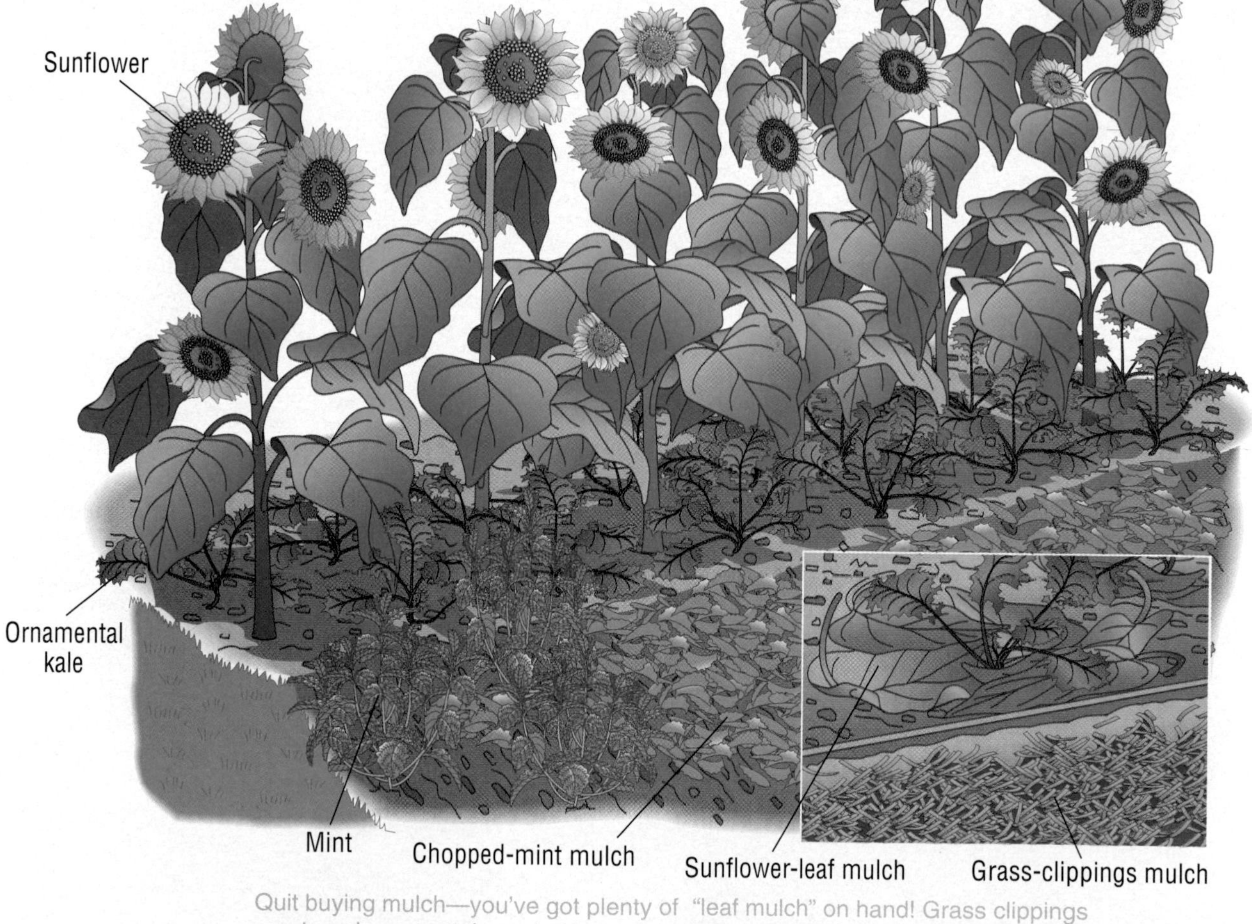

Quit buying mulch—you've got plenty of "leaf mulch" on hand! Grass clippings create a dense mat through which weeds have a hard time growing, and large leaves from vegetables or ornamental plants make quick thick mulches. Chopped herbs suppress weeds and also repel and confuse pest insects.

Big leaves cover lots of ground. Use large leaves from ornamental plants or vegetables as mulch anytime you need to cover bare ground quickly. Place two or three leaves on top of each other wherever you need extra weed control. There are always plenty of big-leaved plants to choose from. Strip the leaves off sunflowers after you harvest the seeds and use them to mulch fall crops of broccoli and cauliflower. Or cut large leaves off ornamentals such as bear's-breech (*Acanthus mollis*), bronzeleaf rodgersia (*Rodgersia podophylla*), and fingerleaf rodgersia (*R. aesculifolia*) for quick mulches.

If you need mulch early, before big-leaved ornamentals get growing, check out the leaves of a spring vegetable like rhubarb. I harvest the succulent red stems of my rhubarb in spring for strawberry-rhubarb pie. But instead of throwing out the leaves, I use them to mulch around bush squash. I grow several rhubarb plants around the garden because they make great ornamentals as well as excellent pies. Just be aware that the leaves are not edible and are, in fact, poisonous.

Once you try whole-leaf mulch, you'll see your plants in a new light. Whenever ornamental plants grow beyond their boundaries, you'll see mulch materials instead of overgrown plantings!

Lawn leaves smother weeds. Ordinary lawn clippings make one of the all-time-great mulches. They keep weeds away, hold in soil moisture, and add nitrogen and other nutrients to the soil as they break down. You can pile the clippings 4 to 6 inches deep around plants, depending on how bad your weed problem is. They'll mat down to a dense layer just a couple of inches thick.

In your planting beds, shake grass clippings over the bed so that the clippings fall helter-skelter, crisscrossing one another. When you've got a good 2 inches on the bed, move the mulch aside as needed to set in your plants. When you finish planting, tuck the clippings back around the transplants. Leave a little space between the clippings and plants so the stems get good air circulation—the air will help discourage diseases.

Stalks stop pests. You can turn corn leaves and stalks into excellent mulches by shredding them with a chipper/shredder or a lawn mower (see Idea #53 for details). If you can grow enough of them, the aromatic herbs like lavender, oregano, rosemary, sage, and thyme make wonderfully fragrant mulches. The chopped herbs not only suppress weeds, but their aromatic oils can confuse and repel insect pests.

Stick Stalks in the Compost Pile

The stems and stalks of plants make great mulch when you shred them. So what if you don't have a shredder? Leave the stalks whole and add them to your compost pile. The long hollow stems are perfect for getting air into the center of the pile, and that's just what you need for really hot compost.

As you build a compost pile layer by layer, place sunflower or corn stalks crisscross on top of each new layer of material. Cut the stalks so their ends stick out slightly beyond the edge of the pile. The stalks will decompose pretty quickly, leaving air channels from the outside to the center of the pile.

Other hollow-stemmed, fleshy stalks will also work wonders for getting air into the compost pile and promoting rapid decomposition. Try using the stems of bachelor's buttons, bee balm, dill, and fennel to make your compost pile cook.

Sunflower stalks

Layer plant stalks in generously to make your compost fixings quickly turn into black gold.

29 This Summer, Grow Gourmet Baby Vegetables

Miniveggies are all the rage in gourmet restaurants, where their flavor and appearance make them popular—and expensive. But the good news is that these tasty morsels aren't any more difficult or expensive to grow than regular-size vegetables. So don't wait for a night on the town to enjoy fresh miniveggies. Once you know which plants to grow, you can have full-flavored baby vegetables anytime you want.

Miniature and baby vegetable are irresistible in salads and stir-fries, and they make delectable pickles. Try miniature carrots, cucumbers, and tomatoes in salads, or pickle whole baby beets and baby corn for appetizers—you'll be hooked on the flavor and appearance of these tiny treats.

Begin with the basics. Mini-vegetables, like their full-size counterparts, need full sun, fertile soil, and plenty of water. Get them off to a good start by digging ½ inch of compost into the soil before planting seeds. Once the seeds have sprouted, surround the seedlings with 2 inches of mulch to hold moisture in the soil and keep competing weeds away. Use a soaker hose or bubbler as needed to make sure the plants are never drought stressed. When it comes to which plants to grow, you've got two choices—miniature or standard-size vegetables.

Give miniature veggies a try. Some vegetables just don't taste good until they've had a chance to mature and develop their full flavor. That's why many of the great "baby" veggies are miniatures—they're not really babies at all. Miniature vegetables are naturally small and won't grow beyond the size of baby vegetables even when they're mature.

Baby standard-size veggies. Some standard-size vegetables are full-flavored or just plain fun when harvested as babies. Here's a rundown of some of the best.

Beets. Although you can grow miniature beets, most baby beets taste just as good if you harvest them when they're the size of golf balls. You'll get plenty of flavor from baby beets of standard-size cultivars such as 'Chioggia', 'Detroit Dark Red', 'Golden', 'Red Ball', and 'Sangria'.

Corn. Plant any sweet corn cultivar and harvest the ears when the silks start to push out of the corn husks. The baby ears will be just 3 inches long—the perfect size for stir-frying whole or pickling for appetizers.

Potatoes. It's no secret that spuds are even more luscious young than when they're full grown at the end of the growing season. It's a gardening tradition to swipe young potatoes from under the plants while waiting for the main crop to come in.

Summer squash. You'll get great taste from 3- or 4-inch-long green and yellow zucchini, yellow crookneck, and pattypan squash. Harvest these squashes daily or they'll quickly grow beyond baby size.

Both miniature and baby vegetables will give you beautiful, flavorful harvests of tiny fruits, so why not try some of each?

A Gallery of Miniature Vegetables

Here's a sampling of popular miniature vegetables. There are lots of other minis available, so be sure to check seed catalogs for more. See "Sources" on page 228 for ordering information.

Name	Description
'Astrelle' mini filet beans	These choice green beans are mature when they're just ¼ inch in diameter and 3 to 4 inches long.
'Kleine Bol' beets	Harvest baby beets when the rootballs are just 1 to 1½ inches in diameter.
'Partima' carrots	You can grow this little ball-shaped carrot in containers.
'Cornichon' cucumbers	These warty little cukes make great 1- to 2-inch-long pickles, but they're also nice raw and sliced in salads.
'Bambino' eggplants	The round fruits are dark purple and grow 1 to 1½ inches in diameter on 1-foot-tall plants.
'Tom Thumb' lettuce	Use each 4- to 6-inch-tall rosette of leaves for an individual salad.
'Mei Qing Choi' pak choi	Use the vase-shaped heads in salads and stir-fries when they are just 6 inches tall.
'Waverex' peas	Each pod grows 2 to 3 inches long and contains 6 or 7 miniature peas.
'Fingerling' potatoes	Most of these mini-spuds are close to thumb-size when they're mature.
'Little Gem' mini romaine lettuce	Make a gourmet salad from vase-shaped heads that grow only 5 to 6 inches tall.
'Yellow Pear' tomatoes	It's easy to grow all the clusters of 1¾-inch-long yellow fruits you need on these vigorous vines.
'Market Express' Japanese turnips	Pick these white, round turnips when they reach 1 inch in diameter.

30 Harvest Three Foods from One Bean Plant

If you're short on space, you may think you don't have room to grow one type of bean for fresh eating and freezing, and another type for dried shell beans. Well, this is one time when you can have it all—plus a bonus crop! All you need to know is when and how to harvest.

It's summertime and the harvesting goes on and on if you grow pole beans up bean tepees. Make tepees by lashing the tops of six 8- to 10-foot-tall wooden poles together. Stand the poles up, spread the bottoms out, and push the ends into the ground. Plant five seeds around each pole, then thin the seedlings to three plants once they form true leaves. You'll soon reap harvests of flowers, followed by snap beans and dried beans.

Fresh bean pod

Scarlet runner bean flowers

Dried beans

Pick pole beans for a triple harvest. To grow three tasty crops in a small amount of space, choose one or more pole beans with good flavor and short growing seasons. I like the All-America Selection winner 'Kentucky Blue', but other cultivars would work just as well. Plant your beans in mid-June—you can grow them on tepees made of bamboo or wooden poles, or put them in after your pea crop and use the same trellis. (See Idea #11 for trellis-building instructions.)

Pole beans take about 60 days to mature and set a crop. Using typical harvest practices, you'll get two months of bean production before cold weather sets in and shuts the plants down. The harvest season varies a bit depending on where you live—you'll get a longer season in the Sun Belt, and a shorter one in the northerly states. But this trick to extend your harvest works no matter where you live. Just start harvesting before there are any beans on the vine and keep going until frost. Here's how you can get three different harvests from one bean plant.

First, nibble on fresh flowers. Start harvesting bean blossoms as soon as your beans start blooming. That's right, bean blossoms—if you've never tasted them, you're in for a treat. They have a wonderful, light flavor that's like fresh beans, and they're great in salads. For extra color, you can plant scarlet runner beans, which have tasty rich red blossoms—you can get three different crops from them too.

Take a few blossoms here and there from each vine, so that you don't denude the vine of blossoms entirely. (If you take *all* the blossoms, you won't get any beans!)

Second, sup on tender pods. When fresh green beans start forming on your vines, you're ready for your second harvest. Select pods that are young and not filled out, and they'll be nice and tender for fresh eating. Harvest the beans here and there on the vines, leaving the largest and longest pods to mature.

Serve fresh beans steamed or stir-fried, or freeze them for just-picked taste for future meals. Their full beany flavor is better than you'll get from most bush-type beans.

Third, dine on dried beans. The beans you leave on the vines will mature into your third crop—dried beans. You can let the beans dry on the vine, but the pods may still have a lot of moisture in them when the garden begins to shut down in late fall. In that case, dry them inside to get the best results.

To make sure your beans are dry enough for storing, pull up or cut off the bean plants at soil level and hang them upside down in a shed or garage. When the pods are brittle and the beans inside are hard, shell and store them.

When you're ready to use dried beans, soak them in water overnight, then discard the water. They're ready to cook as baked beans, or use them in chili, soups, or any other favorite bean dish.

How to Store Dried Beans

Dried beans need to be really dry—less than 10 percent moisture—or they may mold and rot in closed containers. How do you know when they're dry enough? Try this simple test. Cut a bean in half and press its middle with your thumbnail. It should be perfectly hard and unyielding even with strong pressure.

When the beans are hard all the way through, shell them out of their pods and store them in a paper bag in a warm, dark, dry place for four to six weeks. Then place them in a closed container like a jar and add a packet of powdered milk made by tying up a tablespoon or two of the milk powder in a paper towel. The powdered milk absorbs any moisture the beans give off, so they stay dry and mold-free.

If you can't get your beans dry enough, put them in resealable plastic freezer bags and store them in the freezer. They'll stay fresh and you won't have to worry about mold or rot.

31 Cut-and-Come-Again Broccoli

Bigger isn't always better, especially when it comes to crops that can resprout like broccoli. I start my plantings in summer, harvest big broccoli heads in fall, then coax the plants into sprouting delicious bite-size heads until frost! Those little heads don't look as impressive as the giant-size ones, but hey, you cut them up anyway, and they're just as tasty as the big guys!

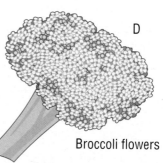

Broccoli flowers

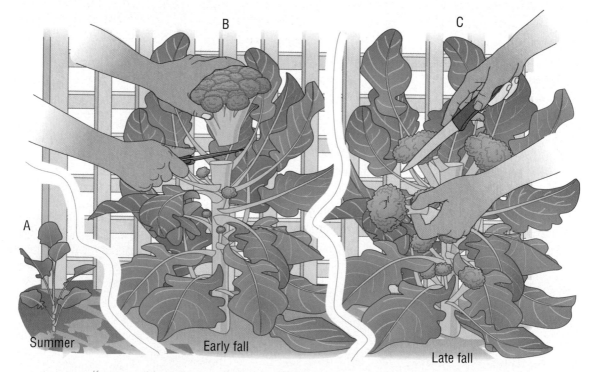

Summer

Early fall

Late fall

If you want to get a second harvest from your broccoli plants, you need to grow healthy, stocky seedlings (A). Take your first harvest in fall, cutting the main head off just below where the stems start to separate (B). Sideshoots will form in the leaf axils providing you with weeks of good eating (C). Always harvest before the flower buds open (D) or the plants will stop producing.

Start sowing in summer. Broccoli, like all the cabbage-family members (brussels sprouts, cauliflower, kale, and so on), prefers cool weather for growing. So why sow seeds in summer? Because, when you do, you'll get a broccoli crop when temperatures cool down in fall. (See the box on this page for tips on keeping summer seedlings cool.)

First, check the cultivar you're planting to see how many days it takes to produce a crop. You want your broccoli to mature in the cooling days of late August or early September. That's the best time to use the cut-and-come-again technique that prolongs your broccoli harvest for weeks. (This system works for spring plantings too, but I think summer plantings taste better.) Depending on which cultivar you choose, you'll plant your crop two to four months before the first frost hits.

After the harvest, let your plants grow. Broccoli has a habit of producing sideshoots from its leaf axils after you harvest the main head. So, instead of pulling the plant out of the ground after the main harvest, let the plants grow and produce sideshoots.

These sideshoots will only be the size of golf balls or small oranges, but there will be lots of them. Harvest the sideshoots before any of the tightly curled green buds open into yellow flowers, and the plants will continue producing broccoli right up until frost. Like me, you may find you actually prefer the smaller heads that mature in cool weather—they're extra-mild and great for eating raw with dips. (You won't have to wait until fall for little broccoli heads if you start a spring crop of broccoli raab. This tasty broccoli relative produces sideshoots the size of quarters.)

Let there be big sideshoots. And what if you can't get over the need to grow big broccoli heads? Not to worry. You can cut off all the sideshoots except for one, to force all of the plant's energy into producing one good-size secondary head. Just remember that letting all the sideshoots grow will produce more broccoli than you'll get from that one big head.

There's another alternative too. Seed companies know that gardeners like big broccoli and second harvests. To meet your needs, they've come up with cultivars like 'Bonanza' that produce secondary heads that can reach up to 5 inches across.

Keep Broccoli from Bolting

The secret to a flavorful main harvest of broccoli and plenty of secondary sideshoots is a stress-free life. (Isn't that what we're all looking for?) Luckily, with broccoli, it's pretty easy to supply. What broccoli plants want is steady, even growth, starting when they're seedlings and continuing through the heading stage. They need plenty of water and nutrients, and temperatures that never get much above 80°F.

Stress of any kind will stop the broccoli plant's growth and cause it to bolt (flower prematurely). The broccoli plant's reaction makes sense—it's trying to hurry and produce seeds before it's too late. But early flowers will put you out of the broccoli business, since the tight green clusters you eat are actually closely clustered flower buds. Once the plant flowers, the flavor and eating quality of the broccoli are ruined.

That's why it's important to raise strong, sturdy seedlings for fall crops and keep them cool. You can sow your broccoli crop beside a crop of tall plants like sunflowers so the plants get afternoon shade. Or, set up a trellis on the west side of the seedlings to help keep them cool. A 6-inch-deep layer of mulch will help keep young broccoli plants from overheating too. Consistent watering is critical, so use soaker hoses to keep the soil evenly moist, but not wet.

Two weeks before you sow broccoli seeds, add 1 inch of compost to the soil to make sure your plants get enough nutrients. After six weeks of growth, work a shovelful of compost into the soil around each plant to keep them well fed until harvest.

32 Tricks for Raising the Tastiest Brussels Sprouts Ever

Brussels sprouts get a bad rap. If you love them, I don't need to say any more. If you're wondering why you'd want those strong, bitter-tasting little green balls in your garden, then you've never tasted truly great brussels sprouts. Try the tricks I use and you'll find out how mild, tender, and flavorful home-grown brussels sprouts can be. And the fact that they're packed with vitamins and other nutrients doesn't hurt either.

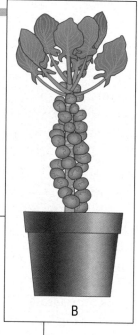

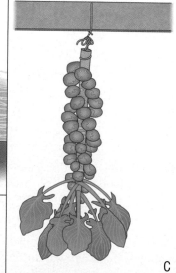

You've got three options for extending your brussels sprouts season. You can cover the plants when freezing weather threatens (A) or pot up the plants in late fall and bring them into a protected, unheated space like a garage (B)—both methods are described on the opposite page. If neither of these methods is to your liking, cut the stalks off at ground level at the end of the season and hang them upside down in an unheated room (C).

Nutrition and timing are everything. You may not believe it right now, but brussels sprouts can be one of the tastiest vegetables around—if they're grown right. What does "grown right" mean? Just that you need to supply the plants with good soil and time your harvests to hit after the first frosts.

Place plants carefully. Make sure you choose a "fresh" spot for your brussels sprouts. Pick a place where you haven't grown a member of the cabbage family (broccoli, cabbage, cauliflower, collards, kohlrabi, or radishes) for a couple of years. Fungal diseases like clubroot can build up in the soil if you plant one cabbage-family crop after another.

Plant 2 crops. It takes 80 to 100 days before brussels sprouts are ready to harvest. It's important to pick your sprouts after the first frost date because, like parsnips and kale, their flavor and quality improve tremendously after they've endured a few frosts. (Call your extension agent to check your first frost date.) You'll need to count back three months from the first frost date to determine the time to plant the first of your two crops.

If the first frost in your area generally occurs on October 15, for instance, you'd plant your brussels sprouts in mid-July. The first sprouts will begin to mature and be ready for harvest at just about the time the first light frosts are hitting.

The first hard, killing frost usually occurs three or four weeks after the first frost date. So plant a second crop of brussels sprouts 90 to 100 days before the killing frost to stretch your harvest. If the first hard, killing frost in your area occurs in mid-November, then you'd plant this late brussels sprouts crop about the first week of August.

Get the soil ready. Like other members of the cabbage family, brussels sprouts need full sun and humus-rich soil. Well-prepared soil will help ensure that your sprouts are flavorful, sweet, and mild. The time to amend the soil with lots of compost and leaf mold is in late June or early July. Two weeks before you plant seeds or transplants, add 30 pounds of compost per 100 square feet of garden space.

In long-season areas you can plant seeds in summer, but if you live where the growing season is short, you're better off with transplants. Mulch the plants with 2 inches of straw or grass clippings to keep the soil cooler and hold in moisture. Always keep the ground evenly moist.

Handy harvest hints. Start harvesting the sprouts from the first planting when they reach 1 inch in diameter. Smaller sprouts taste best, so don't let them get too big. Pick from the bottom of the stem, working upward as the sprouts mature. Remove the lower leaves as you harvest since that seems to speed up the growth of future sprouts.

The sprouts on your first planting will provide meals for six to eight weeks after the first frost. If a really bitter cold snap with lows in the mid to low teens sets in, keep the plants going by mounding leaves up around the stems. You can also bend the plants to the ground and cover them with mulch. And what about that second crop you planted? See the box on this page on storing brussels sprouts.

Storing Winter Sprouts

Your second crop of brussels sprouts will be ready for harvesting sometime in November in Zone 6—earlier in colder zones, later in warmer ones.

You can eat a few of the brussels sprouts fresh then store the rest in pots. Dig up the plants, roots and all, before the ground freezes. Replant the brussels sprouts in plastic pots with good drainage. Store the plants in an unheated, protected place where temperatures won't go much below 20°F—a porch or attached garage works well.

Water the brussels sprouts whenever their potting soil begins to get dry and these plants will supply you with sprouts through the winter..

33 Lettuce Loves Flowers

Midsummer heat can be hard on tender lettuce plants. They can quickly turn tough or bitter, bolt to seed, or even turn to mush. How can you find the cool, moist conditions lettuce likes in the heat of summer? Look no further than your flowerbed!

Place lettuces singly, scattered here and there in a partially shaded garden for protection from midsummer heat. In a sunny flower garden, shade lettuce plants by placing them between larger perennials or annuals.

Find instant shade among the flowers. Providing shade in the vegetable garden, which is situated out in the full sun, can mean some major work. You may have to put up shade cloth or a trellis, or grow lettuce plants in trenches where the soil is cooler.

But the very conditions you work so hard to provide in the vegetable garden may already by available in your ornamental gardens, especially those in partial shade. Under the protection of shade trees, temperatures can be 10 degrees cooler than out in the hot sun! Another advantage to growing greens in the flowerbed is that even in sunny gardens, it's easy to find shade for lettuce down among the taller flowers.

I've been planting lettuces in my ornamental gardens for years. And I've found that not only do the plants thrive, they also add beauty to brightly colored flowers, by setting them off with a background of green or red leaves.

Light frilly yellow-green leaf lettuces like 'Lollo Biondo' make a nice contrast beside the dark leaves of perennials like hostas. The red-tipped leaf lettuces like 'Red Perella' are especially pretty, as long as you grow them in light shade. Enticing little head lettuces like 'Tom Thumb' will tempt visitors to sneak a bite from your flowerbed.

Confuse-a-bug. One of the biggest benefits of growing your lettuces in flowerbeds is the confuse-a-bug effect. Insects have easy pickings in a large patch sown entirely to lettuce. But they'll have a much harder time finding your salad greens when you surround individual lettuce plants with a variety of flowering plants. Some ornamentals like marigolds repel bugs with their strongly scented leaves. Other flowers like yarrow attract beneficial insects.

Take care of baby. Don't worry about your lettuce plants starving among a crowd of hungry flowers. Just give each lettuce transplant a handful of rich compost when you put it in the garden. Planting lettuce transplants, rather than seeds, will also ensure that flowering neighbors don't overwhelm your baby plants. Start your lettuce in small pots or trays, then grow the seedlings to 3 or 4 inches across before you move them into the garden.

Lettuce for All Seasons

These days, you'll find lettuce in every shape, texture, color, and flavor imaginable. Some are much better adapted to heat and cold than others, so keep that in mind when you make your selections. Pick several of the types listed below for variety at the table and in your ornamental beds. (See "Sources" on page 228 for seed catalogs that carry many different types of lettuce.)

Batavian lettuce. These sturdy plants hold up well in the heat, staying crisp and ready for the salad bowl. They look similar to butterhead lettuces but are crisp like romaine. Try 'Nevada' or 'Verano'.

Butterhead lettuce. Soft green or red heads and buttery flavor make these lettuces a must-have. Try 'Capitane' in cool seasons and 'Esmeralda' in summer.

Crisphead lettuce. This very common lettuce is also known as "iceberg." Though it's a staple of the supermarket, crispheads aren't as high in vitamins as other types of lettuce. Most cultivars need cool weather, but 'Summertime' can handle the heat.

Cutting or looseleaf lettuce. Harvest these beauties leaf by leaf over a long time. As long as you pick the outer leaves and let the rest grow, you'll have lettuce for weeks and even months to come. 'Lollo Tossa', 'Red Oakleaf', and 'Salad Bowl' can stand up to the heat. In spring or fall, try 'Valeria'.

Romaine lettuce. These are tall, sturdy lettuces with crunchy, spatula-shaped leaves. They lend a nice snap to salads, have fine flavor, and are very nutritious. Grow 'Rouge d'Hiver' in all seasons, or try 'Apollo' and 'Jericho' in summer.

34 Extend Your Salad Season with Plastic Tunnels

The times I crave garden-fresh salad greens most are in winter when they're just not available. Thoughts of just-picked lettuce, spinach, and other greens (and the taste of store-bought lettuce!) gave me the incentive to find a way to extend my summer crops an extra four to six weeks with homemade plastic tunnels.

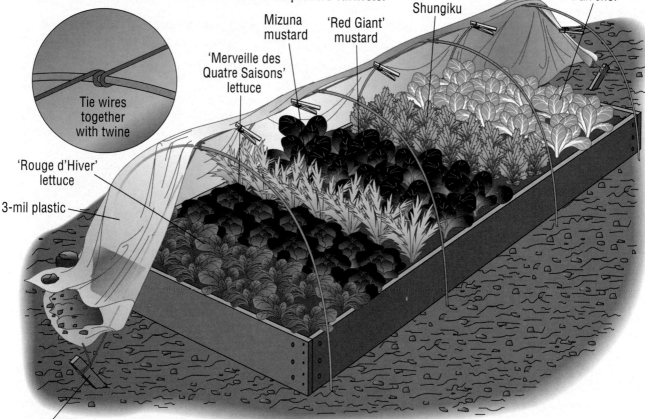

Pak choi

Shungiku

'Red Giant' mustard

Mizuna mustard

'Merveille des Quatre Saisons' lettuce

Tie wires together with twine

'Rouge d'Hiver' lettuce

3-mil plastic

Wooden stake

To enjoy colorful salad mixes from fall into winter, start planting greens in summer, then cover the plants with a plastic tunnel when frost threatens. Plant cold-tolerant greens, such as lettuce and spinach, plus a variety of oriental leafy vegetables for fabulous flavor. Oriental vegetables are great in stir-fries too, so be sure to grow plenty of these spicy greens.

Hold in the heat. Raised beds with wood, cement-block, or stone sides are the perfect place to keep summer crops growing into winter. It's easy to build a tunnel over a raised bed because the sides provide instant support for the frame. If you're building new raised beds, make them 3 feet wide and as long as you like. This technique will work just fine for ground-level beds, but give raised beds a try if you can—they're easy on your back!

Plant late to harvest late. Add ¼ inch of compost to the soil in mid- to late August or eight weeks before your first frost date, then plant the seeds of your winter greens. If you're planting seedlings, they can go in the ground as much as a month later.

Add a little spice. Check seed catalogs for lettuce cultivars that hold up well in cold, wet weather. Choose several different cultivars, including colorful ones like red-leaved 'Rouge d'Hiver', to add pizzazz to your extended-season salad bed. Then plant cold-tolerant oriental leaf vegetables such as Chinese cabbage, mizuna (one of several leaf mustards), chop suey greens or shungiku (*Chrysanthemum coronarium*), and pak choi. (See "Sources" on page 228 for ordering information.) These spicy greens will add some welcome heat to cold-season salads.

Protect your harvest. At some point before the cold frosts hit, purchase 5-foot lengths of bendable, but sturdy wire. If your beds are wider than 3 feet, buy longer wire. Work along one side of the raised bed, and push one end of each wire 8 to 10 inches into the soil. Space the wires 3 feet apart. Then go around to the other side of the bed and draw the free ends of the wire over to you. Push the wires 8 to 10 inches into the soil at the edge of the bed. The wires will form an arc over the raised bed.

Center sturdy stakes at the ends of each bed and drive them into the ground until they're steady. Tie stout twine to one stake, then run it down the center of the bed. Wrap the twine tightly around each bent wire as you come to it, pulling it taut behind you. When you reach the other end of the bed, tie the twine to the other stake. First make sure that the twine is pulled taut all along the length of the bed.

Purchase a 5- or 6-foot-wide piece of 3-mil clear plastic that is as long as the raised bed plus 4 feet. If you use floating row cover on your plants during the growing season, you can use it instead of the plastic.

Lay the plastic over the wires with the excess spread out equally down each side and end of the bed. Bury the ends of the plastic in soil on the side of the bed that faces the prevailing winds. Make sure the plastic is well anchored so the wind can't get underneath and tear it off the wires.

Now, uncover the bed by rolling up the plastic sheet and weighting it down with rocks on the anchored side of the bed. As long as there's no frost danger, you don't need to cover the bed. When frost does threaten, cover the bed in the afternoon by drawing the plastic over the wires, and weigh down the free side with stones or soil. Close off the ends too, so cold winds won't blow the trapped heat out of your plastic tunnel.

If the sun is out the next morning and frost danger is past, roll the plastic up and secure it to the anchored side again. Temperatures under an enclosed plastic tunnel can quickly reach plant-damaging levels, so be sure to roll back the cover during warm, sunny spells. If the day is too cold to completely remove the cover, fold the plastic back halfway, clipping the fold to the twine with clothespins. Anchor the free end to the ground with stones just as you do when opening the cover up completely.

This easy-to-make tunnel can extend your growing season by weeks. Bring the plastic inside when the winter harvest is over, and it will be ready to use again in spring to get your salad greens off to an extra-early start.

35 Bug Juice Blows Pests Away

Turn insect pests into bug juice, and you get an effective spray for fighting pests with pests. One explanation of why bug juice works assumes that in any population of insects, some will be diseased. By spraying a solution of troublesome insect pests on your plants, you can spread diseases specific to that pest. It works for me! Try these simple steps that will make it work for you.

Aphids

Bug-juice spray is another tool for your organic grower's kit. It's made from the insect pests that are bothering your plants. When you spray bug juice or any other pesticide, dress for the occasion. You want to keep all sprays off your skin and out of your eyes and nose.

Identify the problem pest. See the box on this page.

Dress for success. No one knows exactly how bug juice works, so it's best to play it safe. Keep the stuff off your skin and out of your eyes and lungs by wearing rubber gloves, long sleeves, pants, goggles, and a respirator when you mix and spray the juice.

Pick your pests. When you're properly dressed, go to the plants that are under attack and collect ½ cup of the pests—or as close to that as you can manage—in a quart jar. Be sure to collect any insects that appear to be off-color, sluggish, dying, or dead.

Juice 'em. Add 2 cups of water to the jar of pests and pour the mix into a blender. (Check garage sales for a used blender—this isn't something you want to mix up in your kitchen blender! And make sure you label your bargain blender "Bug-Juice Blender" so the kids don't accidentally use it for food.) Mix the bugs and water thoroughly.

Strain the solution through cheesecloth and save the liquid. Pour ¼ cup of the insect/water mix into your sprayer and dilute it with 2 cups of water. You can store any leftover insect/water mix in a plastic container in your freezer, but make sure you label it well! Make sure you clean your blender and sprayer thoroughly after each use—day-old bug juice is putrid stuff.

Add a few drops of liquid dishwashing soap to the sprayer and shake it up. The soap helps spread the solution and makes it coat the leaves. Use pure soap without detergent or additives if you can find it. As a second choice, use dishwashing detergent without additives.

Soak susceptible plants. Cover the leaves of infested plants thoroughly, top and bottom, with the bug-juice spray. Any bacteria or viruses in your bug juice should spread to the healthy pests on your plants. Once infected, the insect pests will sicken and die. Apply the spray once a week if needed.

Name That Pest

No matter what kind of insect pest control you rely on, identifying the pest first is the most important step. You need to find out exactly which insect is pestering your plants before you try any treatment or you're wasting your time.

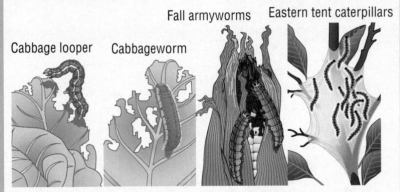

Cabbage looper   Cabbageworm   Fall armyworms   Eastern tent caterpillars

Bug juice works on soft-bodied pests like aphids and those shown here, but it doesn't seem to have any effect on hard-bodied insects like Colorado potato beetles and Mexican bean beetles.

Sometimes when you look closely at the symptoms, you'll discover that insects aren't the problem at all. A disease or cultural problem (like overwatering or underwatering) could be the culprit. Just because there are lots of insects on your plants doesn't mean they're the cause of a plant problem either. With a close look, you may discover that the "pests" are actually beneficial insects that have come to your plants' rescue.

You can become a pest-control sleuth in a hurry with a magnifying glass and a couple of good organic insect-control guidebooks. Look for books with color photos, like *The Organic Gardener's Handbook of Natural Insect and Disease Control*—the photos make it a lot easier to identify insects. (See "Recommended Reading" on page 233 for other good insect identification books.)

36 Plant Juice Foils Garden Pests

It seems like insect pests have a sixth sense for zeroing in on my favorite plants. But the truth is that they just use the same senses to find dinner that you and I do: sight, smell, and taste. You may not be able to change the color or taste of your plants, but you can protect them from pests by masking their scent. Sprays made from aromatic plants are the perfect scent solution—they'll ruin insects' appetites but won't affect your enjoyment.

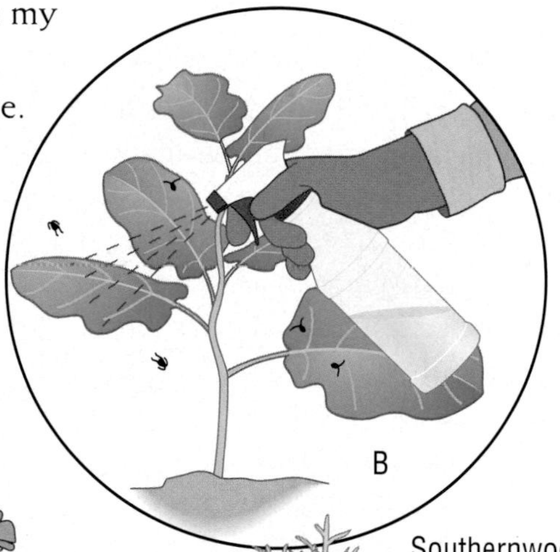

B

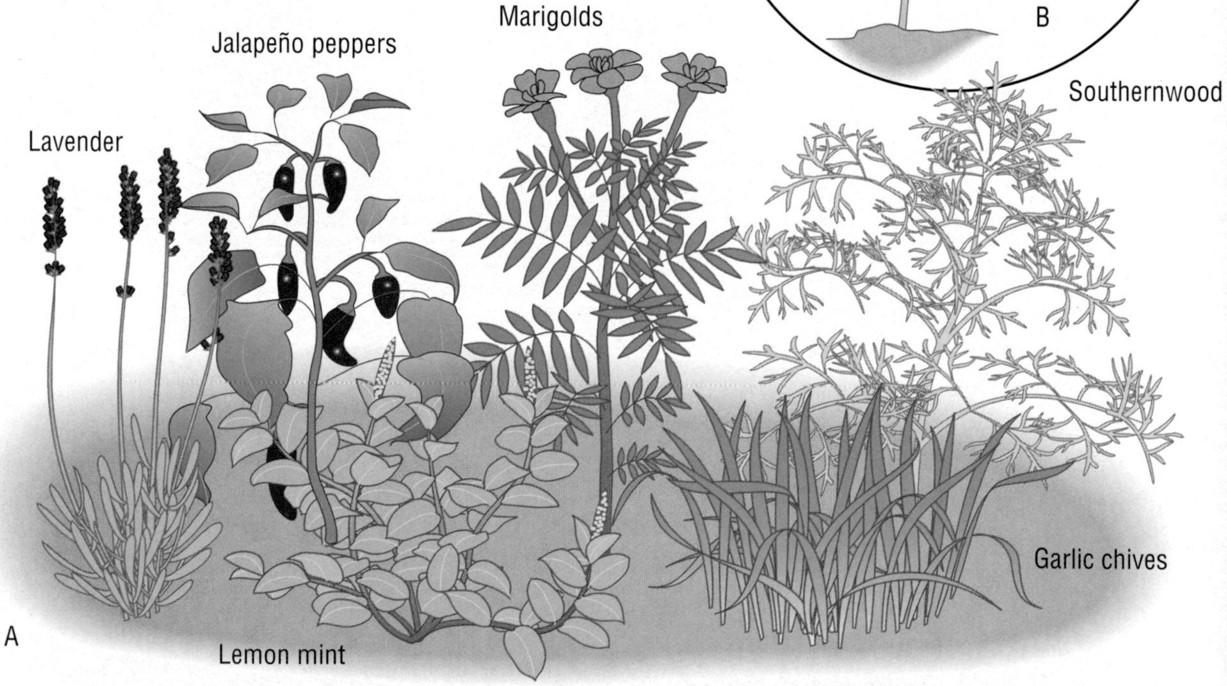

Marigolds

Jalapeño peppers

Southernwood

Lavender

Garlic chives

A

Lemon mint

All you need is a blender to turn aromatic plants (A) into pest-repellent sprays. Buy a used blender to mix your sprays, and label it so no one uses it for food by mistake. The volatile oils in herbs break down fast, so it's a good idea to use plant-juice sprays (B) as soon as possible after making them.

Camouflage plants with perfume. Herbs such as lavender, oregano, rosemary, sage, and thyme rarely have pest problems. The aromatic oils that make these herbs so attractive to us seem to repel garden pests. It may be that strong scents confuse pests as they hunt for a particular fragrance, or maybe there are certain scents insects just don't like.

Do-it-yourself plant juice. It's easy to make homemade sprays that confuse and repel insect pests. You can experiment with juices from a variety of fragrant plants, applying them individually or mixing two or more juices together. Just remember to keep a record of what you're using, because if it works, you'll want to use it again. And most important of all, make sure you never use any plant that is toxic or poisonous. If you don't know if a plant is toxic—don't use it. That said, here's all it takes to make your own plant-juice spray.

1 Collect plant materials from your garden or from the yard or field of a neighbor who's given you permission. Wear gloves and long sleeves to keep plant oils off your skin while you gather leaves and succulent stems.

Take a large cloth sack, like an old pillowcase, and a container the size of a large juice can (about 48 ounces) on your plant hunt. Fill the container loosely with the leaves and succulent stems of the plants you select. Gather 12 canfuls of plant material and mix them together in the sack.

2 Shift the material in the sack to one end and smash it with a baseball bat or handheld sledgehammer. Then turn the sack over and mash the plants some more to thoroughly bruise the leaves and get the plants' juices running.

3 Turn the bag inside out and soak the mashed plants and the bag in a gallon or two of water. You'll need a brewing tub for this—a 5-gallon plastic bucket is ideal. The amount of water will depend on the amount and kind of leaves and stems you've collected. The idea is to just cover the mashed plants and the bag with water. Label the bucket and place it in the sun out of the reach of children and pets. Stir the mix several times during the day.

4 The following day, add a few drops of liquid dishwashing soap to the brew to mix the plant oils evenly throughout the water. The soap also helps the plant-juice solution spread and stick on plant leaves. Stir the mix thoroughly.

5 Pour the brew back through the bag into a clean bucket or container to remove most of the leaf and stem matter. Wear rubber gloves, long sleeves, pants, goggles, and a respirator, just as you would when working with any other spray. Wring the bag as dry as you can to get as much of the liquid out as possible. Then strain the liquid through clean cheesecloth to remove all the little particles that can clog the sprayer nozzle.

Pour the clean liquid into a sprayer and spray it on a test plant of the crop you want to protect, coating the top and undersides of the leaves. You should be able to tell fairly quickly if the spray repels the pests—they'll move off the plants you've sprayed and onto neighboring ones that haven't been sprayed. If the spray works, apply it to the rest of your crop. You'll need to apply the spray each time it rains.

Plants with Pest-Repellent Potential

For effective plant-juice sprays, use plants with strong aromatic oils. Use the leaves and stems of the plants unless otherwise indicated.

Bee balm	Oregano
Cedar	Pennyroyal
(leaves only)	Peppers, hot
Garlic	(fruit only)
Garlic chives	Pines
Horehound	(needles only)
Lavender	Rosemary
Lemon balm	Sage
Marigolds	Santolina
Mints	Southernwood
Onions	Thyme

37 Clothespins Close Earworms Out of Corn

When I pull back the husk on a just-picked ear of corn, I don't want to see any corn earworm caterpillars munching on the kernels. So I use clothespins or other handy household items to keep the pesky critters off my corn on the cob. Clothespins are my favorite no-muss, no-fuss solution to the problem, but I've listed several other effective earworm-control measures in case you want to try them all.

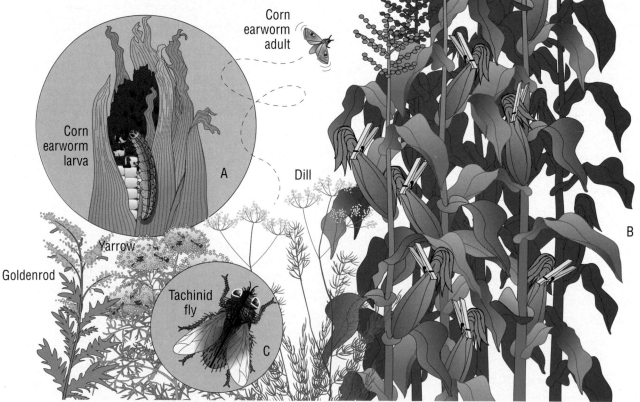

Clothespin

Corn earworm adult

Corn earworm larva

A

Dill

B

Yarrow

Goldenrod

Tachinid fly

C

Use physical barriers and beneficial insects to keep earworms (A) out of your sweet corn. Corn varieties with tight husks create their own pest barrier, or you can pin husks closed with clothespins (B). To attract beneficials like tachinid flies (C), plant herbs that attract pest-eating insects, or let beneficials' favorite weeds grow.

What's eating my corn?
One of the biggest insect problems you'll face when growing corn is corn earworms. The adult pests are moths that lay eggs in the tips of corn ears or on leaves. The eggs hatch into brown, green, pink, or yellowish caterpillars with stripes on their sides. The caterpillars munch on your corn for several weeks before they pupate and turn into moths. Luckily for all of us corn-lovers, there are several good organic techniques that can keep corn earworm larvae from pestering our crops.

Clip corn earworms out with clothespins. This is by far the easiest way to shut the door on these pests. Just gather the husks at the tips, pinch them closed, and hold them that way with a clothespin—your corn will be safe for the season! You can use clothespins over and over again, and they take less time and effort than other methods. But, just in case you're short on clothespins, or you're dealing with really big plantings of corn, here are some other options.

Plant tight-tipped corn. Some cultivars have husks that are tight enough to keep earworms out. Planting those cultivars is a fine solution, but the only corn cultivars I know of with the tight-tipped characteristic are the heirloom varieties 'Calumet', 'Country Gentleman', and 'Stowell's Evergreen', and the modern variety 'Northern Super Sweet'. With so many new delicious sugary sweet corn cultivars around, I don't want to be that limited.

Repel earworms with rubber bands. Gather the husk tips and hold them tightly around the freshly emerging silks, then twist a rubber band fairly tightly over the silks and around the gathered husks. Don't put the rubber band on so tightly that it will damage the silks, however. Obviously this takes more work than clothespins, and rubber bands tend to break so they're not reusable. But you probably have a stash of them around, and you may not have clothespins on hand.

Spray caterpillars away. If you're growing so much corn you don't have time for clothespins, you can apply *Bacillus thuringiensis* var. *kurstaki* (BTK). This product is a bacterial stomach poison that only kills caterpillars. BTK is very effective, but use it as a last resort—insect pests will develop resistance to BTK and other BT products if you use them too often. Apply BTK spray or granules as soon as you notice corn earworm damage on your plants. Follow label directions exactly for good results. When you apply BTK, or any pest-control product, wear rubber gloves, long sleeves, pants, goggles, and a respirator or dust mask to keep from getting the material on your skin or in your eyes or lungs.

Smother pests with an oil slick. Squirting a few drops of mineral oil onto the tips of the ears right where the silks emerge is another time-honored method of controlling corn earworms. It's fairly labor-intensive since you have to place the mineral oil inside the tip of each ear after the silks have wilted.

Get Bugs to Do the Dirty Work

Some beneficial insects eat corn earworms. If you can attract these pest munchers to your garden, you'll find they help control corn earworms and other insect pests. The adults of beneficial insects such as tachinid flies, braconid wasps, and ichneumon wasps lay their eggs on or in caterpillars. As the larvae or maggots (fly larvae) grow, they feed on their hosts and eventually destroy them.

You can attract these insect good guys by setting out plants that produce plenty of nectar and pollen for the adult insects to feed on. Beneficial flies and wasps aren't very big, so they'll look for small-flowered plants to meet their needs. Sow catnip, dill, fennel, hyssop, parsley, sweet clover, thyme, or yarrow in your garden to keep beneficials happy. Goldenrod and Queen Anne's lace are good for beneficials too!

38 Snare Slugs and Snails with Baits, Traps, and Barriers

When I need to control a bad infestation of slugs or snails, I start by thinking like a slug or snail. Keeping your plants slug-free is just a matter of discovering what attracts the slippery critters and what sends them slithering away. Like slugs of the human variety, these garden pests like potatoes and beer and dislike being uncomfortable—and that gives you lots of control options. Use a mix of the methods listed here to keep your garden free of these slimy plant eaters.

B

D

F

E

C

Slug

A

Garden snail

There are lots of options for clearing your garden of slugs and snails. Beer (A) and shady hideaways made of flower pots (B), cabbage leaves (C), or decaying boards (D) will lure the pests to where you can catch them. Or you can use dry-powder barriers (E) and copper (F) to keep slugs and snails from reaching prized plants.

Set a beer trap for slugs. Lure slugs to a drunken death in pans of beer set flush with the soil and placed at 15-foot intervals throughout the garden. The yeast in the beer attracts slugs, and sometimes snails, that crawl into the pans and drown. Renew your beer traps every day since slugs don't like stale beer—who can blame them?

Bait and squish night visitors. Another extremely effective method of disposing of slugs and snails is squishing them flat—but first you have to catch them. Slugs and snails like to eat at night, when the ground is moist with dew and the hot, drying sun is gone. During the day, they hide from the heat in dark, moist areas. Rather than hunting them down, lure snails and slugs to hideouts of your choosing so they're easy to catch.

Take clay pots, soak them in water, and turn them upside down in the garden where slugs or snails are a problem. Dig out an area under the rim so the critters can crawl in. If you don't have spare pots, lay boards or cabbage leaves on the ground throughout your garden. Slugs and snails will crawl under any object that keeps them cool and moist. Every morning, after the sun has been up for a couple of hours, check under the pots, boards, or leaves, and destroy any of the pests you find there.

Lay down a barrier against slimy travelers. Both slugs and snails leave slime trails so they can move easily over the ground. You can disrupt their travel by surrounding plants or garden beds with 2-inch-wide bands of dry materials like lime, wood ashes, and sawdust. Another good barrier is diatomaceous earth (DE)—a white powder that's actually the fossilized remains of algae called diatoms. When slugs and snails touch the powder, the sharp bits of the diatoms' silica shells puncture their skins so they dry out and die. Use DE from garden centers, not the kind used in swimming pool filters—it's a different grade and won't be effective. Renew dry barriers after each rain.

Create a slime-free zone with copper. Slugs and snails won't crawl on copper because they get an electric shock when their wet bodies touch the metal. Some garden centers sell thin copper foil for surrounding beds and borders, but old copper roofing or flashing will work, too.

Mix and match baits, barriers, and traps. So, with all these methods to choose from, which should you use? If slugs and snails are more than a minor problem, try to integrate all of these methods. Copper is too expensive to use all over the garden, so just cover the tops of raised-bed boards with it or place copper strips around your most valuable plants.

In ground-level beds and borders, set out old aluminum pie plates so their lips are flush with the soil surface. Fill the plates 1 inch deep with fresh cheap (yeasty) beer. Halfway between the pie plates, place your upside-down flowerpot traps—with a piece of cut potato inside to lure slugs in. Lay cabbage leaves on the ground here and there, and place boards alongside paths where they won't be obtrusive. Check underneath all the hiding places each morning and collect and destroy the slugs and snails.

Use the diatomaceous earth, lime, or wood ashes in wide bands around seedlings and specimen plants like hostas. Since you have to reapply dry barriers after rain, save these labor-intensive materials for your most valuable plants.

Lime That Slime!

If you're looking for an inexpensive one-step way to stop slugs and snails, try liming your soil in early spring before you see any of the pests. Slugs and snails seem to prefer acidic soils—so sprinkling the ground with lime will make it more alkaline and less appealing to slimy critters. Use about 10 pounds of lime per 100 square feet of garden. Lightly rake the lime into the soil. You'll get good results after one to two years of liming.

39 Fight Plant Fungi with Homemade Solutions

Anthracnose

Black rot

When black spot, downy mildew, and other plant fungi threaten my grapes, roses, or squash plants, I raid my kitchen cabinet for a solution. With three simple ingredients—baking soda, garlic, and liquid dishwashing soap—I can make a safe and super-effective fungus-fighting spray and so can you. Here's how.

Black spot

Downy mildew

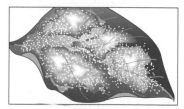

Powdery mildew

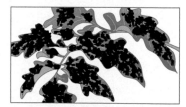

Sooty mold

Common Fungal Diseases

Consult a guide like *The Organic Gardener's Handbook of Natural Insect and Disease Control* to see which symptoms common fungi cause and which plants they affect. If you come up with a match, get out the blender and prepare to do battle with a combination of simple household items such as baking soda, garlic, liquid dishwashing soap, and vegetable oil. (It's a good idea to buy a used blender at a garage sale and use it for all your pest-control needs.)

Garlic spray keeps fungi away. To make an antifungal spray for vegetables or ornamental plants, you'll need a whole garlic bulb. Pull apart the cloves, leaving their papery skins on, and toss them into a blender with 1 quart of water. Blend the mix until the garlic is ground up into a soggy mash that floats to the top. Now add 1 teaspoon of liquid dishwashing soap and stir it in well with a spoon.

You need soap in the mix because the garlic oil and water won't blend together without it. Pure soap that doesn't contain detergents or additives works best. If you can't find pure soap, choose a mild dishwashing detergent without additives—soaps that are too strong can burn plants' leaves. When you've stirred the garlic-and-soap solution thoroughly, strain it through a sieve or piece of cheesecloth into a quart jar, then add 1 teaspoon of baking soda. Stir until the baking soda is dissolved.

If the level of the liquid is less than 1 quart, add water to fill the jar, then strain the liquid a second time so the bits of garlic and skin won't clog your sprayer. Use the spray as soon as you see any sign of fungus on your plants. Cover the tops and bottoms of the leaves thoroughly. Apply fresh spray every two weeks until the disease symptoms are gone. At harvesttime, wash the leaves and fruits of edible plants thoroughly to remove any dishwashing soap that might still be on your plants.

Add oil for a triple-whammy spray. Both garlic and baking soda help control fungal infections. When their combined efforts aren't enough, add cooking oil or horticultural oil to give your spray a stronger antifungal effect. Oil sprays form a coating on leaves that seems to keep fungal spores from germinating. Here's how to make the spray.

Pull apart 2 whole garlic bulbs and put the cloves in a blender with 1 cup of vegetable oil or horticultural oil. Blend the garlic with the oil and let the mix set for 24 hours or more. Then strain the mixture to remove any clogging bits. If there's less than 1 cup of mix after straining, add enough oil to make a full cup.

Now add ⅓ cup of liquid dishwashing soap to the garlic-and-oil mixture, put it in a closed jar, label it, and store it in the refrigerator. This is enough concentrate to make 5 gallons of spray.

Using this recipe, you can mix up 1 gallon of the antifungal spray at a time. Thoroughly dissolve 4 level teaspoons of baking soda in 1 quart of warm water and pour the solution into your spray tank. Next, pour ¼ cup of the garlic-and-oil concentrate into the tank. Stir the mix up thoroughly. Then add 3 more quarts of water to make 1 gallon of antifungal spray, mix well, and apply as needed.

Wait until the time is right. Whenever you use sprays that contain oil, make sure the environmental conditions are right. Plants can be damaged by oil-based sprays if they are drought-stressed, if the temperature is above 85°F, or if the relative humidity is above 65 percent. If you live where the heat and humidity are high through most of the summer, do your spraying in the early morning. Do not apply oil and sulfur within 30 days of each other, since the combination can damage plants.

For vegetables, wait until you see fungal symptoms before you start spraying, then apply the spray every two weeks as needed. For ornamentals—when looks are especially important—prepare the spray ahead of time and use it as a preventive. Spray susceptible plants, such as lilacs, phlox, and roses, every two weeks during the entire hot, wet fungus season—mid-May to the end of July in most of the United States.

Proceed carefully. Before you go in for wholesale spraying, it's always a good idea to try your homemade spray on a plant and wait for two or three days just to make sure that the plant will tolerate it. It takes several days for leaf damage to show up.

40 Fast Apple Thinning for Fuller Harvests

Before thinning

After thinning

├─6"─┤

The harvest

Left to their own devices, apple trees tend to produce a heavy crop one year and a very sparse crop the next year. I don't like being overwhelmed then underwhelmed, so I thin the fruits each summer and get a consistently moderate harvest. Thinning is a great way to get enough apples for fresh eating and baking each year without going through the feast-and-famine cycle.

You can thin apples without climbing up into the branches if you use a long pole. Wave the pole around inside the tree where you see apples spaced closer than 6 inches apart. Gently but firmly strike the branches on the outside of the tree too, until all the apples have enough space to grow. You'll be rewarded with gorgeous apples and trees with unbroken branches.

Natural thinning. When an apple tree blooms, it goes all out and is literally covered with blossoms. If the rains hold off, the temperatures stay warm, and there are plenty of pollinating bees around, the fruit set can be tremendous. Untended trees can get so weighted down with fruit that the limbs will literally fall off, leaving the stubby trunk jutting jaggedly into the air. I've seen it happen!

Apple trees usually try to avoid this fate by dropping excess apples. When a tree produces an extra-large crop, it will drop a whole bunch of apples sometime in early summer, when the fruits are about the size of jelly beans. This natural apple fall will reduce the amount of fruit to a quantity that the tree can ripen without killing itself. But the tree will still produce an enormous crop that will be followed by a shy harvest the next year.

Hands-on work for small trees. Commercial growers sometimes use chemicals to limit the number of apples on a tree. But organic growers use the old reliable, pick-them-off-by-hand method. The hands-on method works fine on dwarf or semidwarf fruit trees since they only grow 8 to 15 feet tall. You can reach every bit of these trees with a small stepladder and thin the fruits to one every 6 to 8 inches apart on the branch. Another way to esti-mate the proper thinning distance is to count leaves—aim for 30 to 40 leaves per apple. (For tips on thinning clusters of fruit, see the box on this page.)

Go to bat for big trees. Thinning a few dwarf trees by hand works fine—it's good exercise too. But what if you have a small orchard, or one or several full-size trees that reach 30 feet tall or more? You'd have to be Superman or Wonder Woman to go over those trees and thin the apples to one every 6 inches!

Fear not. Here's how I learned to thin tall trees by practicing year after year on a mature, full-size 'Gravenstein' apple in my front yard. Get a long pole that will reach to the very top of the tree and wave it around vigorously in the branches, shaking them hard. (A bamboo pole works well since it's tall but light-weight.) Take the pole and hit the branches from outside the tree also. Showers of apples will descend around you until you think you've knocked all the apples off the tree.

Keep an eye on how the fruit is spaced on the branches as you do this. Make your best estimate of when the fruit that's left averages about one for every 6 inches of branch. Many will still be in clusters of two, but that's okay as long as the clusters are about 12 inches apart. This isn't an exact science and the fruits don't have to be exactly spaced every 6 inches. Just try to make it average out.

Rake up the little apples and throw them in the trash so they don't attract flies or provide homes for other insect pests.

Come harvesttime in summer or fall, you'll get all the apples you and your tree can handle. As a bonus, you'll find that picking up little green apples is a lot easier than raking up full-grown apples that are turning to mush. And there's no danger of yellow-jacket stings, either!

Thinning Clusters

Apples will sometimes set in pairs, or groups of three, four, or five, depending on the number of blossoms that arise from a fruiting spur. These fruits are too close together to grow their best, so you'll want to thin them.

Thin groups of five to two fruits. Thin clusters of four apples to two or one, and groups of three to two or one. Leave pairs alone or thin them to one fruit. Do this by pinching off the center fruits with your fingers. Don't pull the little fruits off: you'll break the fruiting spur, or all the apples in the cluster may come off.

How do you know which fruits to remove? Remember the rule that apples grow nicest and largest when they are spaced about 6 inches apart along the branch. Try to thin the clusters of two so they are at least 12 inches apart, and individual apples so they are 6 to 8 inches apart. Always remove fruit with insect damage.

41 Start a Cottage Garden of Self-Sowing Flowers

I like variety in my flowerbeds, and there's no better way to get it than with a cottage garden—an informal mix of several different flowers. Plant your garden using self-sowing flowers and you'll see just how spectacular and varied a cottage garden can be. Flowers that seed themselves tend to move around the garden finding the best spots to grow. As the flowers pop up in new places each year, you'll be surprised and delighted by ever-changing plant combinations.

Once self-sowing flowers get started in your garden, your only task will be to admire them and keep them from growing too far! These perennial flowers are fairly well behaved, but others like bugloss (*Anchusa* spp.) will take over more than their share of space unless you remove the seedheads before the seeds ripen.

Clear the way for a cottage garden. Site your garden where it gets at least four hours of sun a day to provide good conditions for the widest range of plants. Most self-sowers are sun lovers, although a few plants prefer partial sun or shade. Start your cottage garden in late summer by mixing ½ inch of compost into the top 2 inches of soil in your planting area.

Plant your garden informally. Make a planting plan before you start sowing your seeds, grouping plants together in some areas and leaving them out of other areas. Create extra interest by planting drifts (large swaths) of plants or by making a mass planting of one flower that dribbles into a planting of another kind. Rows, regular spacing, and a set planting pattern are for formal gardens, not cottage gardens, so forget about rigid lines and let your imagination go.

Sow seeds in summer, fall, and spring. Once you've prepared the bed, plant it with ripe seeds you've gathered from flowers in your yard or from the yards of willing neighbors. For a wider variety of plants, order seeds from mail-order catalogs. (See "Sources" on page 228 for perennial catalog suggestions.)

When you gather your own seeds, make sure they're ripe—seeds are ready to harvest when they fall easily from their seedheads. Seeds may ripen in

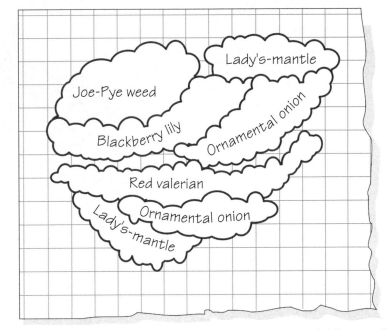

When you plan your cottage garden, use rounded shapes and drifts to outline your planting areas—they'll give your garden an informal look. And leave room for paths so you can reach the plants when they need water or weeding.

summer, fall, or spring, depending on the plant. Start your garden by planting in summer and fall. When spring rolls around, see if there are gaps in your planting—if there are, sow more seeds as they ripen.

Broadcast the seeds over the surface of the soil, then mulch them with ¼ inch of straw. Some seeds may sprout in fall when rain and cooler temperatures make growing conditions favorable, but many will wait until spring to sprout. Some plants will bloom the first year and others will need an extra year of growth.

Take what comes. You need to be flexible when you plan a garden of self-sowing flowers—after you plant them, the flowers will go to seed and come up

wherever they like. This ability to move around is how the self-sower Johnny-jump-up (*Viola tricolor*) got its name.

Once all your self-sown flowers bloom, you're sure to be surprised each year by the color, beauty, and changes in your cottage garden. It's fun to let the plants do their own thing, but feel free to transplant plants to better sites, reseed them in new areas, or yank them out to get the look you want.

Some self-seeding plants like forget-me-nots (*Myosotis* spp.) can be invasive. I let these plants put on their starry display of true-blue flowers, then immediately pull them out by the armloads. Plenty of seeds will fall to the ground as you pull the plants out, and you'll have all the forget-me-nots you need the following year.

If you're not sure how vigorously a plant will reseed in your garden, leave it alone the first year and watch what happens. In the second year, if you get more flowers than you want, cut off and compost three-fourths of the seedheads before any seeds drop. See what happens the next season and cut off more or fewer seedheads to get the number of plants you want.

Reseed freely or fastidiously. Once your garden is established, you can help spread seeds after the flowers turn brown and the seeds dry. Gather the dried seedheads and wander through the garden, broadcasting seeds where you want them. Scatter the seeds as soon as they dry out in the seedheads or they'll quickly sow themselves. For a really informal look, knock the dead flowerstalks to the ground when the seeds ripen. The seeds will scatter in drifts as they fly out of the seedheads.

If any seeds sprout in fall, protect the seedlings by mulching the area lightly with shredded leaves. Fall is also the time when you can move seedlings around in the bed and add seedlings that you've purchased from garden centers or nurseries to your planting. Water seedlings immediately after you move them and surround them with an inch or two of mulch to keep weeds away.

Create natural-looking drifts of plants and take out your frustrations at the same time! Walk through your self-seeding cottage garden in fall, knocking seeds from the dried plants with a stick or your hand.

Sow Seeds That Are True to Their Traits

To make sure your seedlings are just as attractive as the original plants you selected, choose open-pollinated plants (those that pollinate naturally) for your self-sown garden. Hybrids, which are created by cross-pollinating plants, and cultivars, which are varieties of plants that have been selected for special characteristics, will not usually come true from seed. They often revert back to the appearance of the parent plants, leaving you with pale flower colors or other less-desirable features. Check plant descriptions in seed catalogs and books to see if the plants you'd like to grow are hybrids. Cultivars are easy to identify—they have fancy names added to their common or scientific names, such as 'Blue Angel' columbine or *Coreopsis verticillata* 'Moonbeam'.

Be ruthless when plants with weak or washed-out flower colors appear in your garden. Yank undesirable plants out before they go to seed—you don't want to perpetuate those traits.

A Selection of Self-Sowing Flowers

Try any of these reliable self-sowers to get your cottage garden off to a glorious start. Where a specific species is listed, only that species self-sows, rather than the whole genus of plants.

Examples: Ornamental onions (*Allium* spp.)—All species self-sow.

Red valerian (*Centranthus ruber*)—Only the species *Centranthus ruber* self-sows.

Name	Bloom Time	Amount of Sun, Hardiness Zone Range
Hollyhocks (*Alcea* spp.)	Summer and early fall	Full sun, Zones 2 to 9
Lady's-mantles (*Alchemilla* spp.)	Spring and early summer	Sun or partial shade, Zones 3 to 8
Ornamental onions (*Allium* spp.)	Spring, summer, and fall	Full sun, Zones 3 to 9
Bugloss (*Anchusa* spp.)	Late spring	Full sun, Zones 3 to 8
Columbines (*Aquilegia* spp.)	Spring and early summer	Sun to partial shade, Zones 3 to 9
Milkweeds (*Asclepias* spp.) Ornamental milkweeds include swamp milkweed (*A. incarnata*) and butterfly weed (*A. tuberosa*)	Summer	Full sun to partial shade, Zones 3 to 9
Blackberry lily (*Belamcanda chinensis*)	Summer	Full sun to partial shade, Zones 4 to 10
Bellflowers (*Campanula* spp.)	Spring and summer	Sun or partial shade, Zones 2 to 8
Mountain bluet (*Centaurea montana*)	Late spring and early summer	Full sun to partial shade, Zones 2 to 8
Red valerian (*Centranthus ruber*)	Spring and early summer	Full sun, Zones 4 to 8
Coreopsis (*Coreopsis* spp.)	Late spring and summer	Full sun, Zones 3 to 9
Foxgloves (*Digitalis* spp.)	Summer	Full sun to partial shade, Zones 3 to 8
Purple coneflowers (*Echinacea* spp.)	Summer	Full sun, Zones 3 to 8
Sea hollies (*Eryngium* spp.)	Summer and fall	Full sun, Zones 3 to 9
Joe-Pye weeds (*Eupatorium* spp.)	Summer and fall	Full sun, Zones 2 to 9
Cranesbills or hardy geraniums (*Geranium* spp.)	Spring and early summer	Full sun or partial shade, Zones 3 to 8
Lobelias (*Lobelia* spp.)	Summer and fall	Full sun to partial shade, Zones 2 to 9 (For best results, do not mulch the seeds.)
Campions (*Lychnis* spp.)	Spring and summer	Full sun to partial shade, Zones 3 to 9
Catchflies (*Silene* spp.)	Spring and early summer	Full sun to partial shade, Zones 3 to 9
Blue-eyed grasses (*Sisyrinchium* spp.)	Early summer	Full sun to partial shade, Zones 3 to 10
Spiderworts (*Tradescantia* spp.)	Late spring and early summer	Full sun to partial shade, Zones 3 to 9
Violets (*Viola* spp.)	Spring	Sun or shade, Zones 3 to 9

42 Easy-Does-It Dried Flowers

I've looked enviously at the photos of barns with their rafters hung with bundles of colorful flowers and herbs. And I've looked longingly at the expensive dried-flower crafts in stores and catalogs. But not anymore. I've discovered that it isn't any harder—or more expensive—to grow and dry flowers than it is to grow and freeze vegetables. All you have to know is when and where to put them up!

Paper clip hanger

Grow and air-dry your own flowers and you'll be able to create a beautiful flower arrangement or homemade gift on a moment's notice. Flower crafts range from simple bouquets and potpourris to wreaths and table decorations.

Try it, you'll love it! There are lots of benefits to growing your own flowers for drying. Of course you'll save money and you'll have a wider variety of dried flowers to choose from than the florists and craft stores carry. But best of all, you get to enjoy the flowers year-round. In summer, the opening blooms will brighten your garden. Then, after the harvest, you can turn the dried blooms into wreaths, arrangements, and potpourris, to see you through fall and winter.

Start planning in summer. Look over your flowerbeds as they bloom in summer, and decide where you can tuck plantings of easy-to-dry flowers. Since you'll be cutting the flowers down at their peak, you'll want to choose spots where other flowers can disguise their absence. Plan on putting your dried-flower plantings behind bushy perennials like asters. Or place them between flowers like sunflower heliopsis (*Heliopsis helianthoides*) that tend to flop over onto their neighbors. If you want to make lots of crafts, you're better off growing the flowers in cutting beds as if they were vegetables. That way you won't leave big holes in your flower garden when you harvest all the blooming flowers.

Add everlastings to your plantings. Some plants, such as cupid's dart (*Catananche caerulea*), globe amaranth (*Gomphrena globosa*), and strawflower (*Helichrysum bracteatum*), have papery flowers that dry so easily and hold their color so well, they're called "everlastings." Stick with everlastings and other easy-to-dry flowers and you'll get the most color for the least amount of work.

If you want to preserve big delicate blooms such as peonies or fully-open roses, you'll have to bury the flowers in a desiccant (drying agent) like silica gel. You can buy silica gel at hobby stores—the directions are on the container. As for me, I'll enjoy my peonies fresh and preserve flowers that need only air drying to look their best.

Air drying is easy. Harvesting flowers for drying is just like harvesting vegetables for freezing. You don't want the flowers to be too ripe or the results will be colorless. Some flowers dry best if they're picked at the bud stage, while others do better if they are half open, or fully open. Check your flowers' peak stage in the box on page 99 before you start cutting.

Pick a dry day to harvest your flowers and wait until the morning dew dries completely. Leave long stems on your flowers when you cut them down so they're easier to work with. The green leaves make your arrangements more attractive, so don't bother stripping them off the stems. Make small bundles of six to ten stems and hold them together with rubber bands. The stems shrink as they dry and rubber bands will keep them tightly together—strings and twist ties won't.

Choose a dark place that's warm and dry. A garage, attic, or spare room will work if there's some air circulation—open a window or door a crack if the air is too still. Use a piece of wire (try open paper clips or Christmas ornament hooks) or string to hang the bundles head-down from the ceiling. If your room doesn't have rafters, hang the flowers from strings or wires fastened to shelves or nails on the wall. Hang the flower bundles at least 6 inches apart so air can circulate around them.

Most flowers will dry in one to three weeks unless the humidity is really high. To test for dryness, break a piece off a stem. If it's brittle and snaps, the plant is dry. When you turn the flowers right side up, you'll see that they've dried in an upright position and are ready to use for crafts and arrangements.

Once the flowers are dry, you can use them for arrangements and wreaths. You don't have to feel pressured to use them right away—the blooms will keep for weeks if you leave them hanging in a dry, dark room or closet.

(continued)

Step-by-Step Wreathmaking

It's not hard to make your own wreaths—you just need time and a few materials. Growing your own flowers for these decorations is fun and it adds an extra personal touch. But if you don't have the time or space to grow all the dried flowers you need, don't let that stop you from making wreaths. All of the plants and supplies mentioned here are available at craft and hobby stores.

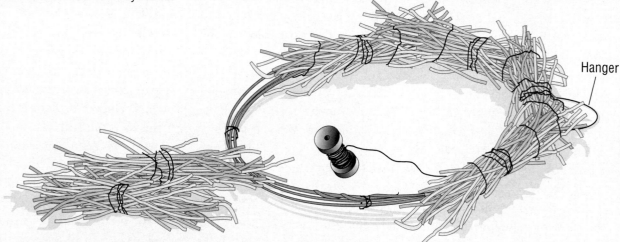

Hanger

Step 1. Buy a 12-inch-diameter wire wreath frame or make one from a piece of heavy-gauge wire. Attach a small piece of 22-gauge wire for a hanger, then create a base by tightly wrapping bundles of straw all the way around the frame with floral spool wire. (Or you can buy a ready-made straw wreath base and skip straw tying all together.)

Step 2. Create a background for your wreath by covering the straw frame with 3- to 5-inch-long bundles of dried foliage plants—sweet Annie (*Artemisia annua*) and 'Silver King' artemisia (*A. ludoviciana* 'Silver King') are good choices. Use floral spool wire or greening pins to attach bundles (made of 5 to 8 stems of foliage) to the straw. Start on the inside of the wreath and work your way around to the outside. Tie the floral spool wire to the frame before you start wrapping the bundles in place. Always work in the same direction so you can cover the stems as you go.

Greening pins

Step 3. Now use greening pins or floral spool wire to attach small bunches of colorful dried flowers to the wreath. Again, each bunch should have 5 to 8 stems cut 3 to 5 inches long.

Arrange the bunches of flowers before you start putting your wreath together to make sure you get the look you want. It's a good way to make sure you have enough materials to cover the entire wreath too!

For a formal look, vary the colors of the flowers around your wreath in regular patterns—blue, then red, then yellow, then white, then blue, then red, and so on. Or mix the bunches together more haphazardly for a cottage-garden effect.

Always work in the same direction, overlapping the bunches so each new bundle of blooms hides the stems of the previous bunch. Keep attaching bundles to the frame until it's completely covered. If you're short on flowers, just decorate the middle of the frame and let the background show along the sides. When you get to the last bunch, you'll need to lift up the first bunch of flowers slightly so you can hide the last group of stems.

Once you're finished, you can use the wreath as is, or add a bow or extra flowers here and there to act as highlights.

Pick Flowers When the Time Is Right

These flowers will hold their colors after air drying if you pick them at the right time. If the flowers you're growing aren't listed here, pick them as soon as they're fully open. Plants marked with an asterisk (*) are everlastings.

Pick when buds show color

*Winged everlasting (*Ammobium alatum*)
*Pearly everlasting (*Anaphalis margaritacea*)
Artemisias (*Artemisia* spp.)
Safflower (*Carthamus tinctorius*)
Joe-Pye weed (*Eupatorium purpureum*)
Roses, for buds (*Rosa* spp.)
Goldenrods (*Solidago* spp.)

Pick when blooms are half open

Ageratums (*Ageratum* spp.)
Bachelor's button (*Centaurea cyanus*)
Delphiniums (*Delphinium* spp.)
*Strawflower (*Helichrysum bracteatum*)
Roses, for flowers (*Rosa* spp.)

Pick when blooms are fully open

Yarrows (*Achillea* spp.)
Alliums (*Allium* spp.)
*Thrifts (*Armeria* spp.)
*Cupid's dart (*Catananche caerulea*)
Celosias (*Celosia* spp.)
*Globe amaranth (*Gomphrena globosa*)
*Everlastings (*Helipterum* spp.)
Hydrangeas (*Hydrangea* spp.)
Lavenders (*Lavandula* spp.)
*Statice (*Limonium* spp.)
Scarlet sage (*Salvia splendens*)
Tansy (*Tanacetum vulgare*)
*Immortelle (*Xeranthemum annuum*)

43 Get Creative with Container Combos

Colorful container plantings are like snack foods—it's hard to get enough of them! I started out with just one plant in a large pot, but pretty soon I was combining two or three flowering plants in the same container. Try your own plant combinations this summer—there's no easier way to brighten an entryway, patio, balcony, porch, or yard. You'll get such spectacular results, you'll be hooked, too.

Brazilian vervain
(*Verbena bonariensis*)

Violet sage
(*Salvia* x *superba*)

Rose verbena
(*Verbena canadensis*)

Shasta daisy
(*Chrysanthemum* x *superbum* 'Alaska')

Colorful plant combinations in pots can light up any spot in a hurry. And they're a great way to try out new perennial combinations for your garden without all the expense. Once you're sure you like a mix, you can confidently plant it in your flowerbed, knowing that the plant shapes, colors, and sizes look just the way you want.

Choose compatible plants. Great combinations start with plants that like the same soil, water, and light conditions. Just think of yourself as a plant marriage broker and try to make the best matches you can. If you're putting together a plant combination for a sunny spot, you'll need plants that like heat and sun. (Mixing a dryland plant like a cactus with a moisture-loving plant like a marsh marigold isn't the way to build a lasting relationship!) You've got to find plants with similar likes and dislikes.

Luckily, matchmaking is a lot easier with plants than with people. You can find out everything about the plants before you try to put them together, so you're guaranteed a successful pairing before you start. If you need information about plants' needs, check flower garden books—many have lists of plants for sun and shade and for wet and dry soils. (See "Recommended Reading" on page 233 for flower gardening books that fill the bill.)

Mix and match. Once you've got a list of compatible plants picked out, head for your local garden center or nursery and see what you've got to choose from. Pick out two or three plants you like and set them beside each other to see how they look. If they don't suit your fancy, keep mixing and matching until you find a combination you like.

As a general rule, place the tallest plant in the center. Set bushy plants in front of or on either side of the central plant to cover its skinny stems and soften the lines of the pot or urn lip. In the areas that are left, plant some trailing or floppy plants that can tumble down from the edge of the pot.

Look for plants with contrasting leaf sizes and colors to make the mix interesting. For example, you could start with a central plant that has light-green compound leaves like cleome. Then surround it with bushy plants like heliotrope with dark-green leaves, and finish with trailing plants with small medium-green leaves like garden verbena. Or add interest by including a plant with variegated foliage or gold, silver, or purple leaves. Study the flower colors of the different plants too, and choose combinations that look pleasing to you.

Give them a good home. For healthy potted plants, make sure the pot or urn you use has one or more drain holes so excess water can drain out. Buy or make your own coarse potting mix to help ensure good drainage and give the roots plenty of air space. Keep the soil evenly moist unless you're growing rock garden plants that need drier soil. Water your container plants with seaweed extract or compost tea once a month during the growing season to give them an extra nutrient boost.

Creative Combos

Here are some uncommon plant combinations that grow particularly well together in large pots or urns. Try either of these combinations to get started, then experiment with your own colorful mixes of annuals or perennials.

A tropical twosome. Combine licorice plant (*Helichrysum petiolare* 'Limelight') with flowering maple (*Abutilon hybridum*—any red cultivar). The bright lime green leaves of the licorice plant will trail over the edge of the pot. The flowering maple grows upright and sets off the lime green foliage with red bell-shaped flowers.

A perennial trio. Mix a pieris shrub (*Pieris* hybrid 'Forest Flame') with 'Beacon Silver' lamium (*Lamium maculatum* 'Beacon Silver') and a clematis vine (*Clematis alpina*). The woody pieris with its bright red new leaves produces dangling clusters of beadlike flowers in spring, while 'Beacon Silver' forms a lush silver and green cover beneath it. The violet-flowered alpine clematis will trail out of the container and down its side if you keep it pinned down with a discreetly placed clothespin. This group needs an acidic soil mix and a shady spot.

44 Change the Color of Your Hydrangeas

Bigleaf hydrangeas are gorgeous plants that have either big puffy flowers or flat lacy ones. The flowers come in beautiful shades of pink or blue, but when you grow them in your yard, the colors can change. Look at your hydrangeas in the summer. If they've changed for the worse (bright blue flowers have turned muddy pink, for instance), you can change the colors back to bright pink or blue by adjusting your soil's pH.

Bigleaf Hydrangeas in Slightly Acid Soil

Bigleaf Hydrangeas in Moderately Acid Soil

A

B

D

C

E

You can change the color of bigleaf hydrangeas by changing the pH of the soil. Add sulfur to the soil to make it more acidic (A) and you can change the color of 'Nikko Blue', a hortensia type of hydrangea, from muddy pink (B) to bright blue (C) and the color of 'Mariesii', a lacecap type of hydrangea, from pink (D) to mauve pink (E).

Keeping track of your soil's pH. Why should you care about the pH (the measure of acidity or alkalinity) of your soil? Well, in addition to having an effect on the flower color of your bigleaf hydrangeas (*Hydrangea macrophylla*), it also affects the growth of all of your plants.

Most plants grow best when the pH of the soil is between 6.5 and 6.8. In that range, soil organisms like worms are happy, and most soil nutrients are available. But some plants, like bigleaf hydrangeas, need a moderately acid soil of pH 5.0 to 6.5 to perform at their peak.

Bigleaf hydrangeas not only thrive at this lower pH, they also let you know if the soil is at the high or low end of their pH range. They'll change their flower color to blue if they're in a soil with a pH of 5.0 to 5.5 and to pink if they're in more neutral soil with a pH of 6.0 to 6.5. That means you can change your bigleaf hydrangea flowers to the bright blue or pink color they were when you bought them by making the soil more acidic or neutral.

Take a soil test. For a really accurate pH measure, send a soil sample to your Cooperative Extension office and ask them to run a soil test. Ask your extension agent for organic recommendations for changing the pH and you'll get specific instructions with the test results.

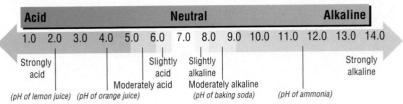

The pH scale runs from 1.0 to 14.0, with 1 being the most acidic, 7 being neutral, and 14 being the most alkaline reading. Soils that are strongly acidic or alkaline won't hurt you, but they are hard on plants. To get an idea of how acidic or alkaline your soil is, compare the soil pH with the pH of the common household items listed.

Start with soil amendments. Your extension agent may suggest using ground limestone or wood ashes to raise the pH, or elemental sulfur, gypsum, or peat moss to lower it. Just don't expect your blooms to change color overnight—the process takes a few months. It's best to amend your soil in fall after the plants go dormant and lose their leaves to get results in the next growing season.

Get to the root of the problem. If your hydrangea is small, you can dig up the plant, shake the soil from its roots, then plunge the roots into a bucket or tub of water to keep them wet while you work. (For a larger plant, amend the soil around the plant without digging it out.)

Once your plant is in the bucket, dig a bigger hole where you took it out and place the soil on a tarp nearby. Mix in the soil amendments recommended for your soil and start filling the hole. Replant the hydrangea and finish filling in with soil. Then water the plant in and pull 4 inches of bark or straw mulch up around it for winter protection.

Change your pH point by point. Aim to change your soil pH by a point or less each year—bigger changes can be hard on beneficial organisms. If you don't get the color you want after the first attempt, repeat the procedure.

pH Pointers

The pH will change at different rates depending on whether your soil has more sand or clay—that's why it's best to follow the extension agent's recommendations. But just to give you an idea of the amounts of soil amendments you'll be working with, here's a general guide for raising pH.

It takes about 5 pounds of lime per 100 square feet to raise pH by 1 point. (It takes 2 to 3 pounds of sulfur per 100 square feet to lower pH by 1 point.) Sandy soils will usually need less limestone and clay soils will need more. For the small amount of soil you'll be dealing with, you'll use much less lime, maybe a cup to a quart depending on your soil type.

45 A Snip in Time Extends Bloom Time

It's tempting to laze around in early summer enjoying your flowers and letting them bloom and go to seed. But if you do, you'll face a colorless garden full of faded blooms in late summer and fall. That's why I use super-quick techniques for removing spent flower heads (a procedure called deadheading). It's an easy way to get a second round of blooms and still have time for life's pleasures.

Save time-consuming hand grooming for flowers like irises that have new emerging buds and spent flowers packed close together. You can deadhead most other flowers quickly and cleanly with hedge shears or a lawn mower. The plants won't mind—they'll reward you with a second flush of blooms.

Off with their heads! Deadheading seems like a daunting task when hot weather kicks in and all your plants are clamoring for attention at once. If you remove fading blooms one by one with hand shears, it is a HUGE job. Luckily, there's an easier way—just use your hedge shears, lawn mower, and string trimmer.

You can use hand-operated hedge shears or electric or gas-powered shears to quickly trim the tops off medium-size or tall flowering plants. Remove the flower heads completely by shearing the flowers and their stems off just above healthy leaves. The leaves hide the cut stems so your plants look tidy. This technique is great for cleaning up perennials such as bee balms (*Monarda* spp.) and chrysanthemums, and it's handy for shearing back large plantings of annuals like marigolds too.

Deadhead low-growing perennial plantings with a lawn mower—set the mower high enough to cut the flowers off the plants without hurting the foliage. Or use a carefully controlled string trimmer to do the job. These tools are especially handy for trimming large plantings of flowering groundcovers such as ajuga (bugleweed) and lamium (dead nettle).

Spare some stems! There are plants like irises and pinks (*Dianthus* spp.) whose new unopened buds are clustered right next to their spent blooms. If you shear these plants, you'll cut off the emerging flowers, so you're better off pruning them with hand shears. Since you'll be able to handle most flowers with hedge shears or a mower, the few that need individual attention won't take up too much of your time.

Plants that self-sow, such as forget-me-nots (*Myosotis sylvatica*), wild columbine (*Aquilegia canadensis*), and foxgloves (*Digitalis purpurea*), are another exception to the shearing rule. Let these plants go to seed so they can re-establish your planting each year.

What do I get out of it? You get more flowers, healthier plants, and a more beautiful garden. Here's how it works. Spent blooms signal a plant that it's time to set seed. So instead of concentrating on flower production, the plant turns its attention to seed production, and the number of new flowers drops off. By removing spent blooms, you delay seed set so the plant keeps producing flowers in an attempt to reproduce.

Since the plants don't have to use their energy to produce seeds, they turn their attention to vegetative growth—the roots, stems, and leaves. Plants with big root systems and strong stems and leaves are healthier. Robust perennial plants have a better chance of surviving the winter. And they'll have the energy to give you more blooms the following year.

Then there's the matter of looks. Your entire garden will look tidier if you keep the dead flowers cut off. Shear the flower stems back just far enough so that they're hidden by leaves. If company's coming, a few snips with your hedge shears can turn a messy-looking planting into a pretty sight in a hurry.

You can make your foliage plants look their best with a flower trim too. The blooms aren't the most important features of plants like lamb's ears (*Stachys* spp.), so cut off the flowers and really show off those fuzzy leaves.

Double Your Blooms by Deadheading

Here are just a few of the many perennial plants that will respond with more blooms if you shear off their spent flowers.

Bellflowers (*Campanula* spp.)
Red valerian (*Centranthus ruber*)
Coreopsis (*Coreopsis* spp.)
Delphiniums (*Delphinium* spp.)
Blanket flower (*Gaillardia* x *grandiflora*)
Baby's-breath (*Gypsophila paniculata*)
Daylilies (*Hemerocallis* spp.)
Catmint (*Nepeta* x *faassenii*)
Phlox (*Phlox* spp.)
Salvias (*Salvia* spp.)
Pincushion flower (*Scabiosa caucasica*)

46 Create Planting Possibilities in Patios and Stairways

The best gardens don't know their own boundaries! Flowers and ground covers come right up to and into outdoor living areas, adding color and a finishing touch. Sometimes this informal decorating scheme is an accident, but more often it's by the design of a clever gardener…like you.

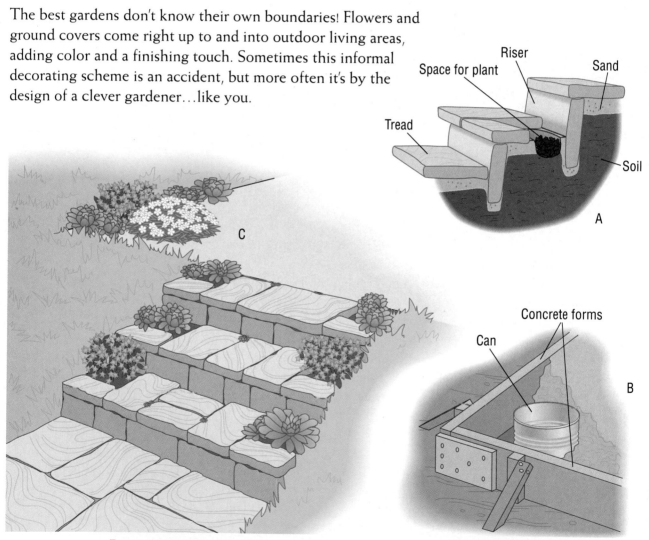

Remember to leave spaces for ground-cover plantings when you build steps (A) and patios (B). The flowers and foliage add color and flair to your hardscape that you can't get any other way (C). Stones and concrete gather and hold summer heat, so remember to wash your stairs or patio down frequently with a hose to water the ground covers.

Invite plants into your living space. Stone or concrete stairways and patios can be pretty lifeless and colorless. Potted plants will soften their hard look, but it's much nicer—and more natural—if the plants are actually growing out of your stairways and patios!

Plan plantings before you pour concrete. Get set to make steps and patios out of concrete this summer. You'll follow the usual procedures, setting up boards to hold the wet concrete in place. But before you pour the concrete into the forms, set cylindrical pots or metal cans on the soil where you want plants to grow—choose the spots where you're least likely to step. Pour the concrete so it flows around the pots or cans.

When the concrete is almost set, remove the cylinders, leaving holes in the concrete down to the soil level. Make sure you use pots or cans that don't have lips on the bottom—lips can snag on the hardened concrete and may be impossible to remove.

Once the concrete has completely hardened, fill the holes with a mix of half compost and half garden soil, then plant them with annuals or perennials. Ground covers that spill onto the concrete look especially nice against that gray background.

Watch your step! If you're making steps using a dry-wall technique—that is, setting stones without mortar—dig out the form of your steps first. Leave risers of from 4 to 6 inches and treads from 18 to 20 inches from front to back. (A riser is the vertical part between two steps and a tread is the horizontal part of a step.) This low, generous profile is inviting-looking and makes climbing the steps easy. On steep slopes, you may need to make the risers 7 or 8 inches high (no higher) and treads from 14 to 16 inches front to back. The rule is, the steeper the rise, the shorter the tread.

Using chunky stones, set in the risers first. Lean the stones back slightly from vertical so they are supported by the soil. Bury the base of each stone a few inches deep to hold them in place. In areas where the ground freezes, dig out 6-inch-deep holes for the riser stones and put 3 inches of sand in the bottom. The sand allows water underneath the stones to drain away, which keeps the stones from heaving out of the ground when the soil freezes and thaws.

Once the risers are in place, they should protrude an inch or two above the level where you'll set the tread stones. Use sand to bring the soil surface for the tread stones up to the top of the riser stones. Another way to prevent heaving is to set the tread stones in mortar that holds the entire step together.

When you place your tread stones, leave an empty space here and there on either side of the central portion of the tread for plants. You can also leave out a tread stone that abuts the riser behind it, so that you can plant low-growing plants where the riser meets the tread. Replace the sand in the planting holes with compost before setting out plants.

Choice Plants for Steps and Patios

These low-growing plants make well-behaved additions to patios and steps.

Geneva bugleweed (*Ajuga genevensis*)

Wall rock cress (*Arabis caucasica*)

Mountain sandwort (*Arenaria montana*)

Common thrift or sea-pink (*Armeria maritima*)

Rock cress (*Aubrieta deltoidea*)

Basket-of-gold (*Aurinia saxatilis*, also known as *Alyssum saxatile*)

Dalmatian bellflower (*Campanula portenschlagiana*)

Cheddar pinks (*Dianthus gratianopolitanus*)

Coral bells (*Heuchera sanguinea*)

Perennial candytuft (*Iberis sempervirens*)

Sedums (*Sedum* spp.)

Hens-and-chicks (*Sempervivum* spp.)

Mother-of-thyme (*Thymus serpyllum*)

Creeping speedwell (*Veronica repens*)

47 Add a Water Feature (without the Water)

Imagine a beautiful stream meandering through your garden. Nice, isn't it? The only problem is there's no natural source of water on your property. Well, don't fret. You can create a dry streambed with all the appeal of the water-bearing kind. All you need is some imagination, a roll of rubber pool liner, and a pile of river rocks.

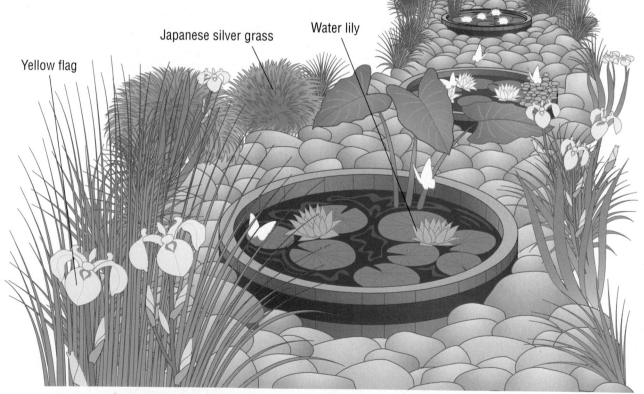

Yellow flag

Japanese silver grass

Water lily

A stream of stones adds beauty to your landscape even when water isn't available. Site the "stream" where water naturally runs off your property, then give it the look of a real watercourse by planting the edges with tall grasses, irises, rushes, sedges, and shrubs. Set tubs of potted water lilies inside the stream for a finishing touch.

A dry stream is a bargain. Locate your streambed in a damp or wet spot in your yard, and you can grow many of the same plants that you would along a creek that's flowing with water. A stream made of stones is a great way to channel excess water away from your yard too. And even if your streambed is dry as a bone, you can give it a watery flavor by setting containers of water plants along its banks.

Look for a low spot. Think of your dry creek bed as a real stream and imagine where water would flow through your yard. Look for the lowest parts of your lawn and for areas where rainwater runs off. Those are the places to locate your streambed since it will look most natural.

Make your stream the shape of an actual flow of water. Imagine that heavy rains sent water flowing through your yard and try to imitate the shape of the runoff. If you have a deep gully in your yard, the stream would run through it and be narrow. If you live on flatter land, your streambed would run through the lowest spot and be wider.

When you do have torrential rains, you'll find that a dry streambed carries off water just as well as a real waterway. Keep that in mind when you place the lowest end of your streambed. Make sure it ends in a site that can handle extra water, not next

to an area like your patio where runoff water would be a nuisance.

Lay down a liner. Remove any brush or vegetation from your future streambed and till or turn the soil to make sure all traces of grass and weeds are buried. (Do your digging in summer when your low spot is driest.) Then cover the area with the thickest black rubber pool liner you can find. (See "Sources" on page 228 for a list of water-gardening catalogs.)

The liner will keep weeds from sprouting in your streambed, so don't try to skip this important step. Forget about using thin sheets of plastic for a liner—they'll disintegrate and turn into bits and pieces that will be impossible to remove. Use rolls of rubber pool liner that are 30 to 45 mils thick instead—this stuff can last for 20 years!

Prepare for water plants. Once you've lined the area, make some places for water-loving plants like water lilies to grow in and around the streambed. The amount of light your streambed gets determines which water plants will grow there. Water lilies need full sun, but cattails and irises will grow in full sun or partial shade.

Half-barrels or large pots, lined with a plastic tub or rubber pool liner, make good homes for many different kinds of water plants. Water-gardening catalogs carry all sorts of water

plants and are great places to look for plant suggestions.

Arrange the half-barrels or pots within the boundaries of the "stream" and along its edges. Then draw a circle on the liner with chalk or flour to mark the location of each container. Cut holes in the liner for the containers, then sink the half-barrels or pots to at least two-thirds of their height into the ground.

Set the stage. Completely cover the liner with a mix of large and small rounded stones to give your streambed a natural appearance. Rounded stones or cobbles are formed in the bottom of streams and rivers, and their shape alone suggests flowing water. You can buy cobbles from building supply stores and landscaping supply firms.

Add the finishing touches. Fill the half-barrels in the stream with water and water-loving plants. If your streambed stays moist, plant the edges with bog plants, moisture-loving grasses like Japanese silver grass (*Miscanthus sinensis*), or water-dwelling plants like yellow flag (*Iris pseudacorus*). In areas that don't carry runoff water, plant the stream edges with Siberian irises and grasses like blue Lyme grass (*Elymus arenarius* 'Glaucus') that don't mind drier conditions. Or continue the illusion of a really wet area by setting half-barrels of water plants along the edges of the stream too.

48 Two Gardens in One

I like to get dramatic results in a short amount of time and this two-for-one garden sure fills the bill. For the same effort it normally takes to build one garden, you can create a rock garden and a bog garden right next to each other. Each hosts a completely different set of plants and the combination creates an intriguing look that will have the neighbors gazing your way with envy, this summer and every growing season to come.

For a wide variety of plants in a small space, you can't beat this combination bog and rock garden. The mixture of wet- and dry-land plants gives you an ever-changing display of contrasting flowers and foliage.

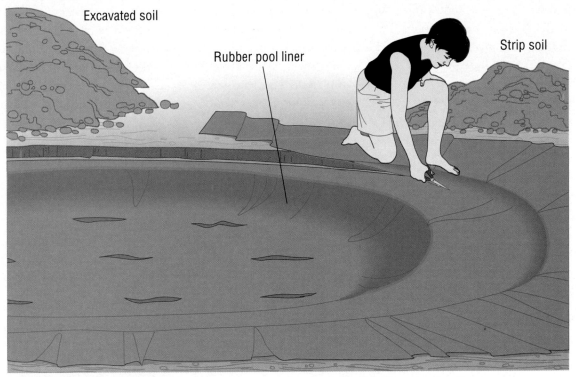

Excavated soil

Rubber pool liner

Strip soil

Line your bog garden with rubber pool liner and trim it so the edge lies flat on the shallow strip. Make foot-long cuts every 3 feet over the bottom of the liner so the water can slowly drain out.

A place in the sun. Choose a spot for your gardens that gets full sun. The idea is to dig out a basin that becomes the bog garden and heap up the soil that you excavate to create a rock garden. You can build the rock and bog gardens on flat or fairly level ground or on a sloping spot. The gardens will fit quite naturally into a sloping site. In a flat area, you can use shrubs to blend them into the landscape. If you can place the bog garden where rainwater runs off, or in an area that stays moist most of the year, so much the better.

Dig a big hole. My plan is for a bog garden that covers a 6-by-10-foot area and is 18 inches deep. Of course you can make a smaller garden, but like I said, I like dramatic results. As you mound the soil to one side, leave at least 1 foot of empty space between the edge of the excavation and the beginning of the mound.

A hole that's 6 feet wide by 10 feet long and 18 inches deep will yield about 90 cubic feet of earth and rocks, or a little over 3 cubic yards. Mind you, this requires some digging, and you might want to hire someone to do the heavy work.

Put a liner in place. Once you've excavated the hole, remove a strip of soil all around the edge that's 1 foot wide and from 4 to 6 inches deep. Put this "strip soil" in a separate place from the excavation soil, because you're going to put it back eventually.

Line the hole with a piece of rubber pool liner that's at least 30 mils thick, making sure the edges overlap the shallow strip. Then trim the liner all the way around so the edges just cover the shallow strip and lay flat. Put the strip soil back where you got it, so it covers the liner and holds it in place.

Make sure the liner leaks. Even a bog garden needs drainage. Get into the hole and,

111

with a sharp knife, cut foot-long slits in the bottom of the liner every 3 feet. That gives you three cuts in the 6-foot direction (two at the edges and one in the middle), and four cuts in the 10-foot direction. Now fill in the excavated hole with compost-enriched topsoil delivered by your local soil supplier (or hauled in by you and some helpful friends or family members using your pickup truck).

When you thoroughly wet the humusy soil in the bog hole, you'll notice that it takes an extra-long time for the water to drain away due to the liner underneath. But because the liner has slits, you don't have standing, stagnant water. In an area that catches some runoff water, you'll have created the perfect conditions for bog plants to flourish. In a drier spot, if rains don't keep it soggy, you'll occasionally need to refresh your bog garden with a hose.

Pile up the rocks. Arrange the soil and stones you excavated from the bog garden to form the rock garden (see Idea #71 for details). If you didn't uncover any good-size stones, you'll need to import some—maybe five to seven big ones and two or three dozen smaller ones.

Using the soil and stones, make several levels in your mound. Set the stones into the soil with one-third to two-thirds of their depth buried, with smaller stones near the top and

larger ones set in at the middle and bottom of the mound. Place the largest stones first and finish up with the smaller stones. Place the rocks so some stand individually and others touch. Create planting pockets where you can tuck plants in among the stones. Put some rocks into the soil so they lay flat, and stand others up for variation. Look at natural rock formations and try to duplicate a favorite

arrangement. Make sure there's plenty of exposed soil in every part of the garden for planting.

Because the rock garden soil is mounded up for quick drainage, it will stay relatively dry, just as the bog garden at its feet will stay relatively wet.

With this two-for-one garden, you've opened up environmental niches for many new types of plants you couldn't have grown before.

Plants for a Sunny Bog Garden

Marsh mallow (*Althaea officinalis*)
Swamp milkweed (*Asclepias incarnata*)
Water arum (*Calla palustris*)
Marsh marigold (*Caltha palustris*)
Green and gold (*Chrysogonum virginianum*)
Summersweet (*Clethra alnifolia*)
Red-osier dogwood (*Cornus stolonifera*)
Dwarf papyrus (*Cyperus isocladus*)
Joe-Pye weed (*Eupatorium purpureum*)
Queen-of-the-prairie (*Filipendula rubra* 'Venusta')
Purple avens (*Geum rivale*)
Yellow flag (*Iris pseudacorus*)
Spotted lamium (*Lamium maculatum*)
Cardinal flower (*Lobelia cardinalis*)
Mints (*Mentha* spp.)
Forget-me-not (*Myosotis scorpioides*)
Cranberry (*Vaccinium macrocarpon*)

Plants for a Sunny Rock Garden

'Silver Mound' artemisia (*Artemisia schmidtiana* 'Silver Mound')
Basket-of-gold (*Aurinia saxatilis*)
Blanket flower (*Gaillardia grandiflora*)
Sweet alyssum (*Lobularia maritima*)
Baby-blue-eyes (*Nemophila menziesii*)
Mexican evening primrose (*Oenothera berlandieri*)
Star-of-Bethlehem (*Ornithogalum umbellatum*)
Moss rose (*Portulaca grandiflora*)
Rock soapwort (*Saponaria ocymoides*)
Hens-and-chicks (*Sempervivum* spp.)
Blue-eyed grass (*Sisyrinchium* spp.)
Lamb's-ears (*Stachys byzantina*)
Thyme (*Thymus* spp.)
Verbena (*Verbena* spp. and hybrid verbenas)
California fuchsias (*Zauschneria california*)

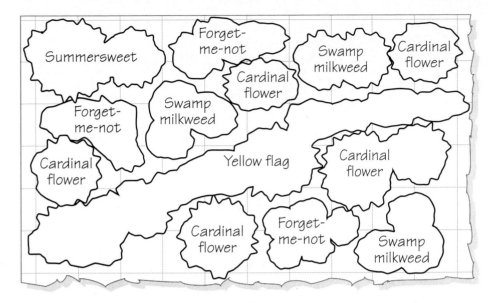

Bog Garden

1 foot

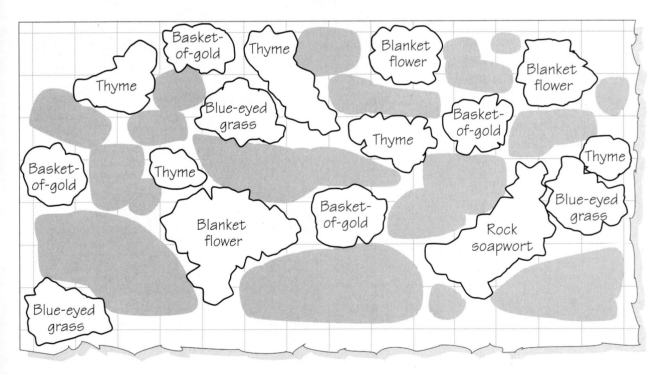

Rock Garden

1 foot

Draw out plans for your bog and rock gardens on graph paper before you get started. These sample plans show how you can arrange the gardens for beautiful floral displays. Consider the eventual size of each plant and the colors of the leaves and flowers when you put your plant combinations together.

49 Bring Life to Your Garden with a Small Pond

A water feature can bring more beauty to your garden than you can imagine. That's what I found out when I installed a small pond and waterfall beside a garden bed. I knew I'd get a nice display of water plants, but I didn't realize what an attraction the water would be for birds, dragonflies, frogs, and water striders. The pond was easier to build than I expected and the results were magical. Start this summer and you can become a pond builder too.

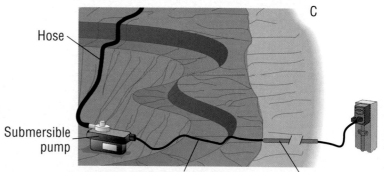

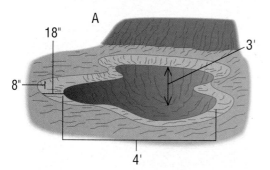

A

18"

8"

3'

4'

D

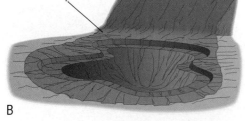

32-mil PVC pool liner

B

Hose

C

Submersible pump

Submersible electrical wires

Conduit

You can build a small pond in a weekend with a little help from your friends. First choose a site against a slope and dig out the hole and a ledge (A). Add a liner (B). Install a pump and a piece of hose to direct the water (C). Then place the rocks and fill the hole with water. Adjust the rocks for good water flow and so the hose can't be seen. Add plants and fish to your pond and watch birds and other beneficials flock to your do-it-yourself water feature (D).

Choose a site—and a shovel. Site the pond at the base of a slope if you can so there's some high ground where you can build a waterfall. (The waterfall will actually be produced by a recirculating pump hidden in the pond bottom.) If you don't have a slope, build one out of rocks and surround the back side with shrubs and trees for camouflage.

Begin by excavating a hole at least 3 feet deep and 4 feet in diameter.

Next, dig out an 18-inch-wide and 8-inch-deep lip all the way around the hole so you have a rim for rocks to sit on. At the back of the hole, shape the slope into a curve where your waterfall will go.

Lay down the liner. Make sure the water stays in your pond by buying a piece of black 32-mil PVC pool liner. (See "Sources" on page 228 for catalogs that carry water-garden supplies.)

To get the right dimensions for the liner, multiply the depth of your pond by 3, then add that number to the total width and length of the pool to get the right size. For example, if your pool is 3 feet deep and 4 feet in diameter, with an extra 18 inches on either end for the rim, then add 9 feet to the total width (4' + 18" + 18" = 7') and length (7') for a total of 23 (9' + 7' + 7' = 23'). You'll need a liner that's 23 feet by 23 feet.

Smooth the sides of the hole and remove any sharp stones or roots from the bottom so they don't puncture the liner. You can put a layer of fine sand in the bottom to prevent punctures. With the help of a friend, flatten the liner so it fits the shape of the hole. Then smooth it into place, starting at the center and working your way to the edges. To do this, take off your shoes and get into the hole barefoot.

Fold the excess liner back onto the shallow rim as you work your way around the diameter so it fits neatly. Trim any excess liner with shears. When you reach the curve of the slope, bring the liner up as far as it will reach rather than folding it over.

Add electricity. Hire an electrician—unless you're experienced with working with electricity and water—to make a small shallow trench from the edge of the pond's rim to your house and install conduit and electric wires.

Place stones all along the shallow pond rim to cover the liner, except at the back where the slope is. Next, take a piece of old garden hose and lay it against the back of the hole from the bottom of the pond up the slope. Run the hose as high as you want your waterfall to be—usually about 3 feet above the water surface—but not higher than the liner.

Finish covering the back part of the pond rim with rocks and place rocks along the curve in the slope so the hose is hidden. Make sure the hose protrudes a bit from the rocks at the top, and that water from the hose won't run back under the liner. Attach the hose in the bottom of the hole to a recirculating submersible water pump and connect submersible wiring from the pump up to the conduit, then through the conduit to electrical service at your house.

Fill it up. Add water to your pond hole until it reaches an inch from the top, then turn on the pump. Arrange the rocks at the top of the waterfall so you can't see the end of the hose and so the water flows down naturally over the rocks. Use several flat rocks with lips for the waterfall—the water will look attractive running down the lips, and it will make a pleasant sound.

Let the water sit for a week before you add plants or fish—it needs time to warm up and let any chlorine escape. You'll need goldfish or mosquito fish to devour any mosquito larvae that hatch in the water. And you'll want a variety of plants too, because they're fun to grow and they keep the water clean. Water-gardening catalogs list all the fish and plants you'll need for a successful pond. (See "Sources" on page 228 for ordering information.)

Great Garden Ideas

for Fall

50 Make Great Compost from Lawn Leftovers

I harvest the grass clippings and leaves from my lawn each year to make fabulous free compost. You can't beat these lawn scraps for making compost—they're easy to handle, they're plentiful, and, did I mention, they're FREE?! As an added bonus, leaves are rich in trace elements that are good for your soil, and grass clippings contain as much nitrogen as cow manure—about 1 percent—which is plenty to heat up a compost pile.

4" grass clippings

4" leaves

4'

6'

You can make beautiful compost with a 50/50 mix of just two ingredients—fall leaves and spring grass clippings. Make your pile 4 feet tall, turn it every two weeks, and in six weeks, you'll have gorgeous compost. A mattock makes turning the pile easier. Just slice the mattock down through the outside of the pile, working your way around the pile and into the center.

Gather the goods. Start the process in the fall when lots of leaves are available. Rake them up and fill as many lawn and leaf bags as you can. (See the box on this page for details.) If you have more leaves than you want to bag, rake them into a big pile in a back corner of the yard and cover them with plastic or a tarp held down with rocks or boards to keep it from blowing off during winter storms. In spring, the leaves will be a little moist and matted, but pretty much as they were when you covered them.

In the spring, put the grass catcher on your mower and start saving all your grass clippings. If you don't have enough clippings, you can usually gather bagfuls from neighbors who put them out to be carted away. If you've ever stuck your hand into a pile of grass clippings that's sat for a few days, you know they get pretty hot. They're perfect for getting compost going because that heat means the clippings have enough nitrogen to fuel the microorganisms that break down plant matter.

Mix it up. Now, build a compost pile in layers, using equal amounts by volume of leaves and grass clippings. Start with a 6-foot square of leaves, about 4 inches thick, on the bottom, then alternate 4-inch layers of fresh, green grass clip-

pings and last fall's leaves, moistening them with the hose as you build the pile. You'll find that these lightweight ingredients will make the easiest pile you've ever built.

Leaves for this pile should be light and fluffy. If the leaves have become dense and matted during the winter, use twice as much of the grass clippings as leaves. To speed decomposition of matted leaves, you can shred them with a shredder or a lawn mower, but this step isn't necessary for fluffy, dry leaves.

After about a week, the pile will get hot. Here's where most people grab a pitchfork and start turning the pile, but I don't like to do lots of lifting, so I use a mattock. The mattock is a root-grubbing tool with a flat square blade. Face the pile with your feet well apart and swing the mattock back over your head, then down in an arc to slice through the layers of the pile. Take slices all around the outside of the pile and rake them to a spot beside the pile to create a new compost heap of mixed materials. You don't have to stir the new pile, since slicing through the layers mixes the materials. If they seem dry, moisten the materials as you build the new pile, or they won't decompose.

Soon you'll have sliced through the entire old pile and built a new one that's nicely mixed and half decayed. Turn the

pile again, in the same way, once or twice more at two-week intervals. You'll find that the result is dark, crumbly, sweet-smelling compost that's surprisingly rich in nutrients due to the many trace elements found in leaves.

Meet plants' needs. This finished compost will have just enough nutrients for most plants to grow healthy, strong, and sturdy. Compost is better than chemical fertilizers that jolt plants with too much nitrogen, forcing them to grow too fast, which results in lush, weak growth that insects and deer like to munch.

Put Leaf Bags to Work

Gathering bags of leaves in fall means you have to find someplace to keep them through the winter. The best storage place is on top of your garden beds. A couple of layers of leaf-filled bags will insulate the soil and keep it soft and unfrozen in most parts of the country, so you can keep root crops like carrots and parsnips in their beds and harvest them through the winter.

You can also pack bags of leaves around brussels sprouts, cauliflower, and kale—crops that will survive through early winter if you give them protection. Use leaves to insulate overwintering plantings of early spring crops like spinach too.

51 No-Work Mulch Gardening

I'm sure that gardeners have been stumbling across this gardening idea for centuries—it's so easy and effective! But it was Ruth Stout who named mulch gardening "The No-Work Method" (see "Recommended Reading" on page 233 for the title of Ruth's book) and popularized the process in the 1950s and '60s. Give mulch gardening a try and you'll see why the name fits—you don't have to till or turn the soil and there's virtually no weeding or watering needed!

A thick layer of mulch on top of your garden means healthy soil and healthy roots below ground. Under the protective layer of mulch, worms aerate the soil and improve soil drainage with their tunnels. They bring soil nutrients up from the subsoil so plants can use them, and worm castings help fertilize the soil. Other tiny soil organisms, including actinomycetes and beneficial nematodes, do their part by breaking down organic matter. Beneficial bacteria transform nitrogen and sulfur into a form that plants can use.

Bacteria

Worms

Actinomycetes

Nematodes

Bury your garden. Ruth's mulch-gardening method is simple. All you have to do is cover the ground. Choose a spot with good garden soil for the quickest results, although any spot in full sun will do. Cover the soil with an 8-inch-thick layer of whatever mulch materials you have on hand. You can use leaves, spoiled hay, straw, grass clippings, and kitchen scraps (no meat, fat, or cheese please, or you'll attract hungry animals).

Move the mulch aside when you're ready to sow seeds or set out plants. When you've finished planting, give the new plants a drink and pull the mulch back around the rows or seedlings.

The mulch will break down as the year goes on, so add more materials from your kitchen or garden as you gather them. Bury kitchen scraps under straw, hay, or grass clippings so they won't attract insects. The mulch will break down even more over the winter, so add more mulch each spring. The goal is to always have a thick layer covering the entire garden.

Watch what happens. After three years, soil microorganisms will break the bottom layers of mulch down into humus. The humus will act as a soil conditioner and fertilizer, improving the soil and adding nutrients that the plants use. You won't

need to add other fertilizers or soil amendments.

Behold the benefits of mulch gardening. Because you keep the mulch layer 8 inches thick with regular additions of organic matter, weeds won't have a chance to sprout. If a few weeds do manage to creep in, they're easy to pull from the mulch and the soft, moist soil.

The mulch soaks up rainwater like a sponge and prevents the hot summer sun from evaporating the water out of

your soil. So unless you live in an extremely hot or dry climate, your plants won't need any more moisture than Mother Nature provides. And even if you do live in a dry climate, with mulch gardening, you won't have to water as often.

And there's more! You'll never need to look for a place to toss your garden wastes, leaves, or kitchen scraps again. You won't need a compost pile because, in a sense, your whole garden area will be a compost pile.

Mulch Gardening My Way

Because I was so familiar with Ruth Stout and her no-work garden, I decided to try mulch gardening at a new property I developed in the hills of eastern Pennsylvania.

The ground for my garden had been planted to corn for many years. There wasn't much in the way of nutrients or organic matter left in the soil. The ground was so hard that I had to use a pick to open a 4-inch-deep channel, which I then filled with compost. Even so, my crops were stunted and failed that first year.

In my first fall there, I discovered that a neighboring farmer had dozens of bales of hay that had been rained on. The bales were spoiled for feed, so I bought them and covered an unused part of my garden with a good 2 feet of the spoiled hay. I amended the rest of the garden with manure and struggled to make it productive.

The next spring, when grasses started sprouting from the hay mulch, I added more hay on top. For two years I kept the area mulched, more to keep the weeds down than with a thought of using the area for planting. In the spring of the third year, I decided to use part of the mulched area for a melon patch. I expected the ground under the mulch to be hard, and brought a pick and shovel to the area.

Was I surprised! When I put my shovel into the soil, it went right in. I pulled back the mulch, and there was a good 6 inches of dark, crumbly, humusy decayed hay on the surface, and dark humus had penetrated a good 8 to 10 inches into that rock-hard soil, loosening it and giving it a fine texture. I planted the area and added more mulch each year. In the end, that mulched patch outproduced the manicured and fancy raised beds I'd made in the rest of the garden.

52 Make on-the-Spot Mulch with Compost and Prunings

When you put in large plantings of trees and shrubs, your yard looks great, but yard cleanup and mulching can be a chore. Rather than haul off my tree, shrub, and grass trimmings, I compost them where I collect them. This on-site recycling not only saves time and effort, it puts nutrients from the yard trimmings back where they're needed. Try it, and soon you'll say "Why didn't I think of this before?"

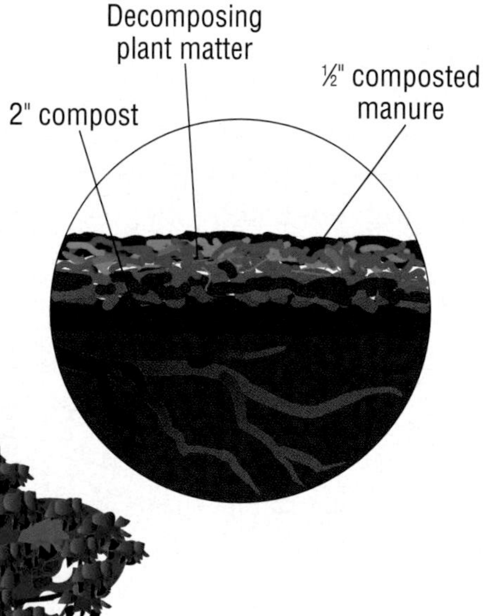

Decomposing plant matter

2" compost

½" composted manure

Make mulching simple around individual trees and shrubs or beds or borders of them. Start with a 2-inch-deep ring of compost. Then, as you collect prunings, trimmings, leaves, and weeds (without seeds), toss them under the trees and shrubs. Fertilize with compost or composted manure and plant annual flowers on top for a colorful show.

You've got to have mulch. That transition area between grass, trees, and shrubs is always troublesome. Mulch is certainly the best way to handle it. A 4-inch-deep layer of mulch keeps grass and weeds from getting too close to plantings. And mulch keeps your mower from getting too close to trees and taking a bite out of the bark. The only problem is, you have to renew mulch each year, which means hauling in load after load of bark chips or compost. Enough work already!

Prepare the planting area first. Here's a simple solution that gives you all the benefits of mulching but cuts down on the work. Start mulch circles as you normally do by removing the sod under trees and shrubs out to the dripline. Then lay on a good 2 to 4 inches of compost.

Put it back where you found it. If a weed sprouts, pull it and lay it down on the composted area. If you shear the shrubs, pile the shearings on the compost. If you prune shrub or tree branches, cut them into 6-inch pieces with your hand shears and toss them under the shrubs on top of the other decomposing matter.

When you grow annual flowers around your trees and shrubs, pull them and leave them on the surface when their bloom time is finished. Rake grass clippings over to the nearest tree or shrub. And when the leaves drop off plants in the fall, don't remove them; mound them up under the shrubs and trees as mulch. (If your site is windy, shred them first.)

In other words, keep all the plant material you gather from your yard in the place you found it. There's no sense hauling all of your organic material to the compost heap if you're just going to haul it back again to use as mulch. Use clippings where they land and they'll suppress weeds, add nutrients to the soil, and decay into precious humus, just like hauled-in mulch.

Proceed to feed. You can still give your trees and shrubs a yearly feeding, despite the un-orthodox mulch. Simply spread ½ inch of compost or composted manure on top of the plant material under your trees and shrubs in spring or fall. These compost additions will not only give the ornamentals a nutritional boost, they'll also add the nitrogen that helps soil microorganisms break down the leavings you're putting under the trees and shrubs.

On-the-spot mulching seems self-evident and simple when you think about it. Try it and see if it doesn't cut down on your work while it beautifies, protects, and feeds your woody ornamentals. You'll probably start a new trend in your neighborhood!

Shade-Loving Annuals Thrive in on-the-Spot Mulch

If you love the shout of color you get from annual flowers, try these selections to beautify the area around your trees and shrubs. Plant these lovelies into the compost-and-clippings mulch. You can toss prunings right on top of the flowers—most will grow back through the clippings as long as they're not completely smothered.

Summer forget-me-not (*Anchusa capensis*). Clusters of blue, pink, or white flowers.

Browallia (*Browallia speciosa*): Showy funnel-shaped white or blue flowers.

Impatiens (*Impatiens wallerana*): Flowers in shades of orange, pink, red, lavender, or white.

Edging lobelia (*Lobelia erinus*): Masses of electric blue, white, or red flowers.

Sweet alyssum (*Lobularia maritima*): Mounds of white, pink, or purple flowers.

Stock (*Matthiola incana*): Fragrant lavender, pink, red, or white blooms.

Garden forget-me-not (*Myosotis sylvatica*): True-blue flowers reseed themselves.

Baby-blue-eyes (*Nemophila menziesii*): Bright blue flowers have white centers.

Pansy (*Viola* x *wittrockiana*): Flowers in solid or patterned shades of blue, purple, red, yellow, or white.

53 Turn Your Lawn Mower into a Shredder

Like most gardeners, I'm always on the lookout for plant materials I can use for mulch and composting. Fallen leaves, grass clippings, and plant stems all work great—if they're shredded. My constant need for chopped materials (and the fact that I don't want to spend a lot of money) is how I discovered that I could use my lawn mower as a shredder.

Mound up the stalks and stems that need shredding and mow over them, aiming toward a fence or wall to keep them in an easy-to-manage pile. If you don't have a fence, you can blow shreds at an old sheet of plywood or at a piece of snow fence or lattice covered with a tarp or cardboard.

124

Make mulch with a mower. The mower is perfect for recycling the remains of herbaceous plants like sunflower and Jerusalem artichoke stalks, faded annual and perennial flowers, old pea and squash vines, and leaves that fall in autumn. I don't use my mower on woody prunings and small branches because that might damage the lawn mower. Also, the mower can fling sharp pieces of wood at high speeds, and these can be very dangerous, even ricocheting off a wall. I know. I tried it...once. Never again!

Ready, set, mulch! Find a spot with a flat ground surface—either lawn or cement. Don't choose a site with bare earth or pebbles. The lawn mower can fling rocks and stones even farther than pieces of wood, and they can hurt even more. The area you choose should also have a wall or fence so that the chopped material doesn't blow out all over the place.

Select the place where you do your chopping with care, because the plant juices and shredded materials that come flying out of the mower will stain what they hit. For instance, you may not want to aim your choppings at a nicely painted white wall that would be disfigured by dark stains.

Always start by putting on goggles. Then rake or pile your leaves and cuttings into a mound.

Bring your lawn mower up to the edge of the pile and push down on the handle so the front of the mower raises up, then lower it onto the materials so the choppings are blown against the wall. Keep moving ahead, raising and lowering the mower, until the pile is chopped into a compact mound. If your mulch is not chopped finely enough on the first pass, rake it away from the wall and repeat the process.

Woody pieces are for the birds. What can you do with the woody prunings the mower can't handle? Stack them in piles where they'll provide shelter for birds and other wildlife. Use them as plant stakes. Build rustic furniture and fences, or try using them in projects like homemade birdhouses.

Remember mower maintenance. After the shredding season is over, give your mower a good going over. Get the blades sharpened, drain and recycle the oil, and change the air filter. That's all it takes to keep your shredding machine in good working order.

What's Right for Chopping

These yard and garden materials make excellent mulch and compost ingredients after you chop them with the mower. For the best results, wait until the materials are relatively dry before you whack them up and always wear goggles when you use your lawn mower as a shredder.

Autumn leaves. These are the very best for shredding into a fine, nutritious mulch and compost ingredient. Ten bags of light fluffy leaves will turn into one full bag of finely shredded leaves. Use leaf mulch where you want a dressy look—in a flowerbed, for instance.

Spent flowers. The stalky stems of sunflowers, daisies, cornflowers, campanulas, Jerusalem artichokes, and annuals such as statice and nicotiana make excellent mulch materials when you shred them. Try this coarser mulch around trees and shrubs, and in pathways and other areas where you don't want to replace mulch very often.

Cornstalks. To turn cornstalks into compost, chop them before they dry out entirely—they should still be a little green. Green plants are better at stimulating the growth of beneficial microorganisms (the ones that break plant materials down into compost) than totally dry ones. For mulch, chop the stalks when they're dry. Coarse mulch is a good choice for pathways, since it provides good drainage and a neat look.

Meadow grasses. Long, tough orchard and meadow grasses like foxtail, timothy, and Johnsongrass work better as a compost ingredient and as a mulch when you shred them. Cut and shred them before they set seed unless you want them to sprout in the mulched area for later use as green manure. Grassy mulches are great for dressing up coarser mulches, or where you want to add some organic matter to the soil.

54 Wipe Out Weeds with White Clover

Weeds in closely planted crops like peas drive me crazy! Mulch is one answer, but it's hard to spread mulch around plants that are growing just 2 to 3 inches apart. My solution is to use a living mulch of clover—it can grow and cover soil in spaces too tight for me to mulch or pull weeds. Clover makes a great mulch in hard-to-weed block plantings too, so it's perfect for your corn or sunflower patch.

B

Nodules

White Clover

A

In the spring, cut 4-inch-wide rows in a clover patch and make V-shaped trenches. Fill the trenches with weed-seed-free compost and plant them with peas. The clover will grow back to the edge of the compost-filled trench, preventing weeds by outcompeting them (A). When the clover starts to flower (B), cut it back. Then, after the pea harvest, turn the clover under to release nitrogen stored in the plants' root nodules to the soil.

Why grow mulch? Clover seed is usually easier to come by than straw bales or other mulches, and there are other benefits too: A living mulch of clover makes a great mud-free path during harvesttime, and since clover is a legume, it adds nitrogen to the soil when you till or turn it into the ground. Get your living mulch started in early September with a trip to your local feed store or garden center.

Sow seeds in fall. Buy white (Dutch) clover seed (the familiar perennial clover with little white ball-like flowers) and inoculant (a powdered seed treatment for legumes). Till up the part of your garden where you'll plant closely spaced crops or block plantings, and get ready to sow clover. You can plant the whole garden to clover if you want to—it's a great way to add extra organic matter and nitrogen to the soil. Plan on 1 ounce of seed for every 100 square feet of area you want to cover, or 8 ounces for every 1,000 square feet.

Wet the seed, coat it with the inoculant, and sow it by hand in the tilled-up patch. Rake the seed in with a steel-toothed rake, then water it well. The clover will have time to sprout and make a nice green ground cover before frost hits. When the really cold weather arrives, it goes dormant.

Start and finish with weed-free plantings. In spring, the clover will start growing again. Make wide rows for planting peas in early April, and prepare blocks for other crops like corn when their planting dates approach.

For pea plantings, take a straight-sided garden spade and dig out 4-inch-wide strips of clover turf. Remove enough soil to make V-shaped planting trenches. Set up trellises over the strips, then fill the trenches to the soil level with weed-seed-free compost and plant your seeds. For a super-sturdy trellis that will support peas and another vine crop, like cucumbers, see Idea #11.

For corn, sunflowers, or other crops, mow, then till the area you want to plant, leaving a border of clover. I don't like to churn up my soil (and weed seeds) too much, so I dig and turn the clover by hand instead of tilling.

In a couple of weeks, the clover will grow right up to the 4-inch-wide strips or blocks where your crops are planted, preventing any weeds from growing. That's all the weed control you'll need for peas. For block plantings, let the crops grow for four to five weeks, then sow clover between the plants at the same rate as your fall planting. The clover grows so thick you won't see a weed.

Outside of the plantings, the clover gets really thick as the weather gets warmer, so I mow it off just 2 to 3 inches tall and use the clippings to mulch other plants or put them in my compost pile. Use a grass-catcher bag if you have one and you won't have to rake the clippings.

When your crops finish producing, till or turn the clover under so it can break down and release nutrients into the soil. Whatever you plant next will get a nitrogen boost!

Working with Clover

Why do you need to treat clover and other legumes with an inoculant? Because the inoculant contains nitrogen-fixing bacteria that legumes need to capture nitrogen from the air and convert it into a form plants can use. Getting the inoculant is easy. It's sold with legume seeds—just make sure you get the right one for the type of seed you're buying.

To use inoculant, moisten the clover seeds, pour them into a bowl containing the inoculant, then shake the bowl to coat the seeds. Plant them right away and your job is done.

The nitrogen-fixing bacteria, called rhizobia, will infect the clover roots and form nodules. Inside the nodules, the bacteria take energy from the plants and give back nitrogen they "fix" or capture from the air.

55 Protect Soil Nutrients with Cover Crops

Snowmelt and heavy winter and spring rains can wash the nutrients right out of the soil. After working hard to *add* nutrients to my garden, that's the last thing I want! So when I add compost, farmyard manure, or other organic fertilizers and soil amendments to my garden in fall, I lock their nutrients in place with a cover crop until spring.

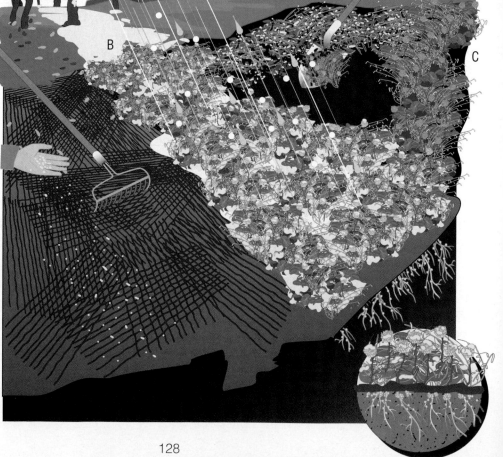

Broadcast the seeds of cover crops such as oats and red clover on a prepared seedbed in fall (A), rake the seeds into the soil, and water thoroughly. The cover crops will protect your soil from weeds and weather (B), until you mow, then turn them under in spring (C). The nutrients and organic matter provided by the decomposing crops will improve the soil—and your future crops.

Save your soil with plants. Cover crops are simply plantings of grasses, grains, or legumes that cover and protect bare soil. The leaves and stems of the plants fend off wind and driving rains that erode and compact uncovered soil. They also crowd out weeds. Roots do their part too, holding the soil in place against the elements.

Sow cover crops in fall. Dig or till your garden in early fall to get the soil ready for planting. Sow cover crops thickly to get as much green matter covering the soil as possible. October and November are the months to sow cover crops in Zones 8 to 10, while August and September are right for starting cover crops in Zones 3 to 7. Early fall plantings give cover crops enough time to blanket your soil before cold weather stops their growth.

Turn your cover crop into green manure. In early spring you'll see the remains of annual cover crops like oats lying across your garden like a protective mulch. Perennial cover crops like winter rye will be putting up new growth.

As soon as you can work the soil, turn annual cover crops into the soil. Wait to turn perennial cover crops under until just before they start flowering—that's when they'll have the most nutrients to put back in your soil. You can use a shovel or a tiller for the task, but either way you don't have to dig deep. Just work the plants into the top 4 inches of soil. Annual crops are easy to work into the soil. Vigorously growing perennials take more digging but won't give you much trouble if you mow them first.

The decomposing leaves, stems, and roots of the cover crops release stored nutrients to your soil, improving the fertility and adding organic matter. At this stage, the cover crops aren't covering the soil— they're improving it and so they're called green manure crops. It takes a month or two for the plant material to break down, depending on the crop, and then your garden will be ready for vegetable plantings.

Mix and Match Cover Crops

Legumes such as clovers and vetches make good green manure crops because they can convert nitrogen from the air into a form that plants can use. It's a handy trick that means vegetables that follow legume plantings get an extra-nitrogen boost. Nonlegumes like oats produce lots of topgrowth and are a good way to build up your soil's organic matter quickly. So which should you use? Both. Mix one legume with one or more nonlegumes, and your soil will get the benefits of both types of plants.

Name	Planting Rate per 100 Square Feet (in ounces)	Description
Legumes		
Crimson clover	¾ to 1½	Annual; helps break up compacted soil. Winter-hardy in southern states.
Hairy vetch	1½ to 3	Annual; helps suppress weeds. Sow with annual ryegrass to provide the crop with winter protection.
Red clover	¾	Perennial; thrives even in poor soil.
Nonlegumes		
Annual ryegrass	1½ to 2	Annual; grows in a wide range of soils.
Barley	3	Annual; fibrous roots hold soil firmly.
Oats	4	Annual; overwinters in southern states and winterkills in the North.
Winter rye	4	Annual; grows best in well-drained soil.

56 Enlist the Help of Volunteer Vegetables

Let self-sowing vegetables go to seed to extend your harvest or to avoid replanting in spring. But be choosy about the vegetables you allow to form seedheads, since the seeds of open-pollinated plants are usually the only ones worth a return engagement. Here are my favorite volunteer vegetables and the tricks I use to keep them coming back.

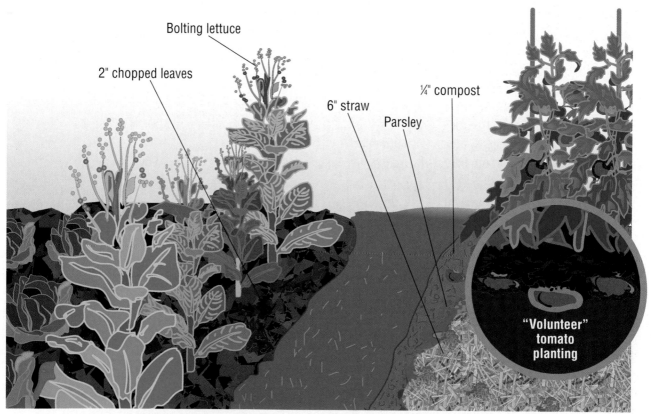

Bolting lettuce

2" chopped leaves

6" straw

¼" compost

Parsley

"Volunteer" tomato planting

When frost threatens in fall, protect self-sown seeds from the cold with a compost, chopped-leaf, or straw blanket. They'll sprout in spring when the weather warms. Remove the mulch from lettuce (and dill) plantings early since the seeds need light to germinate.

Go for the gold. If you plan to encourage volunteer vegetables in your garden, choose open-pollinated seed. Most seed catalogs specify when a vegetable is a hybrid—if they don't say, the plant is usually open-pollinated. (See "Sources" on page 228 for vegetable seed companies.)

Open-pollinated vegetable varieties are real treasures because they come true from seed. That means that the seedlings will grow into plants with the same traits as the vegetable the seed came from.

Hybrid vegetable varieties are produced by crossing two or more plants that are closely related but genetically different. These crosses will either be sterile or they'll produce seedlings with a variety of different characteristics. Instead of getting the traits of the plant the seed came from, you'll usually get less-desirable characteristics from one of the original parents of the cross.

Whenever you let plants go to seed, choose healthy specimens with tasty fruit and growth habits you like. Once your plants have self-sown, make sure you draw a map or use stakes to mark the spot. You don't want to till up your hard-working volunteers by mistake.

Let greens and herbs go. When you're harvesting arugula, basil, lettuce, mizuna (a Japanese mustard), or spinach, remember to let a few of your plants flower and produce seed. With crops such as coriander and dill, there's no memory work needed since they're grown for their seeds.

Lettuce may cross-pollinate unless you separate different varieties with a row of corn, tomatoes, or other tall plants to keep them apart. Other plants, such as basil, need to be separated by 150 feet or more to keep varieties from crossing, but you can avoid the problem by growing only one variety at a time.

When your spring-sown greens and herbs go to seed in late summer, mulch the dropped seed with ¼ inch of compost to plant your fall crop. Let fall crops sow seed for spring harvests, then mulch the planting with 2 inches of chopped leaves for winter protection. (In Zone 8 and warmer, seeds from fall plantings will produce winter crops that will self-sow again for spring.) Move most of the mulch away in spring to encourage the seeds to germinate.

Pile on protection for parsley and Swiss chard. Parsley and Swiss chard are biennials, which means they produce seeds in their second year of growth, then die. The trick to getting these plants to come back year after year is to plant them two years in a row, keeping the first planting alive over winter so it can go to seed.

Protect the first-year plants from winter cold by burying them under a thick (6-inch) layer of straw mulch or chopped leaves before they're frosted. In early spring, uncover the buried plants and let them go to seed—they'll keep you supplied with new seedlings from then on. Plant the patch a second time in spring, sowing new seeds around the overwintered plants. That way you'll always have a mix of one- and two-year-old plants.

Give volunteer tomatoes a hand. Tomatoes are champion self-sowers. Just be sure to plant different varieties on opposite ends of your garden so they don't cross-pollinate.

In summer, set some particularly nice tomatoes on a patch of bare ground and let them rot. Don't wait until fall or you'll be selecting for tomatoes that ripen late in the year. Cover the new planting area with ¼ inch of compost at the end of the season for winter protection. The next spring you'll find tomato seedlings sprouting in the bed when the soil temperature warms to their liking.

As the volunteer seedlings grow, thin them to stand 6 inches apart in all directions. Protect the plants with plastic-covered tomato cages or floating row cover if a late frost threatens or you want them to get off to a faster start.

57 Overwinter Greens for Your Earliest Spring Salads Ever

For tasty, tender harvests of greens such as kale, spinach, and oriental mustards, you need cool weather. Spring planting sounds like a good idea, but before you know it, the summer sun is baking your spring-sown greens and turning them bitter. Don't let your harvest end just when it's getting started. Plant early—the fall before the spring harvest—and you can beat the heat, extend your harvest, and create a bonus crop of compost.

Leaf-filled bags

6"

1' of leaves

Fill a raised bed or cold frame with cool-season greens, such as spinach and oriental mustards, in early fall for an extra-long harvest season in spring. (Oriental mustards are mild enough to eat raw when they're young; cook older, stronger-tasting leaves as you would cabbage.) Sow plants closely— just 6 inches apart in all directions. Use leaves or hay bales for winter protection and your greens will survive the deepest freezes.

A short spring will do greens in. The seeds of cool-season greens will sprout when the soil temperature reaches just 50°F in spring. The seedlings look like they're off to a quick start, but the plants will grow slowly in the cool spring air. By the time your greens reach eating size, the weather is usually turning warm, even hot.

Hot temperatures encourage greens to bolt (go to seed). Instead of putting their energy into leaf production, the plants concentrate on developing seeds. In the process, your once-tasty greens produce a bitter sap and you end up with a bitter harvest.

Sow slow crops in fall. Give your greens a head start by planting seeds in fall, then protecting the plants over the winter. In spring, you'll have plants that are ready to grow salad-size leaves while the weather is still cool.

Make a raised bed for your greens by adding lots of compost to the soil and building a mounded planting bed. The bed should be 3 to 4 feet wide so it's easy to reach across. It can be as long as you like. You can frame the bed with bricks, cinder blocks, or rot-resistant wood like cedar to help hold the soil in place. But the frames aren't necessary if you'd prefer less permanent beds.

Sow your spinach, mustard, or other greens seeds in the first week of September in the northernmost parts of the country (Zone 3), in mid-September in Zones 4 and 5, in the third week in September in Zone 6, and in late September or early October in Zone 7. In Zones 8 and warmer, grow your greens during the winter when temperatures are cool.

Plant your greens seeds 6 inches apart in all directions over the entire surface of the bed. The seeds will germinate and the seedlings will form little rosettes of leaves before the really cold weather sets in.

Mulch for winter warmth. Just before the first killing frost, mulch your greens bed with a 1- to 2-foot layer of fall leaves. Then completely cover the bed with a double layer of leaf-filled plastic bags, or use straw or hay bales. Make sure the edges of the bed are covered to insulate the bed from the deep freezing that can kill the young plants.

Let the sun shine in spring. Uncover the beds when the ground thaws out, removing the bags of leaves or bales of hay and all but 2 inches of the leaf mulch. Wait until the ground dries out enough so it isn't muddy before you start working in the bed.

Check out the contents of the leaf bags as you remove them from the pile, and you'll see they've already started to break down into compost. Empty the bags out wherever you need composted mulch.

Fluff up the remaining mulch around the little greens plants so they're still protected. They'll look kind of squashed and ratty at this stage, but they'll begin to grow, perk up, and put out new leaves quickly. Soon you'll be eating the tenderest, tastiest fresh and cooked greens around!

Keep Greens Warm over Winter with a Cold Frame

Short on space? If you don't have a raised bed to spare for greens, plant a cold frame with traditional greens or oriental mustards such as mizuna and tatsoi in early fall. The plants will be up and growing by early winter, which is when you should mulch the little greens with a 1-foot-deep layer of leaves.

The leaves and a standard glass or plastic cold-frame cover are all the protection cool-season greens need during the winter. In late winter or early spring, prop open the cold-frame cover with a stick or brick on warm days to let excess heat escape. Remove the cover completely on really hot days.

Once the weather turns mild and night temperatures don't go below freezing, remove all but 2 inches of mulch and let the greens grow freely.

58 Deer- and Raccoon-Proof Garden Fencing

You don't have to live in the country to be plagued by raccoons and deer in your garden. They're living in cities and suburbia these days, since there aren't many other areas available. Deer, raccoons, and other furry critters have to eat something, but you can make sure it's not *your* flowers and vegetables with this pest-proof fence.

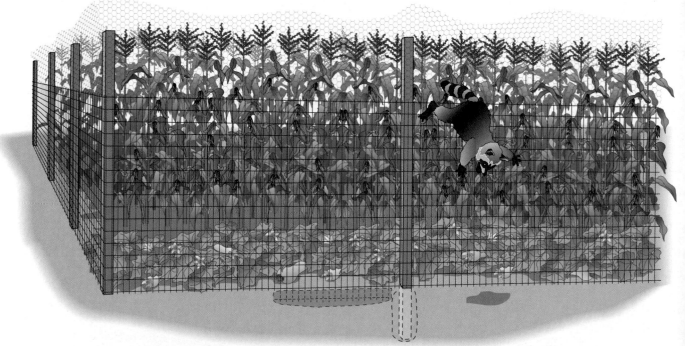

An 8-foot-tall fence is high enough to keep deer out, but it won't stop a determined raccoon. Add a floppy top to your fence and raiding raccoons will get dumped off when they try to climb it. As you are putting the top course of fencing on, it will be apparent how much extra you'll need to make it floppy enough to dump the raccoons off.

Build it to last. Fall is the best time for fence building since the soil is usually moist and easy to dig. Better yet, a fall fence means your spring crops are protected from day one.

Start by setting sturdy 10-foot-tall rot-resistant posts at 10-foot intervals around your garden—black locust posts are a good choice. Set the posts 2 feet into the ground and anchor them with concrete if possible. Finish with the last post about 3 feet from your first post, so you can make an entranceway for yourself. (See the illustrations on page 137 for directions for making a gate.)

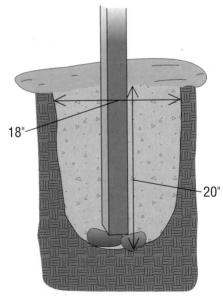

Set your fence posts deep so they're sturdy enough to handle the pull of the stretched fence. Start by digging a bowl-shaped hole 18 inches in diameter and 20 to 24 inches deep for each post. Set a stone or two in the bottom of each hole, then set the post in and fill the hole with concrete mix.

Dig a shallow trench all around your garden, just outside the posts. Next, attach 6-foot-tall welded wire fencing to the posts. Using sturdy staples, nail the welded wire fencing to the posts, keeping it stretched tight. As you attach the welded wire to the posts, bury the bottom 2 to 3 inches of fencing in the trench and you'll keep dogs, opossums, rabbits, and woodchucks out of your garden in addition to the deer and raccoons.

Outsmart pests with chicken wire. This 6-foot-tall fence is a good start, but you still need 2 more feet to keep deer from jumping in—and a way to deter the raccoons. That's where chicken wire comes in. Attach a piece of 3-foot-wide chicken wire to the top of the other wire, leaving an extra 8 to 10 inches of the chicken wire sticking out above the top of the posts. Make sure there's plenty of slack in this top course of fencing—you want it to flop out away from the garden. Now if a raccoon climbs the fence, the floppy chicken wire will sag over and drop him right off.

Finally, you need to securely tie the bottom of the chicken wire to the top of the welded wire fence so the little bandits can't crawl between the two types of fencing. You can do this by running a flexible wire along the whole course and weaving

Materials List

10-foot-long, rot-resistant posts (Buy as many as needed to surround your garden with posts set 10 feet apart.)

Bags of concrete mix (You'll need two 40-pound bags or one 80-pound bag to set each post.)

4 2 × 4s (These will form the gate.)

Rolls of 14-gauge welded wire fencing (Choose wire that's 6 feet tall, and buy enough to surround your garden.)

Boxes of staples (You'll use staples to attach the wire to the posts and gate.)

Chicken wire or plastic mesh fencing (Buy enough 3-foot-wide wire to go around your garden twice.)

1 long piece of flexible wire, or many twist ties or plastic ties (The wire should be long enough to stretch all the way around the garden—you'll use it to fasten the welded wire and chicken wire together. If you use twist ties or plastic ties instead, buy enough to fasten the two wires together every foot or so.)

the fences together, or by using twist ties or plastic ties.

Protect your garden once and for all. Fencing may seem like a lot of bother, but unless you deer- and raccoon-proof your garden—and keep out possums, rabbits, and woodchucks at the same time—you'll lose a lot of time, effort, and expense to these critters. Not to mention food! With a fence, the job is once and done.

(continued)

Easy Fencing Options

If my sturdy, critter-proof fence isn't your style, or doesn't fit your pocketbook, use one of these other effective methods to protect your garden.

Zap pests with an electric fence. Electric fencing works for scaring off both small animals such as rabbits, raccoons, and woodchucks, and larger animals like dogs and deer. It takes less work to set up an electric fence, but more work to maintain it.

Use lightweight metal posts to surround your garden, then install three strands of electric wire—a bottom one just 3 inches off the ground, one about 8 inches above that, and a third wire at 4 feet off the ground. The first two are for small animals, the top one for deer. Hook the fence up to an electic fence box, plug it in, and you're in business.

The problem with electric fencing is that if weeds or grasses grow up to touch it, and they're wet, the fence will short out. You can keep the area mowed or trimmed with a string trimmer, or set boards or plastic on the ground under the wires so weeds and grass can't grow.

Fend off freeloaders with plastic. Building a heavy-duty fence can be a daunting task, but you can make it easier with substitutions. Use metal fence posts instead of heavy wood ones and plastic mesh fence instead of wire. The plastic mesh fence is a favorite idea of Dr. David Benner of Benner's Gardens in New Hope, Pennsylvania. He likes it so much he started selling rolls of the plastic (see "Sources" on page 228 for ordering information). You can use the plastic mesh just like I use welded-wire fencing, but make sure to add an extra-floppy section of plastic mesh on top to keep raccoons out.

Put Fido on patrol. If you have a good dog, you really don't need a fence. Set up an overhead wire and chain run so your dog can patrol the garden perimeter at night. Faithful Fido will keep away deer and any other marauding animals that come by. (Make sure his rabies vaccination is up to date!) Or, use an invisible fence (a buried wire) to keep your dog in your yard but out of your garden. Radio waves from the invisible fence send a signal to your dog's collar and let him know where he can and cannot roam.

The drawback to this system is, of course, that you'll have to listen to your dog barking at 2 A.M. when night raiders come looking for garden treats. If barking bothers you, or your neighbors, choose one of the quieter options above.

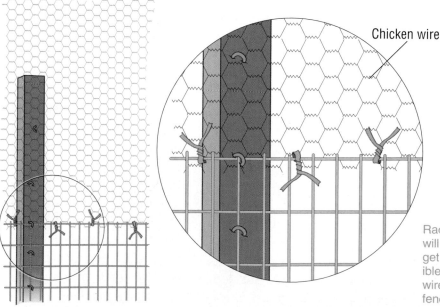

Chicken wire

Raccoons are persistent critters who will sneak through your fence if they get a chance. Use twist ties or flexible wire to securely tie the chicken wire and welded wire parts of your fence together to keep them out.

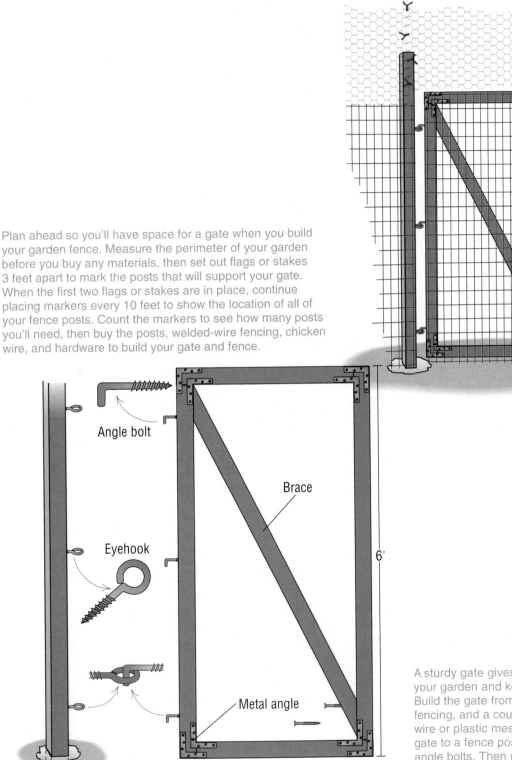

Plan ahead so you'll have space for a gate when you build your garden fence. Measure the perimeter of your garden before you buy any materials, then set out flags or stakes 3 feet apart to mark the posts that will support your gate. When the first two flags or stakes are in place, continue placing markers every 10 feet to show the location of all of your fence posts. Count the markers to see how many posts you'll need, then buy the posts, welded-wire fencing, chicken wire, and hardware to build your gate and fence.

Angle bolt

Brace

Eyehook

6'

Metal angle

3'

A sturdy gate gives you easy access to your garden and keeps critters out. Build the gate from 2 × 4s, welded-wire fencing, and a course of floppy chicken wire or plastic mesh on top. Attach the gate to a fence post with eyehooks and angle bolts. Then use a hook and eye-hook to keep the gate closed.

59 Grow Semitropical Fruits in the North

Imagine growing your own luscious figs, kiwis, and even wine grapes. Everyone knows you can't grow them north of Zone 7, where winter temperatures go below 0°F. So how is it that gardeners have grown tender fruits like figs as far north as Montreal, Canada? All it takes is determination—and a lot of extra winter protection. You *can* grow tender fruits in cold country! Here's how.

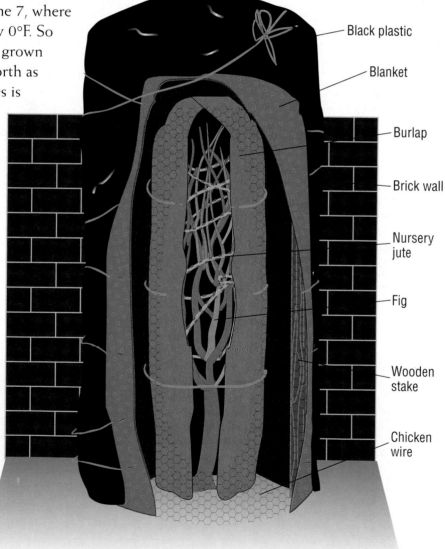

Black plastic

Blanket

Burlap

Brick wall

Nursery jute

Fig

Wooden stake

Chicken wire

Tender fruit trees (and vines) can survive deep freezes if you provide them with extra heat. Plant trees beside a south-facing stone wall so they benefit from the heat the stone collects during the day and releases at night, and wrap them in winter. If you don't have a stone wall, wrap the trees (or vines) and bury them under a protective layer of soil and insulating covers.

Back figs against a warm wall. If you have a south-facing wall of stone or brick, plant your fig next to the wall. When the tree drops its leaves and goes dormant in the fall, tie up the branches, pulling them close together with nursery jute or narrow rolls of burlap (see "Sources" on page 228 for a list of companies that carry garden supplies). Make the fig into as small a cylinder as possible without breaking the branches. Then wrap the plant with several thicknesses of blankets or sheets of untreated burlap.

Next, drive two long wooden stakes into the ground beside the wall and on either side of the wrapped tree. Make the stakes 1 foot longer than the tree. Then cut a long piece of chicken wire and attach it to the stakes with a staple gun so it forms a half-cylinder around the wrapped tree. Make the cylinder 6 inches taller than the tree. Cover the chicken-wire cylinder with an old rug or blanket and tie the fabric in place. Finally, wrap a piece of black plastic over the insulating material so the fabric stays dry.

Bury freestanding figs for winter safety. If your fig isn't close to a wall, dig a trench extending from a point 1 foot from the trunk outward to a length that equals the height of the tree. When the tree is dormant, tie up its branches into a tight cylinder and wrap the tree in burlap.

On the side of the tree opposite the trench, cut downward with a sharp garden spade in a semicircle about 1½ feet out from the trunk, cutting all the roots on that side of the tree. Now gently push the fig tree over, cutting any roots that are still holding it up on the side opposite the trench. When the tree lies down flat in the trench, the roots on the trench side will still be intact.

Cover the tree with an old rug or more burlap, then with a layer of black plastic. Finish the job by covering the trench with several layers of leaf-filled plastic bags or hay bales.

Uncover your tree treasures. In the spring, about two to three weeks before the last frost date, take the insulation off your tree and unwrap the limbs. If your tree was buried, hoist it to a vertical position and tie it to a stake so it stays upright. There will be enough roots on your root-pruned tree to keep it growing until it puts out new roots during the growing season.

Make a sandy bed for vines. Grapevines and fuzzy kiwis respond well to being buried and are easier to handle than trees. Prune the vines hard after they go dormant in fall, then gently remove them from their trellis. Prune grapes as shown in the illustration on page 200.

For kiwis, cut the fruiting arms (also called cordons) of young plants back to leave just 2 feet of growth from the previous season. Cut the cordons on older, mature plants back to 7 feet and the side branches growing off the cordons back to 1½ feet.

Lay the pruned vines in a shallow trench lined with sand and cover them the same way as the trees. In the spring, a week or two before the last frost date, uncover the vines and gently tie them up to their trellis.

Head Off Trench Troubles

Two problems can occur when you overwinter fruits in trenches, but both are simple to solve. The first problem is mice or voles that decide to live in the winter insulation surrounding your tree. Keep these little invaders from gnawing fig bark by wrapping the tree with a fine-meshed wire like window screening.

The other problem is bad drainage, and it affects both trees and vines. If water stands in the trench, it can rot the plant's bark, destroying the cambium (a thin layer of living tissue) underneath. Make sure your plants get good drainage by sloping the end of the trench down from the tree or vine, so that winter rains are immediately carried away.

60 Graft Variety onto Your Fruit Tree

Need a little variety in your life and your fruit bowl? Follow the example of the great early-twentieth-century plantsman Luther Burbank who managed to graft a cherry tree so it produced 500 different kinds of cherries! You don't have to be a plant wizard like Burbank to make grafting techniques work for you. Simply follow the steps here to grow several varieties of a single kind of fruit on one tree and impress your friends and neighbors.

Why settle for one apple variety when you can grow five or more on a single tree? Use a simple technique called T-budding to grow your favorite apples without wasting space.

140

Get ready to graft. August and September are the right months for grafting plants using a technique called T-budding. This grafting technique involves taking a bud from one tree (the donor tree) and inserting it into a branch of another tree (the stock plant). In early fall, the stock plant will still be actively growing and the bark should "slip" or separate easily from the wood when you cut it.

Start by selecting the type of tree you want to graft to produce multiple varieties of the same kind of fruit—apples, cherries, and pears are all good choices. The stock tree should have ¼- to 1-inch-diameter branches that are within easy reach. If you don't have a good candidate for grafting, plant a tree that's at least 3 feet tall this fall and it will be ready to graft in two or three years. Choose a semidwarf tree so you'll end up with an easy-to-manage 12- to 15-foot-tall plant.

To get buds for grafting, take cuttings from the trees of willing friends, or contact the North American Fruit Explorers (NAFEX), Route 1, Box 94, Chapin, IL 62628, for possible sources. (See the "Fruits and Nuts" and "Garden Supplies" listings on page 228 of "Sources" for mail-order suppliers of budsticks and grafting materials.) If you cut your own budsticks, choose healthy

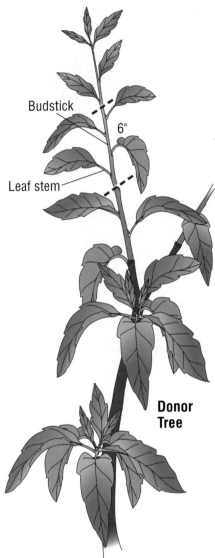

Budstick

6"

Leaf stem

Donor Tree

To graft an apple variety onto another apple tree, cut 6-inch-long budsticks from the middle portion of the current year's growth. Remove the leaves from each budstick immediately but leave the leaf stems— you'll need them later. Wrap the budsticks in damp paper towels and put them in the shade while you prepare the stock plant for grafting.

branches with leaf buds. Avoid branches with flower buds, which are usually larger and fatter than leaf buds.

Prepare the graft site. Choose an upright branch on the stock tree, and strip the leaves from the current year's growth at the point where you want to make the graft. (See the illustration on page 142.)

With a sharp knife, make a T-shaped cut in the branch to prepare it to receive a bud. Clean the knife with alcohol before using it. Make a 1-inch-long vertical cut close to the point where the new growth started in spring. Cut through the bark and cambium (the thin layer between the bark and the wood), but no deeper. Next make a horizontal cut at the top of the vertical cut to form a T. Twist the knife slightly to open the bark flaps.

Cut the bud loose. Cut a bud from the budstick so it just fits inside the bark flaps on the stock tree. Make a horizontal cut through the bark and cambium ¼ inch above the bud. Now place the blade ¾ inch below the bud and cut off the bark and bud, slicing upward until you reach the horizontal cut. You'll end up with a bud surrounded by a shield-shaped piece of bark. Using the bit of leaf stem as a handle, lift out the bud chip.

Insert the bud chip with care. Peel back the flaps of the T-cut with the point of your knife, then slide the bud chip down into the T-cut. Push the

To use the T-budding technique to graft one apple variety onto another, choose a ¼- to 1-inch-diameter upright branch on your stock plant and strip the leaves from the current year's growth at the point where you want to make the graft.

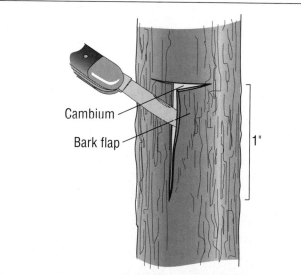

Leaves stripped off

Stock Plant

bud chip down until the top is even with the top of the T-cut and replace the flaps. If the top of the bud chip is too long, you can cut it off. Make sure you insert the bud in the same position it grew on the donor tree. If you insert it upside down, the graft will not grow properly.

Hold the graft tight. Once you've inserted the bud, hold it in place with rubber budding strips or grafting tape. Start wrapping the rubber strips or tape around the bud chip, leaving the bud uncovered. Wrap the bud securely but don't stretch the rubber or tape extremely tight.

The rubber will break down and fall off as the graft heals. You'll need to remove plastic

Cambium

Bark flap

1"

Prepare your stock plant for grafting by making a T-shaped cut in the center of a branch using a very sharp pocketknife. Make a vertical cut first, then a horizontal cut. Use your knife to pull back the bark flaps when you are ready to insert a bud chip.

tape (or other wraps that don't break down) ten days after budding, since they'll restrict the growth of the graft.

Three weeks after grafting, check the bud to see if it looks plump and healthy. The leaf stem should have dropped off by that time and the bark should be its normal color. If the bud and bark are healthy, the graft was successful. You can increase your chances of success by grafting more than one branch at a time.

Make the final cut. Just before the grafted bud starts growing in spring, cut off the rootstock above the new bud. Make a slanted cut ½ to 1 inch above the bud that slopes away from the bud.

Write it down. Add as many different varieties to your tree as suits you, but write down their names and make a drawing of the graft locations on the tree. That way you can remember which variety is which come harvesttime.

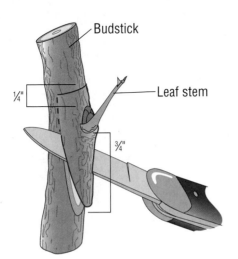

Before you cut a bud from your budstick, measure the T-cut on your stock plant carefully. The bud should fit neatly inside the flaps of the T-cut, and it will if you mark the measurements on your budstick with a marking pen.

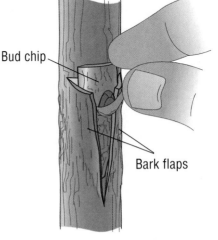

Carefully pull back the bark flaps on your stock plant and insert a bud from another variety of apple tree.

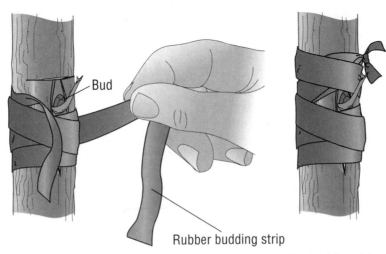

Once the bud chip is in place, wrap the branch with rubber budding strips to hold the bud and bark flaps together until the wound heals.

61 Espalier Fruit Trees for Good Looks and Top Yields

There are so many wonderful apple and pear varieties that you'd need a huge orchard to try even a quarter of them. Or, you could experiment with a technique called espalier so your trees take up just a little space and you can plant as many different varieties as you like. Need more reasons to try this tree-training technique? When you espalier fruit trees, you not only get a great harvest of beautiful big fruit, you also turn your trees into unusual and attractive landscape focal points. Here's how.

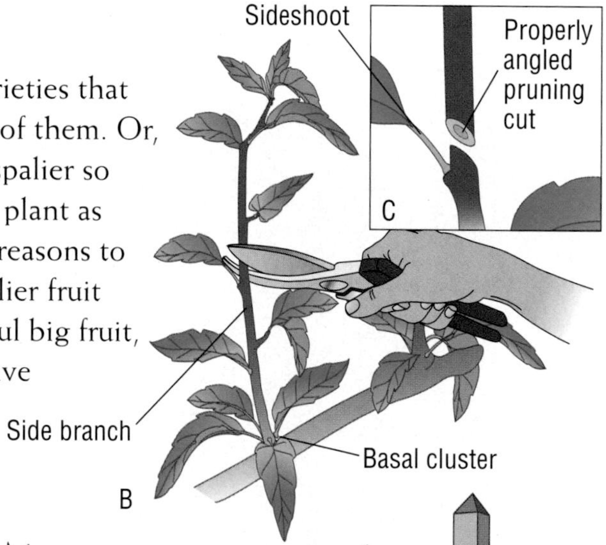

Sideshoot

Properly angled pruning cut

C

Side branch

Basal cluster

B

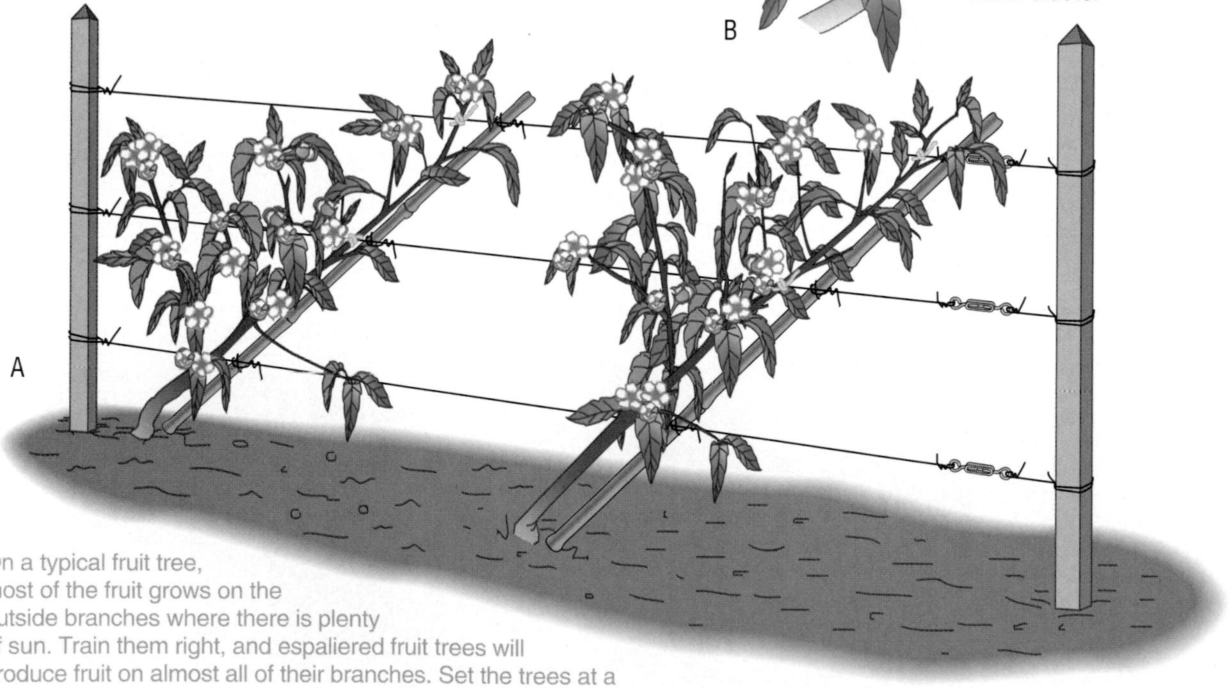

A

On a typical fruit tree, most of the fruit grows on the outside branches where there is plenty of sun. Train them right, and espaliered fruit trees will produce fruit on almost all of their branches. Set the trees at a 45-degree angle when you plant them in fall and tie them in place (A). In midsummer, prune all 12-inch-long side branches back to three leaves above the basal cluster, cutting at an angle just above a bud (B). Cut back any sideshoots growing from side branches to the first leaf above the basal cluster (C).

Start out simple. Train your fruit tree to grow flat against a fence and you've got an espalier. You can train the tree's branches to grow in all kinds of fancy shapes such as fans, U-shapes, or V-shapes, but I go for the easiest system: oblique cordon. Don't let the name scare you off; it simply means that the tree is growing at a 45-degree angle. The sharp angle helps the trees produce more fruiting buds because every bit of the tree is exposed to the sun.

Put your fence in place in fall. If you already have a fence in a sunny spot, you're ahead of the game. If not, put up a post-and-wire or wood-rail fence in an area that gets at least six hours of sunlight a day. The fence should be 6 feet tall and have at least three horizontal wires or railings.

To build a post-and-wire fence, use 4 × 4 oak posts and 14-gauge, vinyl-covered wire with turnbuckles to keep the wires tight. Place the first wire 18 inches off the ground, then add two more wires, each 18 inches above the one below it.

For each tree you're going to plant, wire one 8-foot-long bamboo pole to the fence at a 45-degree angle. Set the poles 3 feet apart since that's how far apart you'll set the trees.

Tilt your trees. Buy two or more whips (young branchless trees) of dwarf apple or pear trees from a local or mail-order nursery

in early fall in Zones 6 and south, and in early spring in Zones 7 and north. Choose two kinds of apples or two kinds of pears that make good pollinators for each other so you'll get lots of fruit.

When the trees arrive, plant each one 10 inches from the fence in front of a bamboo pole and set them at a 45-degree angle. As you plant, turn the trees so the graft union faces up—it's the knobby area toward the base of the tree, where the top was grafted to the root system.

After planting, water the trees thoroughly, then tie each tree to a bamboo pole using a soft string, like twine. If you plant in fall, that's it for training until spring, but you should place 2 inches of mulch around each tree after the ground freezes in late fall or winter. If you plant in spring, mulch immediately after planting.

Snip off long shoots. Spring training is the same whether you plant your trees in fall or spring. The first year, remove any flowers that appear so each tree puts all of its energy into growing. Cut side branches that are 12 inches or longer back around mid-June, leaving just three leaves above the cluster of basal leaves (the group of leaves growing right beside the tree trunk). This encourages the tree to produce fruit spurs for next year instead of more vegetative

growth. Leave all shorter branches alone since they will most likely have fruit buds. Let the leader grow without pruning too, but keep it tied in the proper position.

The side branches will continue to grow after the mid-summer pruning. To keep them from getting too long, cut any new growth back to just one bud and leaf in early fall. In cold-winter areas like the Northeast, prune in late summer.

Repeat the side-branch pruning each summer to keep the limbs short and productive. When the side branches put out sideshoots, cut those back to just one outward-facing leaf above the basal cluster.

Once the tree is mature and starts to grow beyond the top wire or rail, you can remove the bamboo poles. Prune the new tip growth back to ½ inch long each year in late spring, leaving one upward-pointing bud to act as the new tip.

Thin excess fruit for a high-quality harvest. By pruning the trees hard every year, you'll end up with more flowers and fruit than leaves! In fact, you'll end up with so much fruit that you'll need to thin some so each piece has room to grow. When young apples form, pinch off some of them to leave one fruit for every 6 inches of wood. The remaining fruits will grow big and beautiful.

62 Plant Disease-Resistant Apples for Chemical-Free Crops

Harvesting delicious tree-ripened apples in the fall is an absolute pleasure, unless your fruit has been spoiled by fungal diseases. So how can you grow beautiful apples and avoid elaborate and unhealthy spray schedules? Plan before you plant, and choose trees that are resistant to the fungal diseases that plague apples.

Apple scab

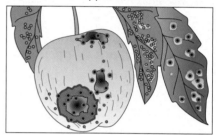

Cedar apple rust

Fire blight

Powdery mildew

Common Apple Diseases

'Goldrush' 'Williams Pride' 'Liberty'

The easiest way to avoid apple diseases is to plant disease-resistant apples. Three of my favorites are 'Liberty', 'Goldrush', and 'Williams Pride'.

Select against scourges.

Before you plant apple trees (or any other fruits), find out which plant diseases are the worst in your area. Your local Cooperative Extension agent can give you specific information for your location as well as recommendations for resistant varieties.

Know your enemy.

The most serious disease problem for apple growers is scab—a fungal disease that causes cracked fruit with ugly, corky lesions. Scab starts growing on rainy spring days when the temperature ranges from 58 to 76°F. Fungal spores that have overwintered on old leaves germinate and infect the new leaves and developing fruit. (You can reduce infections by disposing of fallen leaves.) You'll begin seeing scab lesions 9 to 17 days after an infection occurs. Scab will continue to infect susceptible apples through the spring and summer.

Avoid the sulfur solution.

You can combat the fungus with sulfur sprays, but spraying can be a real pain. You have to apply sulfur before a scab infection occurs so the sulfur can act as a barrier between scab spores and susceptible fruit and leaves. That means you'll be out there spraying your trees before every rain. Sulfur sprays may also be harmful to several beneficial insects. By choosing scab-resistant apples, you can make sulfur sprays a thing of the past.

Choose which apples you'll use.

When you start looking for trees, don't limit your search to apple varieties with scab resistance. Some varieties also offer resistance to other apple diseases such as cedar apple rust, fire blight, and powdery mildew. Check the box on this page for recommendations.

Order and plant resistant trees in early fall if you live in Zone 6 or south. Place your order in winter and plant in early spring if you're in Zone 7 and north. (Remember to plant at least two different apple varieties to ensure good pollination or graft several varieties on a single tree, as shown on page 140.)

Premier Scab-Resistant Apples

Before you place your fruit tree order, look for the latest developments in disease-resistant apple varieties. You'll find there are new developments occurring all the time. And one of these new trees may have exactly the resistance (and flavor!) you're looking for. Here are some great choices to get you started.

'Dayton': This is a crisp, juicy, mildly tart red apple with yellow flesh. It makes a good dessert apple, but has a short storage life. Harvest in early September. Moderate resistance to fire blight and powdery mildew. Moderately susceptible to cedar apple rust.

'Enterprise': Choose this mildly tart red apple for fresh eating and storage. Harvest in mid- to late October. Resistant to cedar apple rust and fire blight. Moderately resistant to powdery mildew.

'Freedom': Large crispy red fruits are good for fresh eating, cooking, and cider. Harvest in late September to early October. Resistant to cedar apple rust, fire blight, and mildew.

'Goldrush': This yellow 'Golden Delicious' type is excellent for fresh eating and storage. Harvest in mid-October. Resistant to powdery mildew; moderate resistance to fire blight. Susceptible to cedar apple rust.

'Jonafree': Round red fruits with a slightly spicy flavor are similar to 'Jonathan' apples. Harvest in mid-September to early October. Resistant to cedar apple rust and fire blight, and somewhat resistant to powdery mildew.

'Liberty': A popular 'McIntosh'-type apple that's good for both fresh eating and cooking. Harvest in late September through early October. Good resistance to cedar apple rust, fire blight, and powdery mildew.

'Macfree': Tart, 'McIntosh'-type apple is good for fresh eating and storage. Resistant to cedar apple rust and fire blight. Moderate resistance to powdery mildew.

'Pristine': Yellow apples with crisp flesh are great for eating and baking. Harvest in August. Moderately resistant to cedar apple rust and powdery mildew. Somewhat resistant to fire blight.

'Williams Pride': Deep red large fruits have a spicy, tart flavor and are wonderful for fresh eating. Harvest in early to mid-August. Resistant to cedar apple rust, fire blight, and powdery mildew.

63 Surefire Ways to Keep Birds and Squirrels from Eating Your Fruits and Nuts

Unless you do something to protect cherries, peaches, pears, and other fruits, birds and squirrels can munch their way through most of your harvest in just a few days. And when nuts like filberts are ripe, it's always a race between you and the squirrels to see who gets there first. Are you tired of fighting off these feathered and furry fiends? Then read on for a few simple harvest-saving tricks.

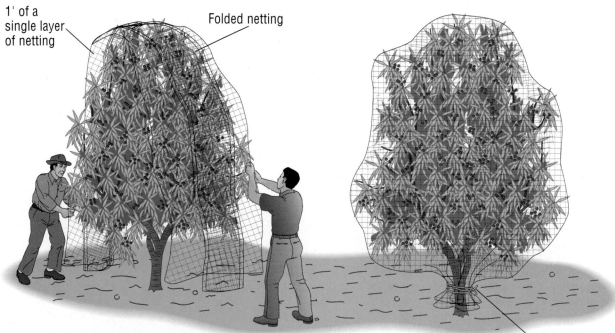

1' of a single layer of netting

Folded netting

Twine

Plant dwarf fruit trees 10 to 12 feet apart so you have room to cover them with bird netting. Fold the netting up so it's easy to handle, then, with the help of a friend, lift the cover onto the tree. Pull the free ends out and down, then bunch the ends together around the trunk. Tie the netting securely in place.

Prevention is the best medicine. As with most things in life, preventing the problem works better than finding a cure. This is especially true when it comes to preventing damage to your fruit and nut crops. The best preventive measures start before you plant the trees.

Small is beautiful. At planting time, choose dwarf or semidwarf fruit trees rather than the larger (18- to 25-foot) standard size. The smaller trees grow 8 to 15 feet tall at maturity, so they're easier to protect than the big boys. You get more fruit from each square foot of orchard space with dwarfs and semidwarfs, and since they're smaller, pruning and harvesting are easier too.

Fruits need space. No matter what kind of trees you're planting, spacing is important. Set standard-size fruit trees 25 to 30 feet apart, semidwarfs 12 to 15 feet apart, and dwarfs 10 to 12 feet apart. The extra room means you can work around the trees with a ladder if you need to, and it ensures good air circulation. Crowded trees are just more trouble. They're not just harder to reach, they're also more stressed and more susceptible to disease and insect damage.

Net yourself a full harvest. Before your fruit starts to color up, buy pieces of 1-inch plastic-mesh bird netting at your local garden center or from a mail-order nursery. (See "Sources" on page 228 for ordering information.) The mesh comes in several sizes so you can use it to cover dwarf, semidwarf, and standard-size trees.

As soon as your fruit shows some color, cover your trees with the netting. Obviously, this technique is easier to perform on smaller trees, but with ladders and a little help from your friends, you can even cover a large tree.

To cover a small or large tree, lay the netting out on the ground so it's folded, with a foot or so of the edges protruding. Now lift the netting over the tree (it helps to work with a partner) and set it on the top middle of the tree. Then pull the free edges out and down to cover the tree.

Gather the bottom of the netting tightly around the trunk and tie it in place with twine so there are no entry points for birds and squirrels. A bird may peck a fruit on the outside of the tree where the netting touches the fruit, but the bulk of your crop will be protected.

Make sure the netting is tight against the trunk, or birds and squirrels can sneak inside the netting. Squirrels can find their way out, but birds can get tangled in the mesh and you'll have to let them out.

Make nut trees unattractive. Netting works fine for protecting small nut trees like almonds and filberts—cover them exactly like fruit trees. But netting won't work for keeping squirrels away from large nut trees such as hickories, walnuts, and pecans, which can grow 30 to 100 feet tall. Here are two solutions to protect even the tallest tree.

• Fence in your nut orchard and keep your dog in the orchard when the nuts are ripening. You can use woven wire or invisible fencing, which works by radio signals, to keep your dog on patrol. Be sure to give Fido food, shelter, and water while he or she is on guard duty.

Space small nut trees where squirrels can't jump on them from larger trees nearby. This forces the squirrels to cross open ground to get to the trees, and that's where you—and your dog—have the advantage. Squirrels can jump long distances, so leave at least 15 feet between your nut trees and larger surrounding trees. Inside the orchard, space large nut trees 25 to 30 feet apart and the smallest trees 5 feet or more apart.

• Train thorny climbing roses up the tree trunks to the lowest limbs, which should be at least 5 feet above the ground. A barrier of thorn-covered rose canes completely encircling each tree will stop squirrels from climbing the trunks to get to the nuts—as long as you've spaced the trees far enough apart!

64 Plant Perennials in Fall to Spruce Up Bulb Foliage in Spring

There are few sights more beautiful than colorful bulbs flowering in spring. And there are few garden sights uglier than the yellowing foliage on those bulbs when the show is over. Luckily, there's an easy fix you can use to hide fading daffodil and tulip foliage—when you plant your bulbs in fall, simply interplant all the bulbs with perennial flowers. Fall interplanting is an easy project that makes your spring and summer garden look marvelous.

Late Spring

Early Spring

Plant perennial plants like peonies and daylilies over your bulb beds in fall. In early spring, the perennials are just breaking out of the ground and they show off the blooming bulbs to best advantage. In late spring, as the bulb foliage fades and looks unkempt, the perennials provide a beautiful cover of leaves and flowers. In warm areas where peony leaves fade in the heat, plant daylilies in front to give the peony leaves summer cover.

Leave those leaves alone.
Wouldn't it be easier just to cut down the fading bulb foliage when bloom time is over? No, no, and no! After the bulbs bloom, the leaves get to work using sunlight, carbon dioxide, and water to photosynthesize and produce the energy the bulbs need to bloom again next year. If you cut off the foliage too soon, the bulbs won't have time to store enough energy and you'll get leaves but few flowers next spring.

It's best to wait until the leaves yellow completely before you cut bulb foliage down. There's no arguing that the spent leaves look unsightly in the meantime, and that's where perennial plants come in.

Mingle perennials with your bulbs. Most perennial flowers emerge slowly in spring so they don't interfere with your bulb show. After the bulb flowers are gone, the perennials' leaves spread out and hide the dying bulb foliage. All kinds of perennials make good partners with bulbs, but here are a few of the best. Plant them in fall, right after you set your bulbs out.

Depend on daylilies. One of the best cover plants is the common daylily (*Hemerocallis* spp.). Its straplike leaves start growing around the time the big bulb show begins. As the bulbs fade, the daylily leaves grow 1½ to 5 feet long, de-

pending on the variety, and that's long enough to hide even the tallest tulip.

Daylilies bloom in spring and summer in full sun to partial shade, and come in every color but white and blue. They'll grow in Zones 2 through 9. Space daylilies 12 inches apart throughout your bulb bed.

Get help from hostas. The broad leaves of hostas are perfect for camouflaging bulb plantings under deciduous trees. Choose Siebold's hosta (*Hosta sieboldiana*), with blue-green heart-shaped leaves, to hide tall tulips and daffodils—the leaves grow 1½ feet long! Space large-leaved hostas 2 feet apart and medium-size hostas like August lily (*H. plantaginea*) 18 inches apart. Look for white or lavender flowers in summer and fall. Hostas thrive in Zones 3 through 8.

Figure on using ferns. Mix several different kinds of ferns together for a beautiful effect. As a general rule, space ferns as far apart as their mature width. In a partially shaded area, mix hay-scented ferns (*Dennstaedtia punctilobula*) with shield ferns (*Polystichum* spp.). In sunnier spots, mix polypody ferns (*Polypodium* spp.) and interrupted ferns (*Osmunda claytoniana*). Many ferns are hardy to Zones 3 or 4, so there are lots to choose from no matter where you live.

Complete bulb plantings with peonies. Bulbs and peonies are one of the truly great plant combinations. Peonies' pointy red leaf buds push out of the ground in early spring and open into beautiful 1-foot-long leaves. Large pink, red, or white flowers open in spring and early summer to carry the bloom season along without a pause. Try the popular Memorial Day peony (*Paeonia officinalis* 'Rosea Superba') or any of the many cultivars of the common garden peony (*P. lactiflora*). Set peonies 3 feet apart. They'll grow in Zones 2 through 8.

"Bury," Don't Bunch, Bulb Foliage

Some gardeners try to hide fading bulb foliage by gathering the leaves together, folding them over, and tying them up in a bunch. But tying the foliage together prevents light from reaching the leaves and creates a dark, wet place where molds and other fungi can grow.

Plant a carpet of perennials like common vinca (*Vinca minor*) and avoid bunching problems. Vinca makes a particularly nice bulb cover because it's evergreen. The plants are short but trailing stems create mounds of dark green that can hide shorter bulbs. Blue or white flowers cover the plants in spring to extend the bloom season in Zones 4 through 9.

65 Colorful Companions for New Perennial Gardens

There's an old saying about perennial plants, "First year sleeper, second year creeper, and third year, gangbusters!" But I don't want to wait three years for my new perennial beds to look sharp, so I put in annuals, bulbs, and biennial flowers to fill the empty spaces between growing perennials.

Bring on the annuals, biennials, and bulbs to make your newly planted perennial garden look colorful and full. Bulbs carry the garden in spring. They're followed in summer by annuals, such as nasturtiums and sunflowers, and biennials, such as foxgloves and Sweet William.

Leave plenty of room.
Perennial flowers need room to grow, which means you should space plants 8 inches to 2 feet or more apart. That leaves a lot of room between plants, particularly if you're planting small, economical seedlings that come in four- or six-packs.

Little plants take off and grow fast, but they look like dots of green in a sea of brown soil or mulch. You won't even get much color at first, since many perennials spend their first year developing a strong root system instead of flowers.

Fill beds with bulbs in fall.
Start out by planting bulbs with your perennials. Work 1 to 2 inches of compost into your garden spot before planting perennials in fall. Set the plants out at the proper spacing so they have room to spread, then fill in the gaps with drifts of spring bulbs. Crocuses, daffodils, and tulips will give you welcome spots of color in spring while your perennials are just waking up. As the perennials grow, they'll hide the bulbs' fading foliage, which makes them perfect partners, each hiding the others' weaknesses.

Add annuals and biennials in spring. When the bulb flowers fade away the first spring, add lots of annuals and biennials in between the new perennials. The annuals will spread and flower right away. The biennials will concentrate on growing leaves

and strong root systems so they're ready to bloom in year two. That's why they're called biennials—they bloom and set seed in their second season.

Many perennials flower during their second year, but it will be a meager display compared to years to come. That's why the biennials make good fillers during the second year—

they'll not only take up extra space between the perennials, they'll also burst into full bloom.

After the biennials bloom, pull them out so the perennials will be able to complete their growth without competition. Leave the bulbs in place. They'll manage to find their way through the perennial foliage for their yearly spring show.

Filler Flowers for a Young Perennial Bed

Here's a mix of annuals and biennials that spread out to give you a big blast of color in sun or shade.

Annuals

Vinca or Madagascar periwinkle (*Catharanthus roseus*): Pink, rose, and white blooms decorate upright or trailing plants. Full sun.

Sunflowers (*Helianthus annuus*): Plant from seed. Look for dwarf cultivars that produce many heads on a single stem. Sun to partial shade.

Impatiens (*Impatiens wallerana*): Makes neat low mounds in shade with colors in all hues except true blue; blooms summer to frost. Full to partial shade.

Sweet alyssum (*Lobularia maritima*): Produces neat low mounds of rose, violet, or white flowers all summer to frost. Sun to partial shade.

Petunias (*Petunia* x *hybrida*): From summer until frost, petunias pump out lots of color in every hue imaginable, plus there are many interesting bicolors. Full sun.

Nasturtiums (*Tropaeolum majus*): Red, yellow, and orange blossoms on shrubby plants or trailing vines from summer to frost. Sun to partial shade.

Verbena (*Verbena* x *hybrida*): Clusters of pink, red, violet, white, or yellow flowers on upright or trailing plants. Full sun.

Biennials

Hollyhocks (*Alcea rosea*): Saucer-shaped blooms come in white and shades of pink, red, and yellow on tall (3 to 6 feet) plants. Full sun.

Canterbury bells (*Campanula medium*): Large, pink, purple, blue, or white bell-shaped flowers bloom in early summer. Sun to partial shade.

Biennial wallflower (*Cheiranthus cheiri*): Flower spikes are densely covered in fragrant red, crimson, or yellow blooms. Sun to partial shade.

Sweet William (*Dianthus barbatus*): Rounded heads of blooms, bicolored or with "eyes" in shades of pink, red, purple, and white. Sun to partial shade.

Foxglove (*Digitalis purpurea*): Tall spikes are covered in white, pale lilac, pink, purplish, and yellow tubular flowers in early summer. Sun to partial shade.

66 Mix and Match Plants for Quick Landscaping Effects

When I plant a few shade trees, a foundation planting, or a new tree and shrub border, I know it will take years before the woody plants are full grown. But it's still a shock to see just how small those new plants look. Rather than wait for the youngsters to reach their mature size, I fill in the gaps with several fast-growing temporary trees, shrubs, and perennials for a finished effect instantly.

Mix a few tall and fast-growing trees and shrubs into a new landscape to fill extra space while slower-growing plants mature. Use clematis vines like 'Superba' (*Clematis jackmanii* 'Superba') and large perennials like Joe-Pye weed (*Eupatorium purpureum*) to add quick color.

Plant a quick solution. Fall is the time to plant fast-growing filler plants—they'll give your landscape a finished look during the 10 to 15 years it takes for slower-growing plants to mature. Be sure you remove the filler plants in 8 to 10 years, or they'll crowd your slower-growing trees and shrubs and spoil their mature shapes.

Why not just grow the trees and shrubs that give you instant results? Quick-growing woody plants tend to have weaker wood than slower-growing types and they're short-lived. These fast-living plants make great fillers, but the trees particularly aren't long-term material.

While you wait for slow-growing trees and shrubs such as hollies (*Ilex* spp.) and witch hazels (*Hamamelis* spp.) to hit their stride, enjoy the company of fast-growing plants like those in the box below. Since they grow fast, nurseries can sell them cheap—they won't make much of a dent in your landscape budget.

Perennial plants, like asters, and quick-growing vines, like clematis, make good fillers too, since they'll grow large in a season or two.

Cut out the crowd. As your plantings grow, reduce the number of fast-growing trees, shrubs, and perennials. The slower woody plants will crowd the perennials out naturally, but don't wait for that to happen. Crowded plants get less air circulation and are more susceptible to fungal diseases and insect attacks.

Fast-Growing Plants to Fill a Young Landscape

Try these shrubs and trees to make your plantings look mature in a hurry.

Name	Hardiness Zone Rating	Description
Shrubs		
Butterfly bush (*Buddleia davidii*)	Zones 6 to 9	Versatile plant can be temporary or permanent. Arching habit with pink, purple, or white bloom spires. Butterflies love the flowers. Grows 15 feet tall.
Tatarian dogwood (*Cornus alba*)	Zones 2 to 8	Open, upright branching habit. Young stems turn bright red in winter. Reaches 10 feet tall and wide.
Forsythia (*Forsythia* x *intermedia*)	Zones 4 to 9	Upright plant with bright yellow flowers in spring. Grows 10 feet tall and wide.
Bigleaf hydrangea (*Hydrangea macrophylla*)	Zones 5 to 8	Rounded plant with large pink or blue flowers. Can reach 6 feet tall and 10 feet wide.
Winter honeysuckle (*Lonicera fragrantissima*)	Zones 4 to 8	Tangled branches spread to 10 feet tall and wide. White, scented flowers in early spring.
Trees		
Boxelder (*Acer negundo*)	Zones 2 to 9	Rounded head. Can grow 15 feet in 4 to 6 years. Mature height is 50 feet.
Catalpa (*Catalpa speciosa*)	Zones 4 to 8	Open habit with large leaves, white and purple-spotted flowers, and long, thin seedpods. Can grow 15 feet in 8 years and will reach 40 to 60 feet.
Lombardy black poplar (*Populus nigra* 'Italica')	Zones 3 to 9	Narrow, upright growth. Can grow 5 to 8 feet a year, up to 90 feet.
'Newport' cherry plum (*Prunus cerasifera* 'Newport')	Zones 3 to 8	Purple-leaved, rounded twiggy plant; grows to 15 feet.

67 Blend Native and Exotic Plants for the Best of Both Worlds

Native plants are perfectly suited to their home sites—they're adapted to the climate, they can resist attacks by local pests and diseases, and they know how to hold their own against other local plants. But what if you can't resist the lure of exotic plants? You don't have to. Put natives' years of evolution to work for you by adding them alongside your exotic plants. You'll create a low-maintenance landscape that suits your taste and your site.

Create the feeling of a woodland in your backyard by growing native plants on the outskirts of your yard for good looks and lower maintenance. Use tall trees like oaks to make an upper level canopy, then add smaller understory trees and shrubs such as flowering dogwoods and spicebush. For the bottom level, plant wildflowers such as bloodroot, Canada wild ginger, and wild geranium (*Geranium maculatum*).

Tuck natives in around the edges. I'm not advocating tearing out all the plants in your existing gardens—that's too much work. Just start bringing native plants in gradually each fall along your property's edges, where they can act as a backdrop for your exotic plants.

What you see is what you can get. Notice how the native landscape around you looks. In most areas, you'll see woodlands, but perhaps you live in an area where grasslands or bogs are a part of the scene. Look at the whole picture rather than individual plants. Try to re-create the feel of the native plants surrounding you by buying and planting groups of native plants. *Don't dig up plants from the wild—many are endangered.*

In much of the eastern United States, you'll see large trees underplanted with shorter trees, shrubs, vines, grasses, and wildflowers. A typical native landscape in the East might consist of maples, oaks, hickories, and maybe a few evergreens like Canada hemlocks. Underneath the tall trees you might find flowering dogwoods and shrubs such as witch hazel (*Hamamelis virginiana*) and spicebush (*Lindera benzoin*).

As you add some of these plants to your landscape, plant a few shade-loving wildflowers at their feet. Natives such as bloodroot (*Sanguinaria canadensis*), great

Solomon's seal (*Polygonatum commutatum*), and Canada wild ginger (*Asarum canadense*) are good choices, and they're available from mail-order nurseries.

Water the plants in well and keep them mulched with compost or chopped leaves.

Keep exotics close at hand. As you move toward the more well-used portion of the yard, let the natives take a backseat and bring in your favorite low-maintenance exotics. (Exotics are those plants that originated outside the United States and Canada.) Keep high-maintenance exotics like roses close to the house where they're near water and handy for deadheading and other care. Match the arrangement of your exotics to your natives so the two landscapes blend in together. By all means, use the plants you've already got. Just add whatever plants you need to create the upper and lower story effect of the native landscape.

For example, if your gardens are made of flowers only, add a few tall and small exotic trees and shrubs. You could include trees like European hornbeam (*Carpinus betulus*) and Japanese snowbell (*Styrax japonicus*). Or you may want some imported flowering shrubs such as butterfly bush (*Buddleia davidii*) and fragrant winterhazel (*Corylopsis glabrescens*) to add color and fragrance. If you need plants underneath the trees

and shrubs, plant perennials such as hardy begonias (*Begonia grandis*) and hostas (*Hosta* spp.).

Live in harmony. Now look what you've got. Layers of native plants form a beautiful, easy-care background for your yard, and equally beautiful exotics are close at hand. This arrangement saves you time and effort and makes your yard and home look more like a beautiful part of the natural landscape.

Go Native

Many native plants are just as beautiful as imported exotics. Since they're handy, we sometimes take them for granted, but all of these eastern United States natives are worth looking for.

Flowering Trees

Downy serviceberry (*Amelanchier arborea*): Zones 3 to 8.

Eastern redbud (*Cercis canadensis*): Zones 4 to 9.

White fringe tree (*Chionanthus virginicus*): Zones 5 to 8.

American yellowwood (*Cladrastis lutea*): Zones 5 to 8.

Flowering Shrubs

Bottlebrush buckeye (*Aesculus parviflora*): Zones 5 to 8.

American beautyberry (*Callicarpa americana*): Zones 7 to 10.

Carolina allspice (*Calycanthus floridus*): Zones 4 to 9.

Dwarf fothergilla (*Fothergilla gardenii*): Zones 5 to 9.

Oakleaf hydrangea (*Hydrangea quercifolia*): Zones 5 to 8.

68 More Lilies Four Ways

Lilies are among the most beautiful (and underused) perennials in the garden. These spring and summer bloomers come in just about every color except true blue, plus there are striped, spotted, and bicolor versions. Buying lily bulbs can cost you a pretty penny, but growing them won't cost you much time or money. With four ways to propagate these plants, you can have a gardenful in just a few years for the price of one lily bulb.

Whether you start lilies from bulbils (A), bulblets (B), bulb scales (C), or seeds (D), they're easy to grow. Plant the baby bulbs in a nursery bed or cold frame until they reach full size, then move them into your garden.

Start stock plants. You should plant lilies like most bulbs, when they're dormant in fall. Buy one of each type of lily you'd like to grow and plant it in an area with well-drained soil. Plant lily bulbs three times as deep as they are high, except the Madonna lily (*Lilium candidum*), which you should plant just below the soil surface. Keep lily roots cool by mulching them or by covering them with low ground covers like St.-John's-wort (*Hypericum calycinum*).

Bury bulbils and wait. The following summer, as your lilies grow, you'll notice that some of them, like the tiger lily (*L. lancifolium*), will produce small black pea-size objects in each of the leaf axils. If you plant these seedlike structures, called bulbils, they'll grow into flowering plants identical to the parent lily. You'll need some patience, since it may take three or more years for the lilies to grow big enough to flower.

Pick the bulbils when they start to come loose in the leaf axils and sow them outdoors in summer or fall, just below the soil surface.

Break off bulblets. Another way to propagate lilies is by separating any bulblets that grow from the stem just at or under the soil surface. If you see bulblets in fall—they look like suckers around the bottom of the plant—cut them from the stem with a sharp knife. Plant the bulblets in a cold frame to overwinter, then move them to the garden in spring. Bulblets will usually flower the year after you remove them from the mother plant.

Snap off some scales. One of the easiest ways to propagate any type of lily, even hybrids, is by removing and growing bulb scales. Lift the whole bulb out of the ground in fall. You'll see that the bulb is made up of many scales that you can peel off like the leaves on an artichoke. Snap off four or five of these scales as close to the base of the bulb as you can, then replant the bulb.

Let the scales dry in a shady spot for a day, then place them in a plastic bag filled with moist vermiculite. Punch a few holes in the plastic bag for ventilation and put it in a warm (70°F), dark place. By spring, the bulb scales will have sprouted tiny bulblets that you can set out in a nursery bed until they're large enough for the garden.

Sprout lilies from seeds. A final way to propagate lilies is from the seed produced by their flowers. Seed-produced plants will not be identical to the parents—you may get a plant that looks better or worse than the original.

Gather the seeds when the seedpods begin to split open and sow them in a cold frame in fall or spring. Some lily seeds sprout right away, but others may take a year or more to germinate. Most seed-produced plants take several years to grow into bulbs large enough to flower, but the regal lily (*L. regale*) is an exception that produces flowers in 9 to 15 months.

Great Lilies for the Garden

Light up your garden with a variety of lilies to grow in sun or partial shade.

Name and Hardiness Zone Rating	Description
Goldband lily (*Lilium auratum*): Zones 4 to 9.	White, starlike flowers have yellow stripes and red spots. Height: 2 to 6 feet.
Madonna lily (*Lilium candidum*): Zones 4 to 9.	Long, white, trumpet-shaped flowers. Height: 2 to 4 feet.
Asiatic hybrids (*Lilium* hybrids): Zones 4 to 7.	Starry blooms in shades of orange, red, yellow, pink, purple, and white. Height: 2 to 4 feet.
Tiger lily (*Lilium lancifolium*): Zones 3 to 9.	Orange, spotted flower petals curve backward. Height: 4 to 6 feet.
Regal lily (*Lilium regale*): Zones 3 to 8.	Long, fragrant, trumpet-shaped blooms are purplish on the outside and white on the inside. Height: 4 to 6 feet.

69 Roses Bloom Better Lying Down

You'll be amazed how many more flowers your roses will produce if you tie or peg their stems so they're horizontal. Train the stems along fences, trellises, or any other horizontal surface—even the ground! The trick is to start with roses that produce long, flexible stems, like the climbing roses and certain shrub roses. (See the box on the opposite page for some choices.) Start your own stunning rose display with these simple training tips.

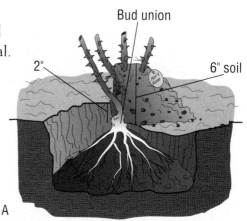

A

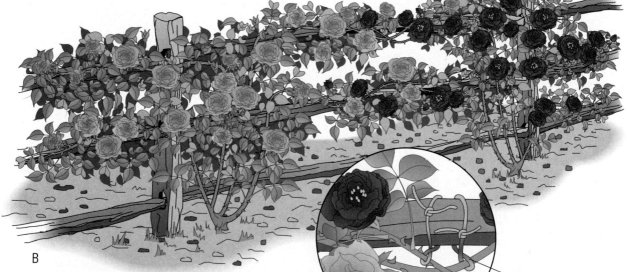

B

Figure-eight tie

C

For bushels of blooms in summer, plant a flexible-stemmed shrub or climbing rose in fall (A) and provide it with winter protection. Train the rose horizontally along a fence or trellis during the next growing season (B), using a figure-eight tie to hold the rose canes close to the fence without injuring them (C). Split rail, picket, woven-wire, chain-link, and post-and-wire fences all make excellent supports for roses.

Choose a place in the sun.

For gorgeous roses, you've got to have at least six hours of sun a day. Pick a spot beside a fence or trellis if you have one, since they make good supports for training roses horizontally. You can also peg flexible-stemmed rose canes down to the ground—just put them in spots where you need a ground cover.

Prepare for planting in fall.

Life in the garden usually isn't as hectic in fall as in spring, so that's when I plant roses. Order bare-root plants from a mail-order nursery or buy them at a local garden center. The plant stems should be a healthy green.

Soak the rose roots in a bucket of water for two to three hours before planting. While the plant is soaking, dig a hole big enough to easily accommodate the roots. Work a couple of shovelfuls of compost into the soil you took from the hole. Then use the mix to make a mound in the bottom of the hole. Set the plant on top of the mound and spread the roots out around the sides.

The bud union (the knobby area where the rose was grafted to the rootstock) should be 2 inches below the soil surface. If it's not, adjust the soil mound until the height is right. Fill in the hole and water the plant in well. Then mound soil over the bottom 6 inches of stem to protect the graft from winter cold.

When the rose starts to put up new growth in spring, gently move the mounded soil away from the canes. In two or three weeks, mulch the ground around the rose with a 3-inch-deep layer of compost.

Train rose canes sideways.

When your rose develops long canes, it's time to bend them for better blooming. Training the canes horizontally encourages more sideshoots to form and exposes the entire stem to sunlight. Remember, more stems and more light mean more blooms!

For roses growing on a trellis or fence, stretch the canes out horizontally, tying them in place with jute, raffia, or string. To cover a bank or slope with roses, weed the area, then cover it with a ¼-inch layer of newspaper topped with 4 inches of straw or leaf mulch. Plant one or more flexible-caned roses and peg the canes to the ground as they grow.

Feed a lot, prune a little.

After your rose blooms, give it a dose of organic fertilizer. Lightly work 3 ounces of alfalfa meal, 5 pounds of compost, or 3 pounds of composted manure into the square-yard area surrounding the rose. Repeat the fertilizer application in about four weeks after another bloom cycle ends.

Long-stemmed shrub roses aren't too picky about pruning.

As with all roses, remove dead or diseased canes at any time. Prune off old blooms as soon as they start to fade and cut the canes back to fit the space you've set aside for them.

Trim out old or weak canes from once-blooming climbing roses after they bloom, leaving three or four good, strong canes. Tie the canes to their support after pruning. For repeat bloomers, cut back the sideshoots to four buds after flowering. Ground-cover roses won't need this treatment unless they stop producing lots of flowers.

Favorite Shrub and Climbing Roses

These are just a few of the fine roses you can train along fences or peg out as ground covers. See "Recommended Reading" on page 233 for books that can supply you with more choices.

'Alchymist', double apricot flowers

'Ballerina', single pink blooms with white centers

'Blaze', semidouble scarlet flowers

'Bloomin' Easy', double red blooms

'Climbing Cecile Brunner', double pink flowers

'Kathleen', single pink flowers

'Nevada', single white flowers

'Sparrieshoop', single pink blooms

70 Grow Six Rose Plants from a Single Bush

I like roses—*lots* of roses. That's why I started exploring ways to grow my own plants instead of buying them. Propagating my favorite roses turned out to be amazingly easy. All it takes is a technique called mound layering, a rose (make sure your plant is at least three years old), a little pruning, a little soil, and a really sharp spade.

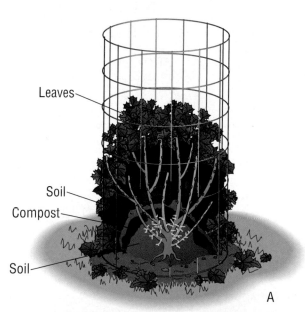

Leaves

Soil

Compost

Soil

A

C

B

Mound layering a plant that's at least three years old is an easy way to get more roses. Cover your rosebush with soil and leaves in fall to protect it from winter. Keep soil and mulch mounded around the plant during the next growing season and the canes will root. Cover your rose as usual in winter (A). In early spring, remove the leaves and split the canes apart before they start growing again (B). Replant the canes, then water and mulch them and watch them grow into beautiful bushes (C).

Get your rose ready early.
You need a healthy rose for successful mound layering, so take good care of your plant in fall. Protect your rose from freezing winter temperatures by mounding a foot of soil up around the base of the plant. When hard frosts threaten, cut back the longest canes so they don't flop around in the wind. Then cover the plant with a tomato cage or a ring of chicken wire and fill it with leaves or straw to bury the rose.

Thin canes in late winter.
Before bud break in spring (about six weeks before the last frost), remove the cage, leaves, and some of the soil from the plant. Leave 6 inches of soil around the base of each rose cane, then add 2 inches of compost or chopped leaves to the mound.

Next, remove all the canes that are at least three years old. The older canes will be larger and woodier than the younger canes. Next choose the six best-looking canes left and prune out all the rest. The canes you leave on the plant should be sturdy, free of disease, and set as far apart from each other as possible. Cut the six remaining canes back to healthy green growth. The canes should then be at least 1 foot tall. If the canes were killed back to less than 1 foot, remove the soil, let the plant grow and recover, and try again next year.

Keep the plant from getting thirsty in summer. If all is well and your rose survived the winter in good shape, keep the base of the plant covered. During warm weather, make sure your rose gets enough water. Each cane will be sprouting roots of its own under the soil mound, but if the soil dries out, the new roots may die. So make sure that the soil stays moist (but not sopping wet) during the entire growing season. When you water, check under the mulch to make sure the soil is 6 inches deep over the bottom of each cane. If the soil packs down or washes away, add more to keep the depth right.

Bed the plant down, then wake it up again. In early fall, protect the rose as you did the previous winter, adding more soil to the mound and covering the canes with a tomato cage filled with leaves. In late winter, remove the cage and leaves so you can work on the plant. Next, cut the plant back to the six canes you left the previous winter. Cut off all of the other canes at the level of the soil mound. Prune the six remaining canes back to healthy green tissue so that each cane and its sideshoots have a total of at least three to five buds.

Cut your new roses loose.
Before you make another move, decide where you want your new roses, dig a hole for each

one, and amend the soil in the hole with a shovelful of compost. Once the soil is ready for planting, take a very sharp garden spade and slice straight downward between the canes. Divide the rose into six separate plants each with a single cane. Over the previous summer, each cane should have developed its own roots. If you want to keep a rose in the original spot, slice off only five of the six canes, leaving one to regrow. Now you're ready to transplant your new roses to their permanent homes.

Steer Clear of Grafted Roses

The easiest roses to propagate are those growing on their own roots. (See "Sources" on page 228 for a list of mail-order catalogs that carry own-rooted roses.) Many roses are grafted to the rootstock of another rose because the rootstock plant has more disease resistance or more cold-hardiness than the original plant. Growers also graft plants because it's a faster way to produce roses than by cuttings.

You can try mound layering a grafted rose, but the result will be plants that are identical to the root-system rose instead of the grafted plant growing on top. When you mound layer with a variety that's not grafted, you can be sure that you'll get a group of new plants that look just like the mother plant.

71 Turn a Slope into a Stone-Wall Garden for Plants

A sloping site isn't great for a lawn—it's too hard to mow— but it's a perfect place for a garden. By putting rocks in the right places, you can create tiers for your plants, like the seats at a stadium. The different levels let you see the specimens in the background (up the slope) as easily as the plants in the foreground. View your sloping garden from below and you'll see that a steep angle shows off plants to their best advantage.

C

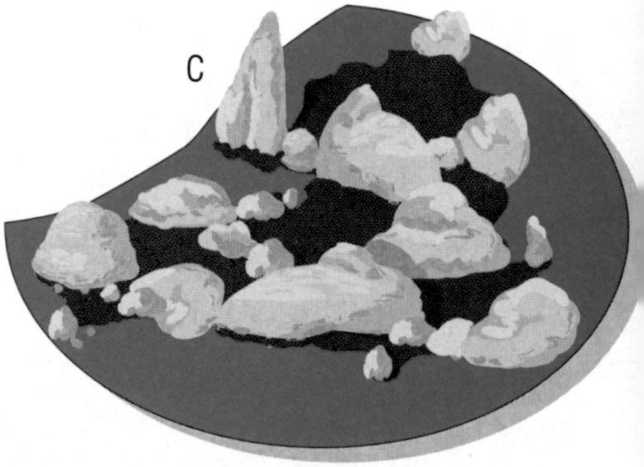

B

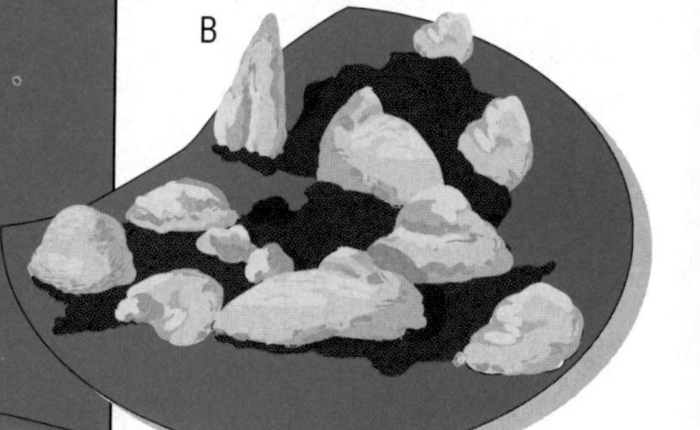

A

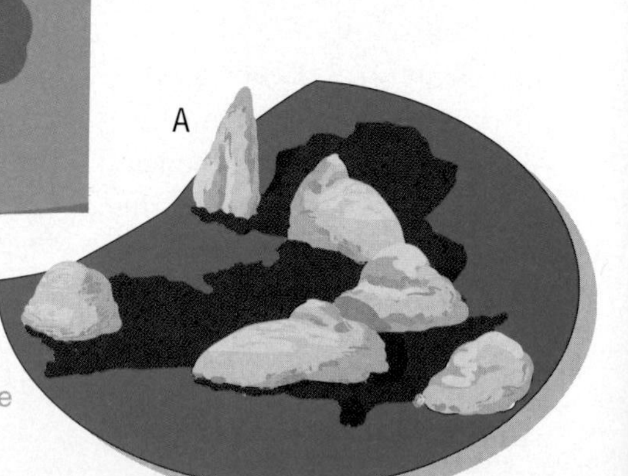

Hold a slope and beautify your yard with a staggered stone wall that's filled with plants. Start by digging holes, then put in the largest rocks and bury them partway with the excess soil (A). Add lots of medium-size rocks to fill spaces between the big rocks, staggering them back up the slope (B). Finish by using the smallest stones to dam places where the soil could erode (C).

Hold the soil with a rock garden. You could keep the loose soil on a slope in place with a retaining wall. But straight walls waste a lot of garden space and destroy the feature that shows your plants off best—the slope.

That's why I devised another method of building a stone wall that holds the soil like a retaining wall but displays plants like a rock garden. It's a project that's made for fall—first, it's a lot easier to move rocks around in cool weather, and second, fall is the perfect time to plant rock-garden plants.

To make your wall look natural, your rocks should all be pretty much the same shape, type, and color. Freshly split, sharp-edged rocks don't mix well with very rounded streambed cobbles. I use chunky rocks for the most part, and a few elongated stones that I can place vertically. The rocks should vary in size from small to large—you'll need more of the little ones than the big ones.

You'll notice that most rocks in nature don't perch on the soil surface—they emerge from the ground. Use the same technique for your rock wall. Bury most of your rocks so two-thirds of each rock's bulk is underground. Occasionally, bury just one-third of the rock to add variety.

Start out big. Place some big anchor rocks at the base of the slope where it flattens out into the yard. Bury a few extra deep so just their tops show and they look like they are emerging from the soil. Stagger other large rocks behind the first group and repeat the process up the slope.

Save a few large rocks to bury near the top of the slope and place them like the others, in a random pattern.

Bring in backups. Now go back to the bottom and put in medium-size rocks, butting them up against the larger ones. Bury these rocks the same way as the large stones, sinking about three-fourths of them deep into the ground and burying one-fourth of them more shallowly.

Put the medium-size rocks in places where they'll hold the sloping soil between the largest rocks. You're basically creating dams with flat areas of soil behind them. Work your way up the slope, positioning the rocks so they seem to belong together and take on an attractive form. Keep things interesting by placing some rocks horizontally and burying other long stones vertically.

Fill in the gaps. Now go back to the bottom and work small stones in between the large and medium-size ones. Just as before, notice where the soil might erode and fashion dams to hold it back. Bury the smallest rocks like you did the larger ones. You can also use the small stones to cover gaps where two larger rocks butt unevenly against each other.

When you're done, the slope will have lots of small planting pockets scattered throughout the rocks. Fill these with small bulbs, rock-garden plants, and succulents.

Rock-Wall Plants

The many small flat areas between and behind the stones in your wall will make good homes for rock-garden plants like these.

Ajuga (*Ajuga reptans*): tough, spreading mats of leaves send up little spires of blue flowers. Zones 3 to 9.

Wild columbine (*Aquilegia canadensis*): red-and-yellow spurred flowers nod above rounded mounds of foliage. Zones 3 to 8.

Common thrift or sea-pink (*Armeria maritima*): dark green grassy tufts of leaves send up short stalks with pink flower balls on top. Zones 3 to 8.

Snow-in-summer (*Cerastium tomentosum*): white woolly leaves and white flowers add contrast beside green-leaved plants. Zones 2 to 7.

'Tiny Rubies' cheddar pinks (*Dianthus gratianapolitanus* 'Tiny Rubies'): spreading grassy mats of foliage set off intensely magenta flowers. Zones 3 to 9.

72 Four Fast Ways to Propagate Succulents

Seed

Indoors or outdoors, succulents and cacti make a delightful addition to your landscape. They come in so many shapes and sizes that it's hard to resist collecting every kind, from fleshy-leaved cacti, hens-and-chicks, and sedums to houseplants such as sansevieria and jade plant. These plants are so easy to propagate, you don't have to hold back. Get started this fall using these four easy ways to expand your succulent collection without spending a dime.

Cutting

String of beads

Snake plant

Aloe

Sedum

Golden barrel cactus

Offset

Division

Propagation Methods

When your plant budget is low, try propagating succulents to increase your plantings quickly and easily. You can propagate these plants from seed, cuttings, offsets (be sure to use gloves and a newspaper collar when handling spiny plants), and division. Always let succulents' leaves and stems dry before repotting them or they may rot.

Let your succulents go to seed. Succulents may flower anytime of year, depending on the species. After flowering, leave the fruits on your plants until the fruits change color. Harvest the ripe fruits—using tweezers to handle prickly types—and remove the seeds. Place the seeds in paper sacks or on sheets of newspaper to dry. Keep the drying seeds in a warm, dry, dark place like an attic, closet, or garage until they separate easily.

Fill a pot or seed flat with cactus potting mix and sow the dry seeds on the surface. Press the seeds into the soil mix lightly, then barely cover the soil surface with grit. (You can buy grit at pet and feed stores.) Set the pot or flat in a shallow pan of warm water until the grit is moist. Drain the pot or flat, then cover it with a plastic bag and place it in a warm spot that gets plenty of light but no direct sun.

When the seeds germinate—this can take a few days or a few months, depending on the plant—remove the plastic cover and move the seedlings into individual pots where they can keep growing. Most seedlings will reach flowering size in two to three years.

Snip off a piece. Cut a stem or the top 2 inches of a leaf off your succulent and let the piece dry in a bright, warm place for a week or more. Before drying, cut stem cuttings back to about 3 inches long, and remove the leaves from the bottom half.

When the wound forms a callus (thickened tissue), set the leaf or stem cutting upright in a pot of dry cactus potting mix. Set leaf cuttings and stem cuttings deep enough to stand upright, then prop them up with grit. Dampen but don't soak the potting mix if the cuttings start to shrivel. When plantlets appear around the base of the leaf, separate them and pot them up. It can take up to a month for the cutting to root.

Break suckers loose. Many succulents form offsets (plants that develop from buds) or suckers (plants that develop from roots) around their base. Choose the largest of these little plants and pry them loose, being careful not to injure their roots.

Let the offsets or suckers dry for a week to ten days, then pot them up in dry cactus potting mix. Water sparingly—only when the soil is very dry.

Divide the mother plant into parts. You can divide succulents like any other perennial. Simply dig up the whole plant and cut or pull clumps of the plant loose from the mother plant. Let the plant pieces callus, then repot them in cactus potting mix. Water when the soil dries out completely.

Propagation Preferences

Here's a list of selected succulents and cacti and the methods you can use to propagate them.

Calico hearts, leopard spots (*Adromischus* spp.): Leaf cuttings, offsets

Aloes (*Aloe* spp.): Seeds, stem cuttings, suckers

Peruvian apple cactus (*Cereus peruvianus*): Stem cuttings, seeds

Crassulas, jade plant, silver dollar, string of buttons (*Crassula* spp.): Seeds, stem or leaf cuttings

Echeverias, hens-and-chicks (*Echeveria* spp.): Stem or leaf cuttings, offsets

Golden barrel cactus (*Echinocactus grusonii*): Offsets, seeds

Hedgehog cacti (*Echinocereus* spp.): Offsets, seeds

Gasterias (*Gasteria* spp.): Division, leaf cuttings, seeds

Haworthias (*Haworthia* spp.): Division, offsets, seeds

Kalanchoes (*Kalanchoe* spp.): Cuttings, plantlets that form on leaf edges, seeds

Opuntias, prickly pears (*Opuntia* spp.): Stem cuttings, seeds

Sansevierias, snake plant (*Sansevieria* spp.): Leaf cuttings, offsets, division

Sedums (*Sedum* spp.): Division, stem cuttings in spring, seeds

String of beads (*Senecio rowleyanus*): Division, stem cuttings

73 Plant a Wildflower Meadow the Easy Way

The biggest obstacles to growing a sunny wildflower meadow are weeds and bad seed mixes. Neither of these problems should deter you from growing a gorgeous meadow, since both are simple to avoid. The easiest way to eliminate weed competition is to solarize your soil. And the best (and cheapest) seed mix is the do-it-yourself kind. Here's what to do.

B

A

Clear plastic

Build a beautiful wildflower meadow the easy step-by-step way. Solarize the soil the first fall by covering the tilled planting area with clear plastic (A). Bake the weeds, then remove the plastic and cover the area with mulch. Plant wildflowers the following fall to give your meadow a healthy, weed-free start (B).

168

Weed the soil with the sun.

Solarizing the soil is an easy and effective way to get rid of weeds. Get started in early fall by using a shovel or tiller to turn over the top 2 inches of soil where the meadow will go. Water the area thoroughly, and cover the soil with a sheet of clear plastic. Bury the edges of the plastic with soil so the heat that builds up can't escape, and let the sun bake the spot for six weeks. Remove the plastic and mulch the area with 4 inches of straw. Let the mulch break down and improve the soil over the next growing season until planting time in fall.

Start out small—an area that's 10 by 20 feet is plenty big. This first miniature meadow will be the nursery and seed-production factory that will supply you with plants and seeds to increase the size of your meadow over the years.

Choose the right plants. If

you want a trouble-free wildflower meadow that you can plant once and enjoy, make a region-specific wildflower mix. There's no use sowing California wildflowers in a Maryland garden, or vice versa.

The best way to get a wildflower mix that's suitable for your area is to mix one up yourself. A mix of annual and perennial flowers and grasses will give you color and interest year-round. Consult your local Cooperative Extension agent and wildflower catalogs to see which wild plants grow best in your climate and soil conditions. Also see the box on this page for recommendations.

Figure on fall planting.

When you plant in fall, your wildflowers get a jump on any weed seeds that may blow in during spring.

Sow seeds in large sweeps to create that splashy meadow look. When the seeds sprout in spring, and the plants grow enough so you can recognize them, mulch to cover any bare soil.

Once your meadow gets established, you can use your own plants to expand it—for free! Gather the seed produced by your wildflowers as it ripens in summer or fall and sow it in newly solarized areas. Rake the soil lightly where you sow to shallowly bury the seeds.

Please don't pick wild

posies. Many of our native wildflowers are becoming endangered because of uninformed and unscrupulous people who collect plants from the wild. To make sure you don't contribute to the disappearance of wildflowers, deal only with growers who sell nursery-propagated seeds and plants. (See "Sources" on page 228 for ordering information.) Never buy from nurseries that sell seeds or plants collected from the wild.

Wildflowers for Sunny Sites

Get a natural look and save yourself lots of fussing by choosing wildflowers and grasses that like living where you do. Match plants to your soil type and climate for great results.

Dry Sandy Soils

Butterfly weed (*Asclepias tuberosa*)

Lance-leaved coreopsis (*Coreopsis lanceolata*)

Rough gayfeather (*Liatris aspera*)

Little bluestem (*Schizachyrium scoparium*)

Indian grass (*Sorghastrum nutans*)

Medium-Moist, Clay Soils

Big bluestem (*Andropogon gerardii*)

New England aster (*Aster novae-angliae*)

Prairie wild indigo (*Baptisia leucantha*)

Purple coneflower (*Echinacea purpurea*)

Switchgrass (*Panicum virgatum*)

Stiff goldenrod (*Solidago rigida*)

Moist Loam Soils

Swamp milkweed (*Asclepias incarnata*)

Bluejoint grass (*Calamagrostis canadensis*)

Spotted Joe-Pye weed (*Eupatorium maculatum*)

Wild geranium (*Geranium maculatum*)

Prairie cordgrass (*Spartina pectinata*)

Great Garden Ideas

for Winter

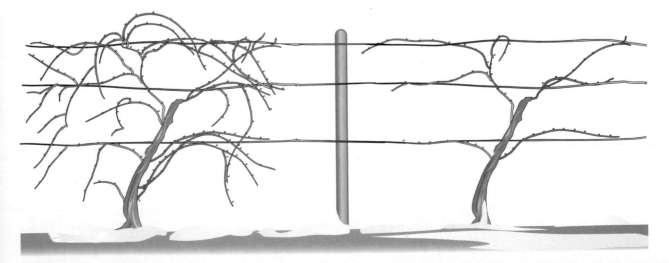

74 Homemade Seed Tapes Save Time in Spring

The days fill up fast in spring—there are all the usual tasks of everyday life, plus suddenly it's time to plant the garden. You may not be able to cut back on working and taking care of the kids, but you can sure save some time and effort planting the garden if you use seed tapes.

Newspaper makes great seed tapes because it's inexpensive and it dissolves easily in wet soil. Tear the paper into 1-inch strips, ripping from the top of the page to the bottom so the strips tear off easily and evenly. The strips of newspaper are about 22 inches long, so it's easy to lay them end to end to fill a row or bed, or glue them together to make longer tapes. Glue seeds in place with flour and water using the correct spacing.

Do-it-yourself seed tapes.
Make seed tapes during the less hectic days of winter, and on busy spring days you can use them to plant straight, perfectly spaced rows without measuring. When you use tapes, you plant just the right amount of seeds and avoid lots of thinning later on. You can buy seed tapes, but it's so easy to make your own, there's no need.

1 Tear sections of newspaper into 1-inch-wide strips. Use only the black-and-white sections of the paper. The inks in colored inserts may contain toxic heavy metals that you don't want in the garden.

2 Make a paste by adding a little water to ½ cup of all-purpose flour. The paste should be just thick enough to coat the seeds—the consistency of a thick gravy.

3 Lay the paper strips out on a table and place a single row of seeds on each strip. Space the seeds at the proper planting distance (check the chart on this page or your seed catalog or seed packet).

4 Glue the seeds to the strips of newspaper by placing a drop of the flour-water paste on top of each seed. Use a teaspoon, Popsicle stick, toothpick, or whatever's handy to drop the "glue" on the seeds.

5 Let the glue dry thoroughly, then roll up the strips and put them in a resealable plastic bag. To keep the seeds dry, wrap a tablespoon of powdered milk or salt in a paper towel and put it in the bag with your seed tapes.

6 Label the bag so you know what kind of seed is inside, or slip the seed packet into the bag to act as a label. Then seal the bag and store it in a cool, dry place until spring.

Planting with seed tapes.
Lay the tapes down in beds or in rows, depending on your style of garden. Cover the tapes with fine soil to the recommended depth, then water them in thoroughly. The newspaper will decompose quickly once it's wet and in contact with the soil.

Recommended Seed Spacing

When you make seed tapes, place the seeds in a single row down the center of each paper strip using the spacing listed below. Some crops may need thinning—it depends on how well the seeds germinate. But you'll still save time, since seeds planted on tapes need much less thinning than seeds sown individually by hand.

Vegetable	Seed Spacing (in inches)
Beets	4
Broccoli	15
Cabbage	15
Carrots	3
Cauliflower	15
Chinese cabbage	15
Collards	12
Kohlrabi	3
Leeks	4
Lettuce, cos or Romaine and head	6 (thin to 8 inches apart)
Lettuce, leaf	6
Okra	8 (thin to 24 inches apart)
Onions	2
Parsley	4 (thin to 8 inches apart)
Parsnips	2 (thin to 4 inches apart)
Peppers	6 (thin to 18 inches apart)
Radishes	1
Rutabagas	4
Salsify	2
Sorrel	4 (thin to 8 inches apart)
Spinach	6
Swiss chard	5
Turnips	2

75 A Simple Seed-Starting Setup with Bottom Heat

The best vegetable plants come from the best seedlings. But without a greenhouse, I had trouble giving seedlings the temperatures and light they needed to grow strong and healthy. That's when I came up with a portable seed-starting setup that warms the soil and provides plenty of light. Now all my vegetable seedlings get exactly the right conditions, so I get great-looking plants and fantastic harvests!

Heating Cable Setup

Timer

Heating cable

A wheeled seed-starting setup with a heating cable for warmth and fluorescent lights to grow on means you'll have bigger, better seedlings than you've ever grown before. When it's time to harden off your seedlings, it's easy to wheel them outside. If your house temperature stays at 60 to 65°F at night, you can get the seedlings ready early by disconnecting the heating coil at night when the seedlings are three to four weeks old.

Start with a cart. You could use a bench to start seeds indoors in winter, but a wheeled cart makes life a lot easier. Check garage sales and garden supply catalogs for carts or make your own by adding wheels to an old bench or table.

Bring home a heat source. Plastic seed flats are handy for starting seedlings, since they're lightweight and reusable. Keep the soil in the flats warm with a horticultural heating cable or heating mat—they're available at garden centers and through mail-order seed catalogs.

Ideally, the cable or mat will keep the seedling tray between 70 and 80°F in the daytime and 55 and 65°F at night. If it's above 80°F, the seedlings will grow spindly, so check the soil temperature with a thermometer. To reduce the heat, stack several flats under your seedling tray.

Once you get the daytime temperature right, the nighttime temperature will take care of itself. As the temperature falls in the room at night, the tray will cool off some too.

Heating mats are easy to set up—you just lay them down. Soil-heating cables take a bit more care, but they're also less expensive than mats. Instructions come with the package, but the main thing to remember is to arrange the heating cables so they don't cross each other or themselves. That's because heat can build up at the crossing points, which could cause an electrical short or a fire.

The results of using heat can be dramatic. I've seen flats of seedlings grown with bottom heat that are just about twice the size of seedlings grown without heat after four to five weeks. But because the seedlings are used to warm temperatures, you'll need to harden them off before you expose them to cooler outdoor temperatures. (For more information on hardening off seedlings, see the box on this page.)

Let in the light. Grow-lights are a must unless you have a sunny climate and plenty of windows. The tried-and-true method—hanging a grow-light holder above the seedling trays by chains—works best. Use fluorescent full-spectrum grow-lights and set them up just 2 inches above the tops of the seedlings. As the seedlings grow, lift the light fixture so the lights stay 2 inches above the plants.

Start out by giving your winter- and spring-planted seedlings 10 hours of light a day. Then, when they are two weeks old, give them 11 hours. When they are three weeks old, give them 12 hours of light, and at four to five weeks old, give them 14 hours. Keep the lights set at 14 hours until your plants are ready to go into the garden.

You can turn the lights off and on manually or get an inex- pensive timer that will do it for you. The advantage of having a timer is that it won't forget to turn the lights on or off, even if you're away from home.

Make the soil ready. Because the seedlings are small, they don't need as much nutrition as they'll need when you transplant them to the garden. A potting soil mixture made of 1 part fine-screened compost and 1 part perlite or vermiculite gives them all the fertilizer they need.

If you have problems with damping-off (a fungus that wilts and kills young seedlings), sterilize the potting soil before you use it. Put the soil mix in a metal pan and set it in a warm (130°F) oven. Just 30 minutes of baking is enough to kill the damping-off organisms. There's no need to roast the potting soil or burn it.

Hardening-Off Hints

Once your seedlings are big enough to move outdoors, you'll need to expose them to the outside air and temperatures for increasing lengths of time each day over a full week.

On day one, set them outside for three hours in a spot protected from high winds. After that, add two hours a day every day until the plants are staying out all day. Then let the seedlings stay out all night too. After that, they're ready to brave the elements on their own.

76 Homegrown Salads in the Dead of Winter

You can grow fresh salads in the dead of winter without a heated greenhouse! How? By planning ahead and growing your own Belgian endive indoors. Belgian endive does take a little extra work—that's why they sell it for big bucks in the gourmet section of the grocery store—but it's worth it. In frozen January, when everyone else is just dreaming of fresh greens, you'll be dining on your own tender, tasty, organic salads.

Leaves

Hay bale

Sand

A

B

C

D

Big witloof chicory roots in fall (A) mean tasty Belgian endive in winter. But first you need to store the roots in a cellar or outdoor pit (B). Then pot up a dozen roots at two-week intervals, starting in January, to force them to sprout the blanched leaves we call Belgian endive (C). Harvest the little heads all winter long for a tasty treat (D).

Plan for gourmet salads this winter. Belgian endive is a crop that takes a little advance planning, so start this winter by ordering witloof chicory seeds. Why chicory (*Cichorium intybus*)? Because when you force witloof chicory roots to sprout new, blanched leaves in winter, they produce pale yellow heads called Belgian endive or "chicons."

Build a bed. You'll need well-drained soil that's free of stones to grow good chicory. If you're not blessed with loose rock-free soil, build a raised bed. Locate the bed in a sunny spot and make the sides out of stones or rot-resistant wood like cedar. Late winter is a great time to start this project so you won't be scrambling to build a raised bed during the spring rush or the heat of summer.

Make the raised bed 1 foot tall, then fill it with good garden soil. Go easy on fertilizer and soil amendments such as rotted manure or compost. You want the plants to produce big thick roots, but if they get too much nitrogen they'll form slender, forked, hairy roots and lots of topgrowth instead.

Sow seeds in summer. Plant the witloof chicory seeds outside 90 days before the first fall frost. Set the seeds 8 inches apart in each direction and water well. Keep the plants watered once they sprout so they'll form big, fat roots.

Dig roots in fall. Just after the first frost, carefully dig up each chicory plant, making sure you don't break the long taproot. Trim off the green tops to 2 inches above the crown and cut the roots to 8 inches long to prepare them for storage. Chicory roots hold up best in a dark place with a temperature near 32°F and humidity at about 95 percent. A cool basement or root cellar makes a perfect storage place for the roots, but an outdoor pit will work just as well. (See the box on this page for pit-building instructions.)

To store the roots, place them in a single layer in a plastic flat, a wooden box, or an outdoor pit and cover them with sand. The roots should not touch each other. Keep adding layers of roots and sand until all of the roots are stored.

Look for roots in winter. In mid-January, remove a dozen roots from your cellar or pit, leaving the rest in storage. Pour a little potting soil into a pot or box that's at least 14 inches deep—make sure the container has drainage holes. Stick the roots into the soil upright, then add more potting soil up to the top of the roots.

Add 6 inches of sand on top of the soil, then water the container thoroughly and put it in a dark place with a constant temperature of 50 to 60°F. (A closet in a cool basement works great.) Check the roots every week to see if they need water—the soil should be moist but not wet.

Harvest heads all winter long. When Belgian endive heads start to poke above the sand (in three to four weeks), pour off the sand and cut off the heads—they'll be creamy yellow to white, tightly wrapped, and about 4 to 6 inches long. Take the harvested heads to the kitchen and rinse them, then slice them lengthwise and serve yourself a winter salad!

Re-cover the potted roots with sand to force a second head from each root. Then keep bringing in new roots to force every two or three weeks until you've harvested Belgian endive from all of them.

Pit Chicory against the Weather

To make a storage pit for chicory roots, dig a trench in the garden that's 18 inches wide and 2 feet deep. The length will depend on how many roots you want to store. Put 2 inches of sand in the bottom of the pit for good drainage, then start layering roots and sand until all the roots are stored. After you cover the last layer of roots with sand, fill the rest of the pit with leaves. Place a 4-inch layer of leaves over the entire pit, then stack bales of hay or straw on top to keep the roots from freezing.

77 Create a Winter Garden

Just because it's cold out and the wind is howling doesn't mean you can't enjoy your yard and garden. Your landscape can be a source of inspiration and beauty even in the coldest months. All you have to do is buy plants with winter color and interesting shapes and add them to your plantings. If you'd rather concentrate winter color in one spot, plan a winter garden for a specific corner of your yard— one you can enjoy from indoors!

American holly

Mugo pine

Red twig dogwood

Christmas rose

Japanese silver grass

Plants with winter berries aren't the only way to create a colorful winter garden. Lure colorful birds to your plantings with seeds and a shallow pan of water— change the water daily. You can use colorful features like a red brick walk to enhance your garden too.

Choose woody plants with winter pizzazz. Not all deciduous trees and shrubs lose their looks when they lose their leaves. As you flip through garden catalogs this winter, look for trees like river birch with textured bark and shrubs with interesting silhouettes like Harry Lauder's walking stick. Keep an eye out for shrubs like winterberry that hold their fruit.

Obviously evergreen trees and shrubs are made for winter gardens. But you can enhance your garden by mixing conifers with broadleaf evergreens for contrasting colors and textures.

Count on great combinations. Ornamental grasses are a wonderful way to add winter interest. One of my favorites is Japanese silver grass, which has showy flower plumes. Set it off with showy stonecrop, which has seedheads that turn an attractive red-brown in fall and winter. And be sure to use evergreen perennials like Christmas roses—their leaves and flowers are a perfect foil for colorful shrubs like red twig dogwood.

Sneak summer preview. The first bulbs peek out of the ground so early that you really can have winter blooms. Plant large drifts of early birds such as crocuses, snowdrops (*Galanthus nivalis*), and spring snowflakes (*Leucojum vernum*) around your trees and shrubs. For delightfully fragrant winter blooms, plant witch hazel or winter honeysuckle shrubs.

Plants to Color Your Garden in Winter

Mix and match these winter gems with a splash of colorful bulbs for a winter garden that just won't quit.

Plant and Hardiness Zone Rating	Description
Trees	
River birch (*Betula nigra*) Zones 4 to 8	Pretty reddish-brown bark exfoliates to reveal layers of lighter-colored bark.
American holly (*Ilex opaca*) Zones 5 to 9	Dull, spiny evergreen leaves set off bright red fruits.
Colorado spruce (*Picea pungens*) Zones 2 to 7	Stiff needles have a color range of green to silver blue.
Shrubs	
Red twig dogwood (*Cornus sericea*) Zones 2 to 7	New stems have colorful red bark. There are also yellow-stemmed varieties.
Harry Lauder's walking stick (*Corylus avellana* 'Contorta') Zones 5 to 9	The stems of this deciduous shrub are twisted into corkscrew shapes.
Witch hazel (*Hamamelis* spp.) Zones 3 to 8	Small yellow to red ribbonlike petals may open anywhere from November to March, depending on the species.
Winterberry (*Ilex verticillata*) Zones 5 to 8	Bright red fruits decorate this deciduous holly until birds eat them.
Winter honeysuckle (*Lonicera fragrantissima*) Zones 5 to 8	Lemon-scented flowers open in January, February, or March, depending on your location.
Perennials and Ornamental Grasses	
Blue fescue (*Festuca cinerea*; also known as *F. ovina* 'Glauca') Zones 4 to 9	Leaf colors range from bright blue to dark green on short, clump-forming plants.
Christmas rose (*Helleborus niger*) Zones 3 to 8	White winter blooms fade to pink. All parts of the plant are poisonous.
Japanese silver grass (*Miscanthus* spp.) Zones 4 to 9	Both flowers and foliage are showy in winter. Depending on the variety, leaves may turn reddish or shades of brown after a frost.
Showy stonecrop (*Sedum spectabile*) Zones 3 to 9	Domes of pink blooms turn reddish in winter against blue-green leaves.

78 You <u>Can</u> Grow Artichokes in the North

Artichokes are the Goldilocks of the vegetable world—they don't like temperatures that are too hot or too cold. Their version of "just right" is a climate that stays between 50 and 75°F. So how can you grow artichokes north of Zones 9 and 10? With a little know-how and a lot of winter protection. Here's how I successfully grew artichokes in eastern Pennsylvania (Zone 6) and how you can do it too.

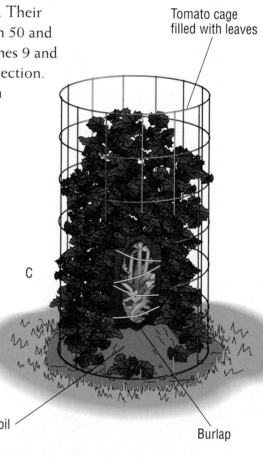

Tomato cage filled with leaves

C

6" soil

Burlap

A

B

Artichokes are worth the effort, whether you grow them for their tasty flower buds (A) or for their beautiful silver-green leaves and fuzzy flower heads (B). Start the plants from seed in winter, then set them 3 to 4 feet apart in flower or vegetable gardens in spring. In cold-winter areas, you'll need to protect your plants from freezing with a burlap wrap and a blanket of leaves (C).

All about artichokes. If you're lucky enough to live in Zones 8 to 10 along the California or Atlantic coasts, you can grow artichokes as a perennial. Just set the plants out in spring, let them grow, and the following spring they'll produce flower buds—the edible part. In cooler parts of the country, you'll need to wrap the plants for winter. It's a little more work, but worth it when you see the look on gardening friends' faces when you serve them tender homegrown artichokes!

Pick the right plant. Start by choosing the cultivar that's right for your area. You'll generally find two artichoke cultivars offered for sale. 'Green Globe' is the most common type and is your best bet for Zones 4 and 5. 'Imperial Star' isn't quite so common and it grows a little differently. It's bred to be treated as an annual, producing flower buds late in its first year in Zones 6 and 7. It's a good choice if you live in an area with an extended growing season—chances are you won't get a crop in cooler zones.

Get growing in winter. Start artichoke seeds indoors six weeks before your last frost date. Harden the seedlings off during the week before the last frost date, and set them in the garden when you're sure all frost danger is past. The plants like a fairly rich garden soil and 3 inches of mulch tucked up to their thistle-like, silvery leaves to help keep the soil cool.

Pick or protect plants in fall. Hot midsummer temperatures will slow artichokes' growth, but they'll start up again when temperatures cool down. If you're growing 'Imperial Star', harvest the flower buds when they develop in fall. Then pull the plants out and start new ones in spring. (In Zones 8 to 10, 'Imperial Star' is usually reliably perennial, so you can let the plants grow.)

If you're growing 'Green Globe', tuck mulch up around the plants when frost threatens—dry leaves are one of the best mulches. When a hard frost hits, the leaf tips protruding above the mulch will get burnt. Then it's time to cut back the center leaves so they're about a foot long and fold the long outer leaves over the crown (the growing point).

Wrap each plant with burlap and tie it snugly. Place tomato cages over the wrapped artichokes and pile some soil up against the burlap for added protection. Fill the cages at least 3 feet deep with leaves, then berm more leaves around the outside of the cages. The leaves insulate the soil so it doesn't freeze and kill the artichokes' roots.

In very cold winter areas, you might need to place bales of hay around each burlap-wrapped plant. Leave just enough space between the bales for the plant, fill in any gaps with leaves, and add a bale on top for a cover.

Harvesting. In the spring, uncover the plants about three weeks before the last frost date. Unwrap the burlap but keep some fallen leaves snugged up against the plants in case frost threatens at night.

Soon the plants will begin to grow, and within four to five weeks, you'll see flower buds forming—harvest them when they're still tight. If the buds are small, amend your soil with rotted cow manure and compost to give your plants a boost.

You can try to keep your plants growing as perennials this way, but I found that starting new plants every year and harvesting their buds in the second season gave me the largest harvests and the best results.

Get the Most out of Artichokes

Once you've tasted a homegrown artichoke, you'll know why I'm willing to make the extra effort to grow them. Steam the just-picked buds until they're tender—the leafy bracts will pull off easily. Dip each one in butter and scrape the flesh off the base with your teeth. When you've finished eating the bracts, scrape off the fuzzy "choke" and treat yourself to the tender artichoke heart.

79 Grow High-Quality Celery Underground

Almost everyone loves celery. You've probably got some in your refrigerator right now ready to use in salads, soups, and stews, or to serve raw (I like mine with peanut butter!) at the dinner table. Celery is a marsh plant that likes wet, nutrient-rich, mucky soils. But there's no reason why you have to turn your garden into a bog if you want to grow celery. Here's how to grow crunchy, succulent celery even if you live far from the plant's native marshlands.

Leaf mulch

6"

8"

A sunken bed, filled with enriched soil, is a great way to give celery plants the nutrition they need and keep the plants cool and moist. (Just remember to rotate the crop to different parts of your garden each year to avoid disease problems.) Pile leaves around the celery stalks to blanch the stems so your harvest is tender, tasty, and a pretty light green. You can harvest an entire plant at once or just a few stalks at a time for really fresh eating.

Soil and compost

Mimic marsh conditions. Growing in a marsh, celery gets plenty of water, nutrients, and organic matter. The plants thrive because temperatures are moderate and there's just enough shade to keep the blazing hot sun from turning their light green stalks dark. All you have to do to re-create these conditions is grow the plants where they'll get a minimum of a half-day of sun. Set the plants underground in rich soil and give them a steady supply of water.

Start seedlings when it's cold. Plant celery seed ten weeks before the last spring frost date. Soak the seeds in water overnight to soften their seed coats, then plant them shallowly in individual peat pots. Soak the peat pots by setting them in a shallow tray filled with water. Then be sure to keep the pots and soil moist, but not soggy, right up until you set the plants outside.

Keep the pots in a bright window (out of direct sun) where temperatures stay at 60 to 70°F—a spot on top of the refrigerator will help keep the sprouting seeds warm at night. Germination is slow, and it may be two to three weeks before the seedlings emerge.

Dig deep to keep celery cool. As soon as the soil outside is thawed and dry enough to work, start digging a trench that's 12 inches wide and 14 inches deep. The trench will provide the shade and cooler temperatures celery plants crave. If you want to cut down on heavy in-ground digging—and who doesn't!—use a raised bed for your celery.

You'll need a raised bed that's 6 inches high to grow celery—any higher and temperatures may get too warm for the plants. Dig out all the soil in the raised bed, then dig down another 8 inches to get the 14-inch depth.

The size of the growing area depends on which digging method you're using. You'll need enough space to hold 6 plants for every person in your family. If you're using the trench method, set plants 6 inches apart. For the raised-bed method, space the plants 6 inches apart in all directions. For a family of three, you'll need 18 plants. That means you'll need a trench 9 feet long or a raised bed that's 2 feet wide and 3½ feet long. (If you need more than one trench, space them 2 feet apart.) Whichever method you use, mix one-third garden soil with two-thirds compost and fill the trench or bed 8 inches deep.

Set seedlings out early. When the seedlings are 5 inches tall, harden them off by placing them outside for two to three hours on the first day, then more and more hours each day for a week. Keep seedlings inside if temperatures go below 45°F, or your young plants may read the cool weather as the onset of winter and bolt to seed.

Transplant your celery seedlings to the garden one to two weeks before the last frost date. Water the soil before planting. Then water the seedlings in with a fertilizer mix of 1 tablespoon of fish emulsion and 2 tablespoons of kelp extract per gallon of water.

Cover stalks to keep them tender. After planting, mulch the stalks (but not the leaves on top) with dry leaves. As the celery grows, keep adding mulch so the stems blanch from the lack of sunlight—this makes them more tender and tasty.

Stretch your harvest into winter. You can harvest the plants as soon as they reach a size that you can use. If you still have stalks in the ground when frost threatens in the fall, dig the celery up, roots and all, and replant them in a box in a cool basement. If you keep the soil watered, the transplanted celery plants will last for several months.

Meet Plants' Needs

Celery needs plenty of water and nutrients through the growing season. An easy way to direct food and water to the plants' roots is to sink a bottomless can between each plant. Fill the cans with organic fertilizer solution once a month, and with water from a hose as needed.

80 Plant Leeks Once, Have Leeks Forever

1" root cutting

A

Sideshoot

6"

B

I came late to leeks, having always been an onion man myself. But once I discovered them, I found more and more reasons to use leeks in the kitchen. I love leeks' mild flavor, their ability to absorb liquid and add substance to casseroles, soups, and stews, and even the look of the fine little ringlets when they're sliced. You'll love the way these plants provide you with tasty harvests year after year without lots of care or fuss.

Keep your leek patch growing by replanting root cuttings (A) and sideshoots (B) from your harvest. Use a mulch of straw to blanch the leek stems during the growing season. Then use a blanket of straw to protect your crop from cold in winter. You'll be able to harvest young leeks in spring and summer and full-grown leeks in fall and winter.

Make your planting last a lifetime. Leeks are easy to grow because they're easy to propagate. They're biennials, so they go to seed and die in their second growing season. But that doesn't mean you'll have to go a season without leeks. If you grow long-season leeks and replant leek pieces as you harvest, you'll have luscious leeks forevermore.

Sow long-season leeks in winter. There are short-season leeks and long-season leeks, but only the long-season ones will provide you with year-round harvests. Short-season leeks mature in 70 to 75 days from transplanting and tend to be extra long in the stem (the usable part). These are fine for growing a crop that you'll harvest by the end of the season, but they won't survive the winter.

Long-season leeks take 100 to 150 days to mature after transplanting, and their stems are usually shorter and thicker than short-season types. But they've got plenty of flavor and they're cold-hardy to boot.

Because long-season leeks take so long to mature, sow the seeds in flats 10 to 12 weeks before the last spring frost date. The seeds take 2 to 3 weeks to germinate and will sprout best if you give them 65 to 70°F temperatures during the day and cooler temperatures (55 to 60°F) at night. Once the seedlings are up and growing, thin them to 1½ inches apart.

Move leeks out in early spring. Plant the seedlings outside just after the last frost date in spring—by then the plants should be 8 to 12 inches tall. Prepare a bed in a sunny spot with weed-seed-free soil that's rich, well drained, and full of crumbly organic matter.

If your soil isn't loose, rich, or weed-free, make a raised bed and amend it with 2 pounds of weed-seed-free compost for every 10 square feet of soil.

Use a dowel, stick, or dibble to make a hole for each seedling. The holes should be about 1½ inches in diameter and 6 inches deep. Set the little leeks 6 inches apart in all directions. The crown of the leek—the point where the leaves unfurl—should be just above the soil level. Put a little loose soil in the hole if you need to adjust the height. Then sift in a little loose compost around the stem to hold it in place, but don't pack it in. Water the seedlings in well.

As the leeks grow, keep straw mulch tucked up along the firm stems to keep out sunlight and blanch the stems white. Blanched stems grow longer and are more tender, so mulching is definitely worthwhile.

Pull and restart leeks. You can harvest leeks young or wait until they reach full size, with stems that are 1 to 2½ inches in diameter. After the first growing season, you'll have leeks of different sizes to harvest in every season.

Whenever you harvest full-size leeks, trim the bottom inch of the stem off along with the roots of each leek. Plant the root-and-stem sections back in the garden under 1 inch of soil. Water the cut pieces in and cover them with an inch of mulch. The root-and-stem sections will regrow, making another crop in five to nine weeks or next growing season.

As you harvest plants in late fall, you'll notice that some of the leeks have sideshoots—small leeks attached to the main plant. Pull these sideshoots off and replant them exactly as you planted the seedlings in spring. The sideshoots will overwinter if you cover them with 1½ feet of straw or leaves.

Pull the mulch aside when you want to harvest leeks in winter, then uncover the plants in spring. You'll have leeks ready and waiting to grow for quick harvests.

Winter-Hardy Leeks

These long-season leeks are cold-tolerant and will overwinter in most parts of North America if you cover them with plenty of mulch.

'American Flag', 130 days

'Blue Solaise', 105 days

'Laura', 115 days

'St. Victor', 145 days

81 Fix Conditions in Your Favor for Really Sweet Melons

No matter how you test for ripeness, you just can't buy a delectably sweet cantaloupe, honeydew, muskmelon, or other dessert melon. That's because melons start losing sugars as soon as they're picked. Even farmers' market melons can't compete with a melon you've grown yourself and picked fresh just before eating. To make sure you get wonderfully sweet melons, just set your plants up to succeed.

Spotted cucumber beetle

Striped cucumber beetle

Powdery mildew

What do you get when you give hardy homegrown melon transplants fertile soil, black plastic mulch, floating row covers, and just the right amount of water? Plants that produce supersweet melons because they're free of pests (top left) and diseases (top right) that sap melons' sweetness.

Enrich the heck out of the soil. Three to four weeks before your last spring frost date, spread 40 pounds of composted cow, goat, horse, or pig manure for every 100 square feet of melon patch. Then dig or till the compost into the top 3 inches of soil. Melons are heavy feeders and will grow big and healthy with good nutrition.

Cover the soil with black plastic. Melons like it warm, and the soil under black plastic warms up faster than uncovered soil. Lay the plastic down any-time after you've prepared the soil—up to one week before planting time. (In very hot areas, black plastic can make the soil too hot. So surround plants with straw mulch right after planting instead of using black plastic.)

You'll get several benefits in addition to the heat from using black plastic. You won't have to water as often, because the plastic keeps water in the soil from evaporating quickly. The black plastic also keeps weeds from sprouting. And a plastic mulch keeps soil from splashing up on the leaves, which helps prevent the spread of soilborne diseases like fusarium wilt.

Start melons inside. Sow seeds of disease-resistant melon varieties indoors one week before the last spring frost date. Then transplant the seedlings to the garden when it's warm. By giving the melons a head start indoors,

you'll avoid that urge to plant melon seeds outdoors too early. Early outdoor planting doesn't mean early melons—it only means setbacks when these heat-loving plants balk at the cold.

When your transplants are three weeks old, harden them off by setting the plants outside in a semishaded spot that's pro-tected from high winds. Leave the plants out for a few hours each day until, by the end of a week, they can take a full day outside. Once they're hardened off, set the plants 2 feet apart in beds that are 4 feet wide.

Keep pests and diseases away. Planting resistant vari-eties is one of the best ways to prevent plant diseases. But when pests threaten or when resistant varieties aren't available, here are some other options.

As soon as your melons are in the ground, cover them with sheets of floating row cover to keep aphids, cucumber beetles, grasshoppers, and leafhoppers away. These pests not only damage plants by feeding, they also spread bacterial wilt and viral diseases like mosaic.

Floating row covers will keep bees off the vines as well as pest insects, so you'll have to hand-pollinate the flowers or remove the row covers when the plants bloom. (See Idea #7 for tips on hand-pollinating.)

If you don't cover crops with floating row covers imme-

diately after planting, insect pests may get trapped inside the covers. If it's too late to cover your melons, try surrounding the plants with radishes—they'll help repel insect pests.

If insect pests are already eating your plants, try attracting them to a plant trap. Cucumber beetles prefer wilted melon leaves, so pull up and make piles out of any extra melon plants. Collect and destroy the beetles early in the morning before they can move very fast.

Water well until just before harvesttime. Melon plants need water while they are growing and forming fruits. But when the fruits are within eight to ten days of being harvested, cut back on the water. This gives the melons a chance to stock up on sugars so they'll develop that extra-sweet flavor.

Wash Powdery Mildew Away

In addition to the viral dis-eases and the insects mentioned on this page, you'll also need to keep a look out for the fungal disease powdery mildew. At first this disease makes melon leaves look like they're dusted with white powder. Then the leaves shrivel and the fruits ripen early—before they accumulate sugars—so they taste bland. You can control powdery mildew by dousing plants with a strong spray of water once a week.

82

Grow Big Onions That Will Keep All Winter

When I first started gardening, a friend told me to plant out my onions and forget them—that his biggest onions always came from the weediest part of the patch. Hah! That advice only got me lots of weeds. I've since discovered that the right onions, weed-free soil, and good storage techniques are the keys to bigger, better onions. Here's how I do it.

Grow your onions in a box so it's easy to give them good soil and keep weeds away and you'll reap a huge harvest. One 3' x 5' box will hold enough onions for a family of three to eat all winter (A). When the plant tops brown in fall, pull the onions and set them on a rack to dry (B). Once the onions have cured, bag or braid them and place them in a closet or other dark spot where they'll stay cool and dry (C).

188

Sow onion seeds. I like to start onions from seed rather than sets or transplants. It's easier to find seeds than sets of the long-keeping varieties that I'm looking for, and seeds give me the flexibility to start growing whenever I like. Choose thin-necked storage onions like 'Copra' because they'll dry quickly. Store them properly and they'll last from late summer to early spring!

When you order onion seeds, pick varieties that are suited for your part of the country. Different onions need different daylengths to form bulbs. Long-day types need 13 to 16 hours of daylight and will thrive in northern areas where days are longer. Short-day onions need less than 14 hours of daylight and will do better in the South. (I know it sounds crazy, but days really are longer in the North and shorter in the South.)

Plant your onion seeds in flats in late January, put them in a cool, bright part of the house, and keep the soil moist but not wet.

Get tough. Harden the plants off four to six weeks before the last spring frost. This process of getting plants adjusted to outdoor conditions simply means moving the flats outside for increasing lengths of time over a five-day period. Start by setting the flats outdoors for a few hours on days one and two, then work the

plants up to staying outside all day and night by the fifth day.

Box your onions. Instead of planting the onions in the garden where they'll have to compete with weeds, construct a rough box from scrap wood that's at least 6 inches deep. A 3-foot-wide by 5-foot-long box is a handy size that can handle not quite six dozen onions—that's enough to last a family of three over winter. If you want twice that many onions, build two boxes or make the box twice as long. Just don't increase the width of the box or you won't be able to reach the middle easily from either side.

Set the box in a sunny spot outside that's within easy reach of a hose. Fill the box with half garden soil and half weed-seed-free compost or well-rotted manure. Onions like a loose, rich soil that drains well. A sandy soil is perfect as long as you amend it with 2 to 3 pounds of compost per 10 square feet of planting area.

Plant your onion seedlings 5 inches apart in all directions. It's okay to space the plants close because the rich soil will support their growth. If any weeds blow in during the growing season, pull them as soon as they show their faces and mulch the soil with grass clippings.

Dry onions out. The bulbs will start to swell as the daylength increases. And after the longest

day of the year is past, the bulbs will size up and mature. Eventually the tops of the plants will begin to turn brown and fall over. When about half the tops have toppled, push the rest of them over with the back of a rake to speed up the drying process. The tops will turn brown in a few days and then they're ready to harvest. Before you start digging, check out the curing directions in the box on this page for the best results.

Curing Onions

Before you store your onions, cure them so they'll keep without rotting. Gently dig the bulbs out of the soil with a spading fork, being careful not to break the brown leaves off. Don't wash the onions, and don't remove the papery wrappers. (When the bulbs are fully dry, you can crumble off any excess soil with your fingers.)

Take the onions to a shady spot and lay them one layer deep on a piece of wire screen set on bricks on the ground, or a picnic table. Let the bulbs dry for about a week, or until the necks are dry—green, moist necks give rots and molds a place to get started. If rain threatens, move the onions into a garage or porch so they don't get wet.

When the onions are cured, cut the tops off, leaving just 1 inch of foliage (unless you're making braids). Put the onions in mesh bags and hang them in a cool, dry, dark room.

83

Grow Organic Potatoes the Quick and Easy Way

Getting a big crop of potatoes doesn't mean you have to do a lot of digging, either to plant your spuds or harvest them. It sounds too good to be true, but you can grow potatoes in mulch on top of the ground! And, if you presprout them before planting, you'll get an extra-early harvest to boot.

Sprouted seed potatoes

Straw

A

Potato planting doesn't get any easier than this! Simply lay presprouted seed potatoes on the soil then bury the patch with straw or hay (A). Your plants will grow through the mulch and form tubers as they flower. After flowering, you can pull back the mulch and harvest a few of the new potatoes forming on or near the soil surface (B). Wait until the potato plants die back before you dig up the main harvest.

B

New potatoes

Prepare the soil early.
Choose a day in late winter to fertilize your potato bed and get it ready for planting. Figure on 30 square feet of potatoes for each member of your family. Make the patch rectangular and no more than 4 feet wide so it's easy to reach the center of the planting at harvesttime.

Before you begin working the soil, make sure it's thawed and moist (not wet) so it's easy to work. Potatoes do best in well-drained soil, but by planting above ground, they'll thrive even if your soil isn't a perfect sandy loam. Add 20 pounds of compost for every 100 square feet of planting area. Then till or use a rake to work the compost into the top inch or two of soil.

Presprout your spuds.
Sprouting potatoes is something you want to avoid in the kitchen, but at planting time it's the key to an early harvest. Unsprouted seed potatoes (potatoes grown for planting) may sit in your garden for weeks without growing, but sprouted seed potatoes will get growing right away.

To presprout seed potatoes, expose them to indirect light and temperatures of 65 to 70°F for two weeks before planting. After this treatment, you'll see the eyes (dormant buds) swell and grow into $\frac{1}{16}$- to $\frac{1}{8}$-inch-long sprouts.

Set your spuds on the soil.
Plant your presprouted seed potatoes in the garden two weeks before the last frost date. There's no advantage to getting them into the garden too early, because a hard frost can nip off their tender growing shoots and cause a major setback.

Some gardeners cut their potatoes so that each cut piece has one eye—but not me. I get more potatoes by planting whole, presprouted spuds.

Space the sprouted seed potatoes 1 foot apart in all directions, then gently snuggle them into the soil surface—you don't have to bury them completely.

Shake straw or weed-seed-free hay over the potato patch until you've covered the potatoes with 10 to 12 inches of mulch. When potato shoots appear, spread more mulch around them so only the top tuft of leaves is visible. After that, leave the plants alone.

Take care of your tubers.
When flower buds appear on the plants, your potatoes will be setting their new tubers. Make sure your potato patch gets an inch of water a week during this stretch so the plants aren't stressed. But when the flowers start to open, back off on the water or you may damage the maturing tubers.

It's okay to jump the gun. As the potatoes finish forming tubers, the vines will start to die back. When about half the vines have died back, you can dig the potatoes with a spading fork. Of course, if you're impatient, like most gardeners, you can pull back the mulch here and there and steal new potatoes weeks earlier. Who could resist that fresh flavor?

For Flavor, Grow Fingerlings

In my book, just about all potatoes are delicious, but for all-around taste, my favorites are the oh-so-delicious fingerlings. These potatoes are called fingerlings because they're long and slender. Some grow only the size of your thumb, while others reach 6 to 10 inches long.

For flavorful potato salad and boiled, steamed, or baked potatoes, try 'Russian Banana', an easy-to-grow yellow fingerling with a waxy smooth consistency. Or grow yellow-fleshed 'Austrian Crescent' or 'German Yellow' fingerlings. The mashed potatoes and hash browns I make from these potatoes are nutty and earthy, with a smooth, dense texture.

Most seed companies list only a few potatoes, so look for potato specialists such as Ronniger's Seed Potatoes in Moyie Springs, Idaho, and Beckers Seed Potatoes in Trout Creek, Ontario, for these special beauties. Both companies offer dozens of varieties. (See "Sources" on page 228 for ordering information.)

84 Sweet Potatoes Forever— Even Up North

I used to think of sweet potatoes as a strictly southern crop like peanuts. But then I discovered that you can grow sweet potatoes as far north as upstate New York, where the growing season is just over 100 days long. You don't need a greenhouse for good results, just short-season slips (rooted sprouts) that you buy or start yourself. One taste of the homegrown flavor of these versatile tubers, and you'll be hooked!

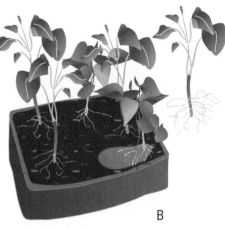

B

A

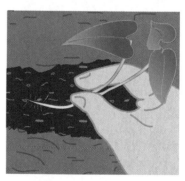

C

Whether you bake them, roast them, mash them, or add them to soups or stew, there's nothing like the flavor and color of home-grown sweet potatoes (A) to brighten up a meal. With short-season varieties, Northerners don't have to miss out on these taste treats. Sprout your own slips in winter, then cut them off the tubers (B) and plant them horizontally (C).

Select short-season varieties. If it's your first time growing sweet potatoes, order slips from a mail-order seed company in winter. They'll ship your order at planting time in spring. Check with local nurseries too. If they grow their own slips, you can buy them in spring. Choose short-season cultivars like 'Centennial' that are ready to harvest in 100 days.

Keep slips warm and watch them grow. If you live in the South, plant the slips in the garden about two weeks after the last frost date in spring. The soil will be warm enough for the slips to thrive by then. If you live in a cooler area with a 100-day growing season, wait until a month after the last frost date before planting. You'll get a big payoff if you prewarm the soil by solarizing it before planting in the North. (See Idea #13.)

The slips will look a bit bedraggled when they arrive, but if you plant them outside right away and keep them watered, they'll revive in a few days. Set the slips in the soil horizontally, 2 to 3 inches deep, so only the top tufts of leaves are above the soil. Sweet potatoes like moderately rich, loose soil, so grow them in raised beds if your soil is rocky or made up of hard clay.

The slips will root and form tubers from each buried node. You can harvest the tubers as soon as they reach cooking size—start checking after 70 days. Harvest what you need and let the rest of the tubers grow until two to three weeks before the first fall frost. Then dig up all of the tubers, cure them (see the box on this page for details), and store them.

Sprout your own slips. Once you've got sweet potatoes on hand, you can sprout your own slips each winter. (Don't try to sprout supermarket tubers—they may be treated with sprouting inhibitors, and they're usually long-season southern varieties that won't produce in colder regions.)

Six to eight weeks before your last spring frost date, bury the nicest, healthiest tubers 1 inch deep in 4- to 5-inch-deep containers filled with good potting soil. A mix of 1 part compost and 1 part sand will work just fine. Water the tubers in well and keep them warm (around 80°F) by using a seedling heating coil to provide bottom heat, or by putting the containers on top of the refrigerator. When shoots appear, move the potted tubers to a warm, sunny window. Always keep the soil moist but not soggy.

After eight to ten weeks (about two weeks after your last spring frost date), your potted tubers will have 8 to 10 inches of topgrowth and four or five nodes. Lift the tubers out of their containers and cut off the largest slips. When you're done, plant the tubers back in the soil mix, leaving the small slips attached so they can grow bigger. Plant the large slips outside immediately and set out the smaller slips when they reach full size.

Cured Potatoes Are Keepers

Once you've harvested your sweet potatoes, set them in the sun for no more than a half hour to dry—any longer and they'll sunscald. Handle the tubers gently, since their skins are delicate when they're first harvested.

Cure the sweet potatoes by placing them in a warm spot in the shade. Use a picnic table or a piece of wire mesh set on bricks to keep the tubers off the ground. Spread the tubers out so they don't touch each other and cover them with newspaper. The paper will keep enough moisture around the tubers to keep them from drying out.

Your sweet potatoes will cure in a couple of weeks, after which you should store them at 55 to 60°F—colder temperatures encourage rot. If you have an unheated cellar, that's ideal. Sweet potatoes like lots of humidity, so if your cellar isn't humid, wrap the tubers lightly in newspaper and pile them loosely in boxes.

Only store sweet potatoes that are free of blemishes, discolored skin, and rot. Cut the bad spots off bruised tubers and eat the good parts right away.

85 Plant Deep to Reap a Heap of Tomatoes

Buying tomato seedlings as transplants should mean an earlier harvest, but lots of times it doesn't. You put store-bought transplants in the garden expecting quick growth, and instead they sit, because they either have too few roots or they're potbound. Either way, it's a struggle for the plants to put out new top-growth. What's the answer? Repot—a lot.

Grow tomato transplants with super-size root systems by repotting seedlings a lot! When the seedlings have four true leaves (A), pinch off the cotyledons and set the plants deep in small paper cups (B). When six new leaves appear, nick off the four old ones and move the seedlings to larger cups (C). Repeat the process whenever six new leaves appear, until the plants have large ready-for-the-garden rootballs.

Big root systems mean big harvests. Grow your own transplants from seed so they'll develop extra-large, ready-to-grow-like-crazy rootballs. All those roots mean your tomatoes can take in enough water and minerals to support a big growth spurt and maintain it. Your plants will soon have green topgrowth equal to their big root systems. You'll get more tomatoes sooner and save money, too. Here's how to do it.

Start seeds in winter. Plant tomatoes ten weeks before the last frost date in flats of sterilized potting soil. Grow the seedlings under lights so they don't get leggy, and you'll have tomato plants that are big enough to plant out a week or two after the last frost date.

Repot once. When the plants show four true leaves (the first two leaves are cotyledons, or seed leaves, not true leaves), dig them out of the flat with a fork or small trowel. Using your fingers, pinch off the cotyledons and pot the plants in peat pots or little paper cups with drainage holes poked in the bottom. Set the seedlings deep so the soil comes right up to their bottom leaves.

Repot twice. Let the plants grow until they produce six new leaves. Then pinch or cut off the four old leaves and repot the plants into a larger paper cup with drainage holes.

Repot three times. When your seedlings grow six more new leaves, nick off the six old leaves and transplant the seedlings to still-larger cups with drainage holes. By pinching off leaves and repotting the plants, you're stimulating them to make giant rootballs with only a moderate amount of topgrowth.

Harden plants off. One week before planting, toughen your plants up by setting them outside during the day in a protected area like a cold frame. Move the plants indoors at night. Once your transplants are used to the stronger light and the wind outside, plant them in the garden. They'll erupt into quick-growing fountains of foliage, and you'll be on your way to plenty of tomatoes while your neighbors are still fiddling with their seedlings.

Why Deep Planting Works

Tomatoes have an advantage over most plants when it comes to producing roots, because their stems can grow roots if they're in contact with the soil. With my supersystem, each time you repot a seedling you bury more and more of the stem. In the process, your transplant grows a bigger root system, plus it develops new roots along the length of the stem for extra grow-power.

Set your transplants deep when you plant them outside, and you'll encourage even more roots to grow. But always remove the leaves that will end up underneath the soil or they'll rot and may cause disease problems.

Tomato seedling

Giant root system

Whenever you plant tomatoes, set them deep in the soil—right up to the leaves. If your transplants are awfully tall, you can lay the plants down sideways in a shallow trench instead of digging a deep hole. Just make sure the plant tops stick out above the ground.

86 Simple Traps Outwit Apple Pests

Apple maggot flies, the adult form of those pasty white larvae that tunnel through and ruin homegrown apples, are attracted to the colors yellow and red. You can take advantage of this fact to trap these apple-eaters and keep them under control. Here are two nifty traps you can buy or make this winter to put apple maggots out of business come spring.

Apple maggot fly

Apple maggot larva

Don't let apple maggots get the best of your apples. Hang sticky yellow panels in your apple trees to find out when apple maggot flies are in the area. Tie the panels to the tree on at least two sides so they don't flop around and stick to the leaves. Then hang red sticky balls in your trees to lure in and trap female apple maggot flies.

Look out for apple maggots.

If you live in the northern half of the United States or in Canada, apple maggots are likely to show up in your apples. They prefer early-maturing and sweet apple varieties, but can also be a problem on apricots, cherries, crabapples, pears, and plums.

How do you know if they're on your trees? The outside of the fruit will look dimpled and be soft and brown from the feeding damage. Inside the fruit you'll see narrow winding brown trails.

The adult apple maggot is a fly—slightly smaller than a housefly—that emerges from the soil anytime between early June and the end of August. The larvae of this fly hatch from eggs laid on the fruit. They tunnel through the fruit for several weeks, then leave the apples and enter the soil to overwinter.

Stop pests with color-coded traps.

To control apple maggots, use two traps that you can buy or make yourself (for instructions, see the box on this page). Start out with yellow sticky panel traps that attract the immature maggot fly when it emerges from the soil. Then follow up with red apple-shaped traps to attract the mature female who is looking for a place to lay her eggs.

Hang the yellow panels in your trees in late May to monitor the insects' emergence. Hang several traps head high and clear leaves from right around the traps. Inspect the traps weekly. When you catch apple maggot flies on the panels, hang your red sticky balls. Hang one trap in a dwarf tree, two or three traps in a semidwarf tree, and six traps in a full-size tree.

The sticky balls should take care of your apple maggot problem. But for added pest control, pick up and dispose of dropped apples once a week beginning in August.

Do-It-Yourself Sticky Traps

The easiest way to get sticky traps is to buy them, since a package of three costs less than $10 and they're reusable. Check your garden center or a garden supply catalog for the traps or the supplies to make your own sticky panels and balls.

If you want to make your own traps, it's really pretty easy. Make the yellow panel traps from ¼-inch-thick wood cut into 5½ x 9-inch pieces. Paint the traps with a white primer coat followed by a coat of bright yellow. Put a screw eye on the top of the trap and one on the side so you can easily hang it out in the tree. Tie a piece of string to each screw eye, then tie each string to the tree. Tying the trap in two places keeps it from moving in the wind and sticking to apple leaves. Coat the panels with Tangle-Trap, a gooey coating for trapping insects.

I've found that plastic oranges and apples work best for the sticky ball traps, but you can use any red apple-size spheres. You'll find these balls in stores that specialize in accessories for the home.

To make a hook for the ball, insert a screw eye into the ball or make a ¼-inch slit in the ball with a sharp knife and insert a nail with a head. (Before inserting the nail, bend the pointed end around with strong pliers to form a hook.) Insert the nail head first by sliding the edge of the nail head into the slit, then straightening it so the nail head flattens out against the inside of the slit and is held securely there.

Next, put the red ball inside a plastic sandwich bag, leaving the hook outside. Tie the plastic bag in place with a twist tie, and apply Tangle-Trap. It's easiest to work with warm Tangle-Trap, so leave the can in the sun for a couple of hours before using it. Smear Tangle-Trap over the whole surface of the ball with a flat-bladed wooden paint stirrer or something similar. Give the ball a thin coating rather than a thick one so the red color of the ball still shows through clearly.

To attach the ball to a tree, tie a piece of string to a branch at eye level. The string should be 2 to 3 feet in from the end of the branch. Then tie the string to the hook on the sticky ball. When the ball becomes thick with dead insects, remove the plastic bag and discard it. Put on a new bag and apply a fresh coating of Tangle-Trap.

87 Balanced Grape Pruning Produces Top Yields

With grape pruning, like everything else in life, a balanced approach is best. Prune off too little growth and you'll get inferior fruit. Prune off too much growth and you may get no fruit at all. So how do you know when you've done just the right amount of pruning? Get out your scale—it sounds wacky, but science shows it really works!

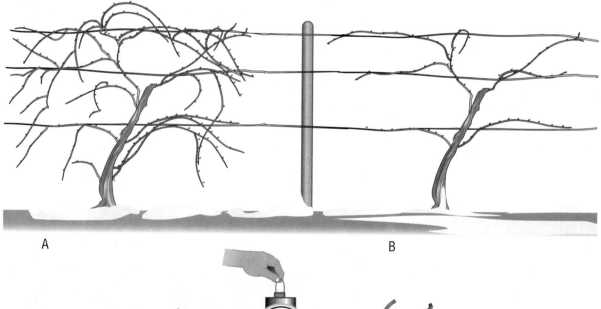

A

B

An unpruned Concord grapevine (A) has so many fruiting buds that, left on its own, next year's growth would be weak from the strain of overproduction. To guarantee healthy plants and tasty grapes, prune your vines (B) and weigh the clippings (C) according to Cornell University's balanced pruning method.

C

Take pruning to new heights.
If the only pruning you do on your grapevine involves cutting it back so it doesn't grow beyond its trellis, you'll still get grapes. But if you want to maximize your grape production and still get the tastiest grapes possible, take your pruning to another level.

Typically, gardeners prune grapes using one of two pruning systems: cane pruning or spur pruning. (See the box on page 200 for details.) Cane pruning works well for American grapes, French-American hybrids, and viniferas and it's the one I like to use to keep my vines in line.

But instead of using general estimates to decide how many canes to leave on a vine, I use a bud-counting system called balanced pruning that was developed at Cornell University. The balanced pruning system helped me turn ho-hum harvests into incredible crops. Here's how.

Use a balanced approach.
Grapevines need a certain amount of leaves and shoots for good health, and of course you want a generous fruit harvest for your efforts. A bumper crop sounds good, but an excessive harvest won't give you high-quality grapes. You'll get the highest quality grapes from a vine that's pruned so its crop and growth are in balance.

When you let your grapevine grow wild, it responds by producing lots of leaves and grapes.

The grapes will be shaded by the excessive leaf growth so they won't grow as large or tasty as grapes that are exposed to full sun and concentrated in fewer clusters. The fruit may use up so much energy that the vine will be weaker next year and you'll get another inferior-quality crop.

So, should you prune off lots of growth to make sure your grapevine doesn't produce too many grapes? No, moderation is the key. If you prune off too much growth, you're just as bad off as if you pruned off too little. Overpruned grapevines will give you few grapes for your efforts and they'll put on a growth spurt to make up for all the wood that was removed.

Turn exacting pruning into simple science. Finding the happy medium between overpruning and underpruning may sound like a formidable task but it's not. Cornell fruit scientists found a way to measure grape prunings for the best results. So pruning, which is usually a technique that's hard to quantify, becomes an easy-to-use formula. The Cornell balanced pruning system involves weighing the one-year-old cane prunings from a vine and using the weight of the pruned wood to determine the number of buds to retain.

To try the balanced pruning system, you'll need a small hanging scale you can hold in your hand. The scale should be

able to hold up to 5 pounds of weight. You'll use it to measure the one-year-old canes that you cut from the vine. To weigh the canes, cut them into easy-to-handle pieces, then tie them together with a piece of twine and hang them from the scale.

Weigh grapevines in winter.
Start balanced pruning when your grapevines are dormant. You'll be working on the entire vine, but only weighing the one-year-old canes that formed last season. Make sure you keep the one-year-old cane prunings separate from the rest to ensure that your calculations are correct.

If you look at your mature grapevine, you'll see that it may have as many as 300 buds on the canes that can produce fruit. By following the balanced pruning formula, you'll end up with less than 70 buds, depending on the weight of the prunings.

Look at your vine and the chart on page 201 before you start pruning. For most vines, use the maximum buds figure in the chart for your initial pruning. If you have a 'Concord' or other American-grape-type vine (*Vitis labrusca*), leave a bit over the maximum bud figure of 60—say 70 to play it safe. Then prune off more buds if the weight of the canes pruned off indicates you should. Use sharp scissor-type hand pruners to make your cuts.

When your initial pruning is done, weigh the canes you've cut off. According to the chart, if you have 3 pounds of prunings, you should leave 50 buds—that's 30 buds for the first pound and 10 buds for each additional pound of one-year-old prunings.

If the prunings weigh 4 pounds or more, just cut the buds back to the maximum number listed in the chart (in this case, 60) and leave it at that. This system is really a way of fine-tuning your pruning to get the best production from your vines.

Give hybrids an extra cut. French-American grapes need some follow-up work after balanced pruning. These varieties have buds at the base of the trunk that you won't be able to see during dormant pruning. Remove these buds and secondary shoot buds when they start to grow in the spring, be-

Standard Grape-Pruning Practices

Different grape varieties respond best to different pruning systems. American grapes (*Vitis labrusca* and hybrids) and French-American hybrid grapes will do fine if you cane prune them. Most European wine grapes (also known as viniferas) respond well to cane pruning and spur pruning. Since Muscadine grapes (*V. rotundifolia*) produce most of their fruit on the first few buds (those closest to the trunk), they respond well to spur pruning.

Cane pruning. Late winter is pruning time since the plants are dormant and you can see the buds easily. Untie the grapevine from the trellis and select new main branches from this year's growth. Choose one pencil-diameter cane near each main branch that's growing near the trunk of the vine. These will become the new main branches.

Just above or below the new main branches, pick out two more branches and cut these back to just two buds (these are called spurs). Remove all the other branches, including the old main branches, by cutting them off flush with the trunk. Tie the new main branches to the trellis every foot or so to hold them in place. Then, use your fingers to rub off excess buds, leaving one bud every 4 to 5 inches. Then cut back the branches so each has just ten buds.

Cane pruning is an effective way to reduce the number of buds on your grapevine to a manageable level. But if you use the balanced pruning method, you'll get even better results.

Spur pruning. For spur pruning, leave the main branches of your grapevine in place, but replace the old ties with new ones. Cut each cane that's sprouted from the main branches back to two buds. Thin the two-bud canes (called spurs) so you're left with one spur every 4 to 5 inches along each main branch.

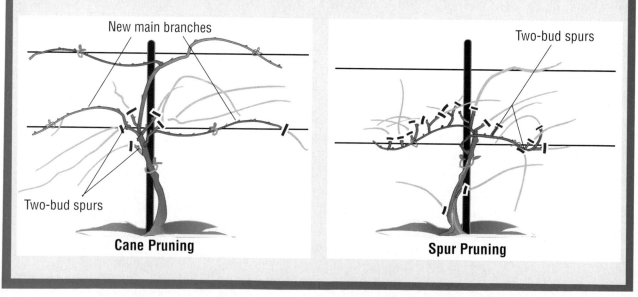

Cane Pruning — New main branches, Two-bud spurs

Spur Pruning — Two-bud spurs

cause they'll also produce fruit and that results in overcropping.

It's also a good idea to thin the flower clusters on French-American hybrid grapes and viniferas to keep them from over-producing. Left on its own, a grapevine will produce three to five flower clusters on each shoot, which is a lot for the vine to handle. By thinning the number of flower clusters per shoot back to two (one for viniferas), you'll get bigger fruits and a healthier plant. That's all there is to balanced pruning. And once you taste the fruits of your labor, you'll agree, it's well worth the effort!

Balanced Pruning for Mature Grapevines

The pruning formula below lets you use a hand scale to determine exactly how many buds to remove from your grapevines for the best results. Give it a try and watch your crop quality improve. This information is the result of the efforts of Cornell fruit scientists. It comes from Misc. Bulletin III, New York State College of Agriculture and Life Sciences, Cornell University, and is based on plants set at a standard 8-foot spacing.

Grape Variety	Number of Buds to Retain for First Pound of Prunings		Number of Buds to Retain for Each Additional Pound of Prunings	Maximum Number of Buds per Vine
American Grapes				
'Catawba', 'Delaware', and 'Niagara'	25	plus	10	60
'Concord'	30	plus	10	60
'Dutchess', 'Elvira', and 'Ives'	20	plus	10	50
'Fredonia'	40	plus	10	70
French-American Hybrids				
Small-clustered varieties such as 'Baco Noir', 'Foch', and 'Leon Millot'	20	plus	10	50
Medium-clustered varieties such as 'Aurore', 'Cascade', 'Chelois', and 'Vidal Blanc'	20	plus	10	40
Large-clustered varieties such as 'Chambourcin', 'Chancellor', 'DeChaunac', 'Seyval', 'Verdelet', and 'Villard Blanc'	20	plus	10	45
Viniferas	20	plus	20	60

88 Change Grape Varieties the Easy Way

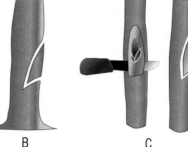

B
Notch Stock Plant

C
Remove Bud Chip

You don't have to live with dud grapes. If you have a mature grapevine that's unproductive or disease-prone, change it to a new variety. Of course, you can dig up the old vine and plant a new one, but then you'll have to wait four or five years for the new vine to mature. By grafting a new vine to your old one using a technique called chip budding, you can get a full harvest of 10 to 20 pounds of grapes per vine in just two years.

D
Insert Bud Chip

E
Wrap Graft

Make the best of a bad grape by grafting on a better vine using the chip-budding method. You'll get a great harvest without a long wait (A). Gather your scionwood in winter, then cut a notch in the stock trunk (B) to receive the bud chip (C). Fit the two pieces together snugly so the cambium layers meet on at least one side (D), then wrap the bud graft with horticultural tape (E). When the bud shows new growth, cut off the stock above the graft and remove the tape.

A

Grafted Vine

Prepare the grafting materials. In the winter, collect cuttings of the new grape that you want to grow. (When you're grafting, cuttings are called scions and the plant you're grafting the cutting onto is called the stock plant.) If you have a favorite grape growing in your yard, this step is easy. If you don't have the new variety on hand, see the box on this page.

Look for canes that grew in the previous summer—they should be as thick as a pencil or slightly thicker. Then locate the nodes (swollen places along the canes where buds are located), and cut 1-foot-long sections of canes so that each piece has one node in the middle. Wrap the pieces in a damp cloth. Put the wrapped scions in a plastic bag, close the bag with a twist tie, and store it in the refrigerator until budding time.

Prune your stock plant during the winter just as you normally would, so that it has several fruiting canes ready for next season's growth. (See Idea #87 for details.)

Make the cut in late winter. Chip-budding time is usually about four to five weeks before the last spring frost date. The buds on the stock vine will still be closed tight at this stage.

First, find a smooth place 2 to 3 inches above the soil line on the trunk of the stock plant. Make a cut at a 45-degree angle downward into the trunk, then make a second cut 1 inch above the first one. The second cut should be at a sharp angle so it meets the first cut about ½ inch deep into the wood.

Repeat these same cuts on the scionwood. Make the first cut downward into the budstick just under a bud, and another 1 inch above it, angled sharply down behind the bud to meet the first cut. The bud chip from the scion should fit snugly into the cut you made in the stock plant.

You may need to practice on two or three buds until you get one that fits the notch on the stock snugly. The idea is to line up the cambium layer on the bud with the cambium layer on the stock plant. The cambium is a row of actively dividing cells between the bark and the wood that looks like a thin green line. It's the area where the pieces will unite and start to grow.

Wrap it up. Once you've fit the bud chip into the stock notch, wrap the area securely with white plastic horticultural or budding tape. The tape keeps the bud chip from falling out or drying out. Start above the bud and wrap down and around it, but don't cover the bud itself.

Encourage the bud by pruning in spring. When you see shoot growth on the stock canes in spring, prune the canes so only two or three buds remain. This will force the plant's energy into the grafted bud. It will also allow you to harvest at least some grapes from the vine in the event that the graft doesn't take and you need to repeat the grafting procedure next year.

When the grafted bud shows ½ inch of new growth (in about two weeks), cut the stock trunk off 1 to 2 inches above the graft. Angle the cut back slightly toward the side of the stock opposite the graft, being careful not to injure the new shoot. Then remove the grafting tape.

As the new shoot grows, gently tie it up vertically to a stake or to the grape trellis. It will become the new trunk for your grafted grape. If you see little roots beginning to grow from the bud graft region, carefully trim them off.

Finding Scionwood

Nurseries don't typically sell cuttings or scions of grape varieties, so you'll need to find your own. Look for grape enthusiasts at local garden clubs, or contact the North American Fruit Explorers (NAFEX), Route 1, Box 94, Chapin, IL 62628. NAFEX publishes a quarterly magazine called *Pomona* and their members meet and swap plants and growing information.

89 Return of the Native (Fruits)

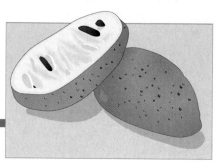

Pawpaw Fruit

Growing fruits and berries can seem intimidating, bringing pruning and spraying schedules to mind—to say nothing of late frosts! But there is an easy-care alternative—native fruits. I plant native fruits in my garden because they're incredibly tasty, hardy, and pest resistant.

Pawpaw

Strawberry

Blackberry fruit

Maypop fruit

Common native fruits such as blackberries and strawberries are too good to do without. Include these berries and more uncommon natives, such as maypops and pawpaws, in your landscape for unforgettable flavor.

Feast on regional favorites.
You may already be familiar with the fruits that are native to your region. If you aren't, visit the fields and forests nearby to see what grows wild in your area. Call your local Extension Service, garden club, or nature center and ask about native plants. Also see the box on this page and *Pomona* under "Fruits and Nuts" in "Recommended Reading" on page 233.

I remember feasting on fruits from spring until fall in the eastern United States where I grew up. In June my friends and I would eat our way through fields of wild strawberries. July would find us harvesting berries of all sorts from fencerows. And then there were wild grapes to munch on in fall.

In the South, treat yourself to black cherries, elderberries, mulberries, persimmons, serviceberries, and wild plums. If the Upper Midwest is your home, you'll have the exquisite pleasure of eating blueberries and wild pawpaws. In the Northwest, plant and pick huckleberries and thimbleberries. There are taste treats for every region!

Plan an outstanding landscape. Native fruits grow on trees, shrubs, vines, and ground covers, so you've got lots of choices when it comes to landscaping. Look over your yard in winter when the leaves have fallen, so it's easy to see where you have space for fruiting plants.

Use native fruit trees for shade and to outline gardens or your property boundaries. Include native shrubs in mixed borders and informal hedges. Grow fruiting vines up trellises or along walls or fences. And though they're tasty, remember that some native fruits can be messy when they drop, so keep those away from sidewalks and patios.

Uncommonly Tasty Native Fruits

See which of these native plants grow in your region, then use them to flavor your garden and wake up your taste buds. Seeds and starts of native fruits aren't hard to find if you know where to look. Check local nurseries and "Fruits and Nuts" in "Sources" on page 228.

For more information on native fruits, contact Seed Savers Exchange in Decorah, Iowa. This organization is known as a source of heirloom vegetable seeds, but it is also a source of fruits. Seed Savers Exchange publishes a book called *Fruit, Berry, and Nut Inventory* that contains a complete listing of all the fruit, berry, and nut varieties available by mail order in the United States. To order the book, write Seed Saver Publications, 3076 North Winn Road, Decorah, IA 52101.

Plant and Hardiness Zone Rating	Description
Trees	
Pawpaw (*Asimina triloba*) Zones 4 to 8	Eat the flesh of these oblong fruits raw or cooked. They have a banana-like flavor.
Persimmon (*Diospyros virginiana*) Zones 4 to 9	Rounded orange fruits have a honey-sweet taste.
Red mulberry (*Morus rubra*) Zones 6 to 9	Juicy blackberry-like fruits start out red then turn dark purple.
Shrubs	
Serviceberries or Juneberries (*Amelanchier* spp.) Zones 3 to 8	The fruits look and taste similar to blueberries. Birds and people love them.
Rugosa rose (*Rosa rugosa*) Zones 2 to 7	The showy orange fruits, called rose hips, are delicately sweet when ripe.
American elder (*Sambucus canadensis*) Zones 2 to 9	Use the clusters of blue-black fruits for jams, jellies, and pies.
Ground Covers and Vines	
Alpine strawberry (*Fragaria vesca*) Zones 3 to 10	Tiny red pointed fruits contain a burst of sweet flavor.
Maypop (*Passiflora incarnata*) Zones 4 to 10	Rounded fruits contain a gelatinous pulp that has a sweet taste.

90
Create a Mini Nut Grove in Your Backyard

A postage-stamp backyard is all the room you need to raise homegrown nuts—hazelnuts, that is. If you have more room, you can expand your nut grove to include favorites such as black walnuts and hickories. Of course nut trees provide good eating (imagine a chocolate hazelnut torte!), but they also look great in your landscape. Start planning this winter and you can start harvesting your own nuts in two or three years.

Husk

Hazelnut

A triangle of filberts makes a perfect private getaway. Site your filbert planting in a sunny spot where a hedge would look nice, like a corner of your yard. In fall, you can harvest your own delicious hazelnuts for fresh eating and desserts.

Landscape your yard with nut trees. You can grow hazelnuts or filberts (*Corylus* spp. and crosses) if you live in Zones 4 to 8. These shrubby trees like a sunny spot with rich, well-drained soil. If your soil needs improving, work compost into the planting area in late winter to prepare for spring planting. Add two shovelfuls of compost to each site where you intend to plant a tree.

Before you plant filberts, check with your Cooperative Extension agent. If eastern filbert blight is a problem in your area, ask for a list of resistant filbert varieties that do well in your area.

Plant at least three different varieties of the trees for good cross-pollination, using the spacing and growing arrangement that fits your yard best. If you're really short on space, plant several trees in a cluster or row, spacing them 3 to 5 feet apart. The filberts will send up lots of stems to form an impenetrable hedge. If you've got a little more room, try growing hazelnuts in a triangular shape. This is my favorite way to grow filberts.

Grow a triangle of trees. Mark out an equilateral triangle that's 15 feet long on each side. Plant one filbert tree at each point of the triangle. In three to five years, these filberts will reach 15 feet tall, and they'll send up many new stems as suckers from their spreading roots.

Cut away all the new shoots that spring up in the center of the triangle, but let the filberts spread out toward each other along the lines of the triangle's sides. Soon the filberts will spread enough to touch each other. Before they completely enclose the triangle, decide where you'd like an entryway and keep the stems clipped away at that point.

From the outside, the filberts will look like a large hedge. But you can place a bench inside the triangular grove and have a wonderfully private place to relax.

Nuts to you. Hazelnuts ripen in fall and are ready to harvest when the nuts come loose easily from their papery husks. At this point, pick the nuts off the tree, husk and all. Set the nuts in a sunny spot and place them on a piece of wire screen that's held off the ground with bricks. Cover the nuts with more wire screen weighted down with bricks to keep squirrels away.

When the husks dry out, remove them and place the nuts in a warm, dry place with plenty of air circulation. Let the nuts cure until they're crunchy. They may be ready as early as Thanksgiving, but will definitely be ready to eat by Christmas.

More Great Nuts for Your Backyard

If you've got the space, try these nuts for some extra-tasty eating.

Name and Hardiness Zone Rating	Description
Pecan (*Carya illinoinensis*) Zones 6 to 9	These trees can grow to 150 feet tall. Plant two cultivars for best pollination.
Shellbark hickory (*Carya laciniosa*) and shagbark hickory (*C. ovata*) Zones 3 to 8	Hickories can grow 100 feet tall and 40 to 60 feet wide. The nuts have a wonderful, delicate taste.
Chinese chestnut (*Castanea mollissima*) Zones 5 to 8	After a blight disease wiped out most American chestnuts (*C. dentata*) in the U.S., it was replaced by blight-resistant Chinese/American crosses and the Chinese chestnut, which grows 20 to 40 feet tall.
Black walnut (*Juglans nigra*) Zones 4 to 8 and English walnut (*J. regia*) Zones 6 to 9	One of these 50- to 100-foot-tall trees will shade a large yard, but you'll need to plant at least two varieties for good pollination.
Almond (*Prunus amygdalus*) Zones 7 to 9	Almonds reach 20 to 30 feet tall and 25 feet wide. Plant two varieties for good cross-pollination.

91 Fresh Peaches for (Almost) Every Region

It's hard to imagine anything more delicious than a fresh-picked peach. The trouble is, peaches are demanding about how and where they like to grow. For example, the trees need some— but not too much—cold weather to do their best. What do you do if your area gets too cold or not cold enough? Pick peach varieties that match your site's conditions.

A   B

Wherever you grow peaches, place the plants where they'll get full sun. In mild-winter areas, site peaches at the bottom of slopes. The cold air that settles in the low spot will give the trees a better chance of meeting their chilling requirements (A). In cold climates, plant your peaches partway up a south-facing slope so they get plenty of heat and protection from winter winds (B).

Science is on your side.
Peaches can generally grow in Zones 5 to 9, but you're likely to run into trouble if you're in the warmest or coolest parts of these zones. Luckily for peach lovers, plant breeders have developed peach varieties that can stand very cold and very warm conditions.

Peaches prefer spring planting, so start your search for trees in late winter. Mail-order catalogs will have the best selection then, and nurseries should be able to tell you which varieties they'll have and when they'll be available.

Give your plants a chill.
When you choose peach varieties, keep their chill requirements in mind. Peach trees need a certain amount of cold (chill hours) each winter to break out of their resting phase and bloom. Specifically, they need to be exposed to 650 to 1,000 hours of temperatures between 32 and 50°F. As soon as their chilling requirements are met, peaches start growing and soon burst into bloom. That's when they can get hit with a late frost. See the box on this page for solutions to this problem.

For the best results, choose peach varieties whose chill requirements match the number of chill hours your area receives. Your Cooperative Extension agent can give you the exact

numbers and plant recommendations for your climate.

Look for low-chill plants down South. In mild-winter areas such as southern California and Florida, head for your local tree nursery and buy low-chill varieties of peaches. (These specialized varieties are not usually available by mail order.) Low-chill peach trees need between 150 to 500 chill hours and include the varieties 'Desert Delight', 'Desert Gold', 'Flordaprince', and 'Florida Star'. Ask nursery workers or local orchardists for more suggestions for your area.

In California, where the terrain tends to be hilly, place your peaches on the lowest part of your property. Cold air is heavier than warm air and it will sink to the lower parts of the landscape. That's where your trees will get the most chilling hours. In Florida, where the terrain tends to be very flat, there's not much you can do about placement, so just grow varieties with low chilling requirements.

Hunt for hardy types up North. Most peaches will suffer winter damage if temperatures frequently fall below -12°F. If you live in a cold area, plant hardy peach varieties such as 'Reliance' and 'Veteran' that can survive winter temperatures that dip to -25°F. Also, choose plants that are grown on standard rootstocks instead of dwarfing

rootstocks—the standard rootstocks are hardier.

Peaches bloom early, so locate your hardy plants partway up a south-facing hillside where they're protected from the wind and are less likely to get hit by spring frosts. Let your plants grow tall, since some of the upper branches may survive frost damage.

If you live in an area that consistently gets hit with late frosts, change your planting strategy. Instead of locating peach trees on the warm south side of a hill, plant them on the upper half of a north-facing slope or 15 feet away from the north side of a building to delay flowering by one to two weeks.

Tips for When Frost Threatens

If you grow dwarf or semi-dwarf peaches, cover each tree with a blanket, floating row cover, or sheet when light frosts threaten the blooms. A covering alone will often be enough to protect the flowers if the frost danger isn't too severe. Another option is to set a 5-gallon bucket full of hot water under the tree to fill the area with warm air, then cover the tree with a cloth.

Standard trees may be too tall to cover, but I've heard of one resourceful grower who strung his peach trees with outdoor Christmas lights, giving them enough warmth to keep frosts away. It's worth a try!

92

Borrow a Landscape— Broaden Your Yard

You don't have to ask permission to "borrow" a neighbor's landscape and make it look like an extension of your property. Simply re-create bits and pieces of the surrounding landscape in your own yard. It's an easy and inexpensive way to make your yard look bigger and more luxurious.

Borrow a landscape by echoing the look of a distant evergreen tree with a series of evergreen shrubs in your yard. Or plant a white fringe tree to expand your vista to the hanging blooms of the black locust next door. Plant red azaleas to repeat the red of a neighbor's birdhouse or to match a neighbor's flowers.

Look at the whole picture.
Start by looking at your yard as a piece of a large natural scene, rather than as a piece of property that ends where the neighbor's yard begins. Using this definition of a landscape, your property doesn't end at your boundary line but continues on into the neighboring yards, fields, and forests. The entire area that you can see from your yard becomes your landscape.

While you have control over how your garden and landscape look, you have little or no control over how the landscape looks beyond your property line. So, before you plant a new flowerbed or a tree or shrub in your own yard, first see what your neighbors have to offer. Winter is a good time to start this project, because you can see all the views around you and notice what you like and don't like.

Watch what blooms and grows in neighbors' yards over the spring, summer, and fall, before you make any major landscape decisions. When winter rolls around again, choose the plants that harmonize best with the near and distant landscapes.

Repeat what you like. If there are attractive trees, shrubs, gardens, or other elements in your neighbor's yard, repeat them in your own yard. You can use the same plants or similar ones to give the impression of repeating forms or colors. Repetition pro-duces a unified look from your garden to the horizon, making your property look as large as the whole area you can see.

For instance, suppose there's a large flowering tree on a neighbor's property that domi-nates the view from your yard. And suppose you just love that tree. You can repeat it in your own landscape. Or, if the tree is too big for your yard, or you don't want to give up that much yard space, plant a smaller tree that gives you a similar effect.

Repeat flower forms. Let's say that the neighbor's tree is a particularly lovely old black lo-cust (*Robinia pseudoacacia*) that's 50 feet tall. It has clusters of white fragrant flowers that hang down like tinsel in the spring. You can repeat the flower effect with a smaller (20-foot-tall) white fringe tree (*Chionanthus vir-ginicus*). Or, if you want the same effect in a different color, plant a golden-chain tree (*Laburnum* × *watereri*). It grows 15 feet tall and has dangling clus-ters of yellow flowers.

How can you find matching plants? Visit local parks and public gardens. These show-places are great for getting ideas, and the gardeners who maintain them can give you ad-vice and suggestions. Don't forget to check with the staff at your local nursery or garden center. Garden books, maga-zines, and catalogs are also great ways to discover plants with matching shapes or colors.

Repeat landscape features.
You can even borrow elements of your neighbor's house or out-buildings to tie your landscapes together. Try repeating the roof lines of neighboring houses in sheds or outbuildings on your own property. They don't have to be exact replicas—after all, you want a landscape that's as individual as you are. Just create an impression of harmony by repeating parts of the landscape you like, not making exact copies of the whole thing.

If there's a rounded hill in the distance behind your house, you can echo that look with rounded berms in your yard. Or you can match the color of an attractive, brightly painted building or feature in the dis-tance with bright flowers of the same color in your garden. For example, bright red flowers in your yard will stretch your view to a bright red barn or bird-house in a neighboring yard.

Avoid Interruptions

A boundary hedge or fence puts an abrupt halt to your ex-panding landscape. Instead of confining your yard and your view, selectively screen out scenes that you don't like. Use a vine-covered gazebo or trellis to hide a messy garage, but leave a more pleasant view open so you can enjoy the scene.

93 Color-Coordinate Your Home and Landscape

Color Wheel

Now I'm not advocating painting your roses red to match your house—in fact, just the opposite. I say, paint your house (or at least the shutters or door) to match your flower colors—it's a simple way to enhance the beauty of your landscape. Or, if you're not planning to paint soon, plant flowers with colors that coordinate with your house or outbuildings.

When you're planning a planting, remember to coordinate the colors of flowers and nearby structures. A color wheel is a handy device that's made to help you pick out the colors that go together best. An easy way to use the wheel is to choose colors that are within eight wedges of each other, counting clockwise.

Color your landscape with plants or paint. It's easy to forget about the background color created by the house, a wall, or a fence when you're designing a flowerbed or shrub planting. The results can be disastrous, like magenta roses in front of orange brick. But what a difference coordinating those colors can make! Decide on your favorite color combinations in the winter so you can try them out in spring.

If you already have structures and plantings in place, paint is the easiest and cheapest way to change your color scheme. A new background will only cost you a can of paint and a couple of hours' work.

If you're just starting a planting, or you just painted your house, pick flowers or flowering shrubs with colors that contrast with the paint color. You want enough of a difference so the flowers stand out against the background.

When you're just starting a building project, you can use the lowest-maintenance approach to coordinating colors. Simply build your walls or fences from colored materials that don't need painting. Gray stone, red brick, or silvery weathered wood all make wonderful backgrounds for a variety of flower colors.

Get wise to color tricks. How do you know which colors will go best with your house, shed, fence, or wall color? Keep a lookout for striking combinations and try these color tips.

Accent your house with flowers. You already accent your house color with trim or a painted door, so why not do the same thing with flowers? Match flower colors to your house trim or a fence or wall.

Mix dark with light. Plant dark-colored flowers against pastel backgrounds and pastel-colored flowers against dark backgrounds. The contrast of dark and light shows the flowers off so they capture your attention.

Use neutral colors near existing plantings. Try beige, black, brown, cream, gray, silver, and tan when you need to color fences and walls. These background colors will help you avoid color clashes. Neutral colors are particularly attractive behind flowerbeds with hot-colored flowers—the reds, oranges, and yellows that make you think of the sun and heat.

Highlight a planting with white. White flowers and green leaves can calm down a busy background planting when nothing else works. But avoid painting a wall or fence white. White does go with anything, but it's so bright that a white wall or fence can draw your eye away from your plantings.

Stop traffic with a lively look. Choose colors that are opposite each other on the color wheel. These complementary colors, like orange and blue, will add extra excitement to your landscape.

Create perfect harmony. Pick a color like blue from the color wheel, then choose a second color that's eight or fewer wedges away from the original, counting the wedges clockwise. You'll end up with a range of harmonious colors that you can choose from.

Great Color Combos

Here are some of my favorite plant and background color combinations. Use them as a jumping-off point for your own color schemes.

• Place 'Blue Wave' bigleaf hydrangea (*Hydrangea macrophylla* 'Blue Wave') against a dark green wall or fence.

• Train pinkish lavender 'Nelly Moser' clematis (*Clematis* 'Nelly Moser') against a pale tan rock wall or painted wall.

• Set a pale yellow Lady Banks rose (*Rosa banksiae* var. *lutea*) beside a red brick wall.

• Grow a light violet Chinese wisteria (*Wisteria sinensis*) on a silvery weathered wood fence.

• Use a purple smoke tree (*Cotinus coggygria* 'Royal Purple') to draw attention to a pastel blue wall or fence.

94 Give Your Trees and Shrubs a Makeover

There's practical pruning—to cut off broken or diseased limbs and suckers. But you already know about that. And then there's artistic pruning—shaping large shrubs and small trees into beautiful forms so they become the stars of your garden. All it takes is you, your pruning shears, a saw, and a fine winter day.

After

Before

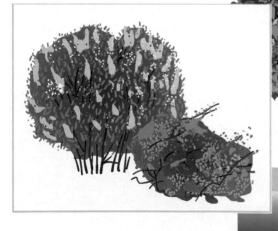

There may be a beauty hiding inside your beast. Reveal the graceful form of a shrubby lilac by removing all but one treelike trunk. And give your quinces a makeover by pruning out most of their tangle of branches.

Prune to reveal branch structure. The easiest way to get beautifully shaped plants is to buy them, but lots of times you have a yard full of plants that got there before you did. Or what you thought was a nice small plant turned into a towering monster. Before you rip out wayward trees and shrubs, see what you can do with artistic pruning. You'll be amazed at the beauty hidden under your hulking giants.

Branches are often a beautiful part of shrubs and small trees, but you'd never know it because they're hidden by leaves most of the year. To see if your deciduous shrubs have beautiful branch potential, take a look at them in late winter. That's the best time to study your plants' form and trim them into shape.

Simplify your plant's structure. First, take out weak, spindly, or broken branches. Then look at the largest stems rising from the base of the shrub. Remove all but three or five (an odd number tends to look best) of the main stems.

Once you've reduced the number of stems, you'll be able to see the plant's shape instead of a jumble of stems and crossing limbs. Then you can remove any remaining limbs that detract from the plant's look. For example, if you see a branch that hides the lower half of the shrub, cut it out. But look the limbs over good

first. Be sure to keep any with interesting curves or crooks.

Turn a multistemmed shrub into a tree. Some plants such as lilacs and summersweet put up lots of stems from spreading underground roots. If you'd like to give one of these shrubs a more dramatic appearance, prune it back to a single treelike trunk and make it a specimen plant.

Start by selecting the healthiest, largest, and most vertical trunk and prune away the rest. The shrub will likely respond by sending up as many suckers from the roots as it can to make up for this attack. Keep after these suckers and don't let them grow. Dig down to the root they're sprouting from and cut them off underground. Cutting them off at the soil line only stimulates the plants to make even more suckers at the stubs. Finish the job by shaping the top so it spreads out in an umbrella-like fashion.

Tip prune for a fuller look. Some shrubs like hollies and azaleas tend to get unattractively spindly as they grow. With tip pruning, you can encourage them to grow lots of leaves and regain their lush, full appearance.

For hollies, prune back each branch tip to a node where several stems arise, and pinch out the growing points of those stems. The plant will respond with lots of new leaves. It may take several years to rejuvenate

your holly, but it's faster than starting over with a new plant.

To rejuvenate azaleas, decide what size and shape you'd like them to be, then prune each plant back to that form. As the shrubs send out new growth in spring, pinch the branch tips back to where you want them again to force the plants to stay within bounds.

Best Plant Makeovers

Show off the graceful limbs of these small multistemmed trees and twiggy shrubs with creative pruning.

Trees

White fringe tree (*Chionanthus virginicus*), Zones 5 to 8

Dogwoods (*Cornus* spp.), Zones 3 to 9

Magnolias (*Magnolia* spp.), Zones 4 to 10

Persian parrotia (*Parrotia persica*), Zones 5 to 10

Japanese stewartia (*Stewartia pseudocamellia*), Zones 5 to 9

Flowering Shrubs

Carolina allspice (*Calycanthus floridus*), Zones 4 to 9

Camellia (*Camellia japonica*), Zones 7 to 10

Flowering quinces (*Chaenomeles* spp. and hybrids), Zones 5 to 8

Summersweet (*Clethra alnifolia*), Zones 5 to 9

Crape myrtle (*Lagerstroemia indica*), Zones 7 to 10

Lilacs (*Syringa* spp.), Zones 2 to 7

95 Keep Cool with Vigorous Vines

There's no faster or prettier way to shade a house than with vines. So stop waiting for those trees to mature! Get beautiful vines to shade and cool hot western and southern walls in one season. You've got lots of leaf and flower colors, sizes, and shapes to choose from. And if you get started in winter, you'll have lots of time to build a support trellis before planting time in spring.

Trumpet honeysuckle

Hop

2 x 4

5'

3'

Freestanding trellises (right) make house care and growing vines compatible. If even this much structure is more permanent than you'd like, support your vines by hanging trellis netting from the eaves of your roof (left)—attach the bottom end to the ground with metal pins.

Grow vines with all seasons in mind. Deciduous vines like clematis are good choices for summer shade, and they won't get in the way of winter heating. When they drop their leaves in fall, deciduous vines let in both light and heat. As an added bonus, many deciduous vines produce beautiful flowers.

Evergreen vines like English ivy have their place too. Their cover of green leaves provides cool relief for a sun-baked stone wall in summer. In winter, those same leaves decorate colorless walls better than a truckload of wreaths. For details on great vine choices, see the chart on this page.

Use trellises to keep vines in line. Growing a vine up a freestanding trellis is one of the best ways to shade your house. You could let vines use their aerial rootlets or clinging discs to climb directly on your walls, but they can be destructive.

The blanket of leaves vines create can spell mold and rot trouble if they're up against a wooden wall. And climbing vines can loosen wood siding and the mortar that holds brick and stone walls as they creep along. You can avoid all of these problems if you train vines to grow up trellises set away from the house.

You'll find lots of ready-made wood or metal trellises in mail-order garden catalogs and at garden centers and nurseries. And if you're a do-it-yourselfer, you can build a sturdy trellis like the one on the opposite page from 2 × 4s and a sheet of lattice. Set freestanding support structures 8 to 12 inches away from walls so you have access to the wall and the plant gets good air circulation.

Shady Vines

The following vines are good choices for creating shade. But don't forget about fruiting vines like grapes and kiwis, berried vines like American bittersweet (*Celastrus scandens*), and vines with flaming fall foliage, like Virginia creeper (*Parthenocissus quinquefolia*).

Name and Hardiness Zone Rating	Description
Dutchman's pipe (*Aristolochia macrophylla*) Zones 4 to 8	Deciduous twining vine can grow 30 feet tall. Greenish yellow and purple pipe-shaped blooms appear in late spring.
Trumpet creeper (*Campsis radicans*) Zones 4 to 9	Aerial rootlets help this deciduous climber reach 30 feet tall. Showy orange-red flowers appear in late summer.
Pink anemone clematis (*Clematis montana* 'Rubens') Zones 5 to 9	Deciduous twining climber can reach 20 feet tall. Pink flowers bloom in early summer.
English ivy (*Hedera helix*) Zones 5 to 10	Evergreen vine comes in a variety of leaf sizes and shapes and grows to 40 feet tall. Climbs by aerial rootlets.
Golden hop (*Humulus lupulus* 'Aureus') Zones 3 to 8	Deciduous twining vines grow to 30 feet tall. Leaves are golden; female plants produce green conelike pods.
Climbing hydrangea (*Hydrangea anomala* subsp. *petiolaris*) Zones 4 to 9	Slow-starting deciduous vine can reach 50 feet tall with the help of aerial rootlets. White flowers open in early summer.
Trumpet honeysuckle (*Lonicera sempervirens*) Zones 4 to 9	Deciduous twining vine will climb to 20 feet or more. Scarlet and yellow summer flowers are showy but not fragrant.
Boston ivy (*Parthenocissus tricuspidata*) Zones 4 to 10	Adhesive discs let this deciduous vine cling as it climbs up to 60 feet tall. Leaves turn bright red in fall.
Silver lace vine (*Polygonum aubertii*) Zones 5 to 7	Deciduous twining vine grows rapidly and can reach 35 feet tall. Airy white flowers cover the top of the plant in late summer.

96 Attract Beneficial Bugs for Natural Pest Control

Beneficial insects are the good guys of the garden—they keep plant-eating pests under control so you don't have to. What's the price of this protection? More reasonable than you might expect. All beneficial insects ask are food, water, and shelter. Add a rock-filled pan of water to your plantings and a few flowers, herbs, or weeds, and you're in the beneficial bug business!

Queen-Anne's-lace

Dill

Catmint

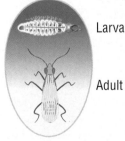

Lacewing

Larva

Adult

Yarrow

Plant a beautiful border of flowers, herbs, and native weeds to give beneficial insects a home. If you want to focus beneficials' attention on a plant like a fruit tree with aphid problems, surround it with dill or other small-flowered herbs and flowers to attract lacewings and their aphid-eating larvae.

A few pests are good for your garden. Beneficials will keep your pest problems under control, if there are pests in your garden to eat. If you wipe out all the pests, you also chase away the beneficial insects that can nip future pest problems in the bud. That's why using pesticides—even organic ones—can be counterproductive. What you want is to create a balance—a mixture of enough pests to feed your beneficials, and enough beneficials to keep your produce and flowers looking good.

Plant a row for the good bugs. Most beneficial adult insects feed on nectar and pollen from flowers, herbs, and weeds. So add their favorite plants to your winter seed order. Many beneficials prefer plants in the familiar Compositae or sunflower family that includes asters, coreopsis, cosmos, dandelions, and marigolds. Beneficials are also attracted to the small-flowered plants of the Umbelliferae or carrot or parsley family. These include herbs such as dill and parsley, vegetables like carrots, and weeds like Queen-Anne's-lace. (See the chart on this page for a list of plants specific beneficials like.)

Let a few weeds grow. Before you pull weeds out of your garden, check to see if they're types that attract beneficials. My personal rule of thumb is to allow 100 square feet of local weeds to grow for every 1,000 square feet of garden space. I cut most of the weeds down before they go to seed, but isn't it nice to have a good excuse not to weed?

Add water and shelter. Insects don't need large quantities of water. A birdbath or shallow pan filled with water will suit beneficials fine. Just be sure to place small stones in the water to give beneficial insects a place to perch.

Weeds, flowers, and herbs will provide your tiny pest patrol with some shelter, but they'll also appreciate straw or leaf mulch to hide in. Cover crops of alfalfa, buckwheat, and clover make good shelters, and so do trees and perennial gardens.

Beneficial Insects' Favorite Plants

Bring beneficials to your garden with the food and shelter of these plants.

Name and Description	Pest Insects Controlled	Favorite Plants
Braconid wasps: Adults are tiny nonstinging wasps that lay their eggs in or on the larvae of insect pests. The wasp larvae are white grubs.	Larvae parasitize aphids, armyworms, beetle larvae, codling moths, European corn borers, flies, gypsy moths, hornworms, and imported cabageworms.	Fernleaf yarrow (*Achillea filipendulina*), caraway (*Carum carvi*), threadleaf coreopsis (*Coreopsis verticillata*), coriander (*Coriandrum sativum*), Queen-Anne's-lace (*Daucus carota*), sunflower (*Helianthus annuus*), sweet alyssum (*Lobularia maritima*), rose campion (*Lychnis coronaria*), baby-blue-eyes (*Nemophila menziesii*), catmint (*Nepeta x faassenii*)
Hover flies: Adults are ⅜ to ⅝ inch long and have yellow and black or white and black stripes. Larvae are gray or green maggots.	Larvae eat aphids, beetles, caterpillars, sawfly larvae, and thrips.	Yarrow (*Achillea millefolium*), New England aster (*Aster novae-angliae*), cornflower (*Centaurea cyanus*), chamomile (*Chamaemelum nobile*), feverfew (*Chrysanthemum parthenium*), threadleaf coreopsis (*Coreopsis verticillata*), Joe-Pye weed (*Eupatorium purpureum*), candytuft (*Iberis sempervirens*), black-eyed Susan (*Rudbeckia hirta*)
Lacewings: Adults grow ½ to ¾ inch long and are green or brown with transparent wings. Larvae look like little alligators.	Larvae feed on aphids, small caterpillars, mealybugs, mites, moth eggs, scales, and thrips.	Yarrow (*Achillea millefolium*), dill (*Anethum graveolens*), angelica (*Angelica archangelica*), threadleaf coreopsis (*Coreopsis verticillata*), cosmos (*Cosmos bipinnatus*), fennel (*Foeniculum vulgare*), sweet alyssum (*Lobularia maritima*), oleander (*Nerium oleander*), tansy (*Tanacetum vulgare*)

97 Plan a Landscape Birds Will Love

If you didn't have birds in your garden, what would you pay to get some? I'd pay a king's ransom! Insect-eating birds help control garden pests, which would be benefit enough if that's all they did. But on top of that, birds increase your enjoyment of the garden by adding color, excitement, and beautiful songs.

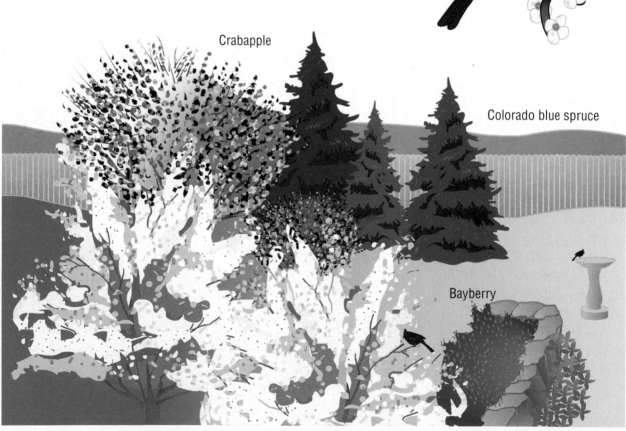

Crabapple

Colorado blue spruce

Bayberry

Flowering dogwood

Virginia creeper

A mix of trees, shrubs, and vines can beautify your landscape and attract birds at the same time. Always remember to give birds fresh water—even in winter!

Plan for birds and plants. With a little planning, you can create a beautiful landscape that's as attractive to the birds as it is to you. The size of your yard doesn't matter. Start small, and keep adding to your planting as you have the time, money, space, and desire.

Just add water. If you do nothing else, provide a bird-bath—water is essential if you want to keep birds around. Hose the birdbath out every time you add water so birds always have clean, fresh water for drinking and bathing.

Take stock in winter. I do all my garden planning in this quiet season 'because that's when I have time to look at the mountains of garden catalogs that arrive. Before ordering for your landscape, think about birds. Are your choices bird favorites? See the chart on this page for plant suggestions, then add trees, shrubs, or vines depending on what you have room for.

Combine trees, shrubs, and vines. If you don't have much space, start by planting a fruiting vine like Virginia creeper on a fence or trellis. If you have room, place fruiting shrubs such as serviceberries beside the vine. Then add smaller trees such as dogwoods that produce berries or berrylike fruits. Surround these small trees with fruiting trees such as crabapples, mulberries, plums, and wild cherries. Then plant groups of three or more evergreens like Canada hemlock near the fruit trees. The seeds and dense foliage of evergreens make them attractive feeding and nesting sites.

Plants Birds Love

Mix any of these trees, shrubs, and vines together in your yard to attract bluebirds, cardinals, cedar waxwings, chickadees, flickers, mockingbirds, robins, titmice, warblers, and a host of others.

Name and Hardiness Zone Rating	Description of Attractive Features
Trees	
Birches (*Betula* spp.) Zones 2 to 9	Seeds, flower buds, and catkins are all food sources.
Dogwoods (*Cornus* spp.) Zones 2 to 8	Berries are an important food source, and the trees provide nest sites.
Mulberries (*Morus* spp.) Zones 4 to 9	Blackberry-like fruits make tasty treats for birds and people. Birds nest and roost in the tree's shelter.
Spruces (*Picea* spp.) Zones 2 to 8	Many birds eat the winged seeds (grouse eat the needles); birds nest and roost in the foliage.
Pines (*Pinus* spp.) Zones 3 to 9	Pine seeds provide food (grouse eat the needles), and large trees make good nesting and roosting sites.
Hemlocks (*Tsuga* spp.) Zones 3 to 9	Seeds are a good food source, and the dense foliage makes sheltered nest sites.
Shrubs	
Serviceberries (*Amelanchier* spp.) Zones 2 to 9	Tasty blueberry-like fruits attract birds and humans.
Bayberries, wax myrtles (*Myrica* spp.) Zones 4 to 9	Waxy fruits are a popular bird food.
Roses (*Rosa* spp.) Zones 2 to 9	Rose hips provide food even in winter. The plants' thorny growth makes a good nesting site.
Vines	
Virginia creeper, Boston ivy (*Parthenocissus* spp.) Zones 3 to 9	Birds love the fruits and leafy shelter of these well-known vines.
Grapes (*Vitis* spp.) Zones 3 to 9	Grapes are a favorite food, and a tangled thicket of grapevines provides nest sites.

98 Bring On the Butterflies

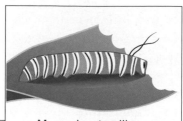

Monarch caterpillar

For a dramatic-looking garden, nothing beats the burst of living color you get when you attract butterflies. It's not hard to lure butterflies to your garden—all it takes is sun, some favorite butterfly plants, a few stones, and water. Adult butterflies like bright colors, so indulge them—and yourself—with a brilliant display. Add food plants to feed butterfly larvae (caterpillars) and watch the color come flying in!

Monarch chrysalis

Butterfly bush

Milkweed

French marigold

Gardening for butterflies means gardening for their caterpillars too. Plant the food plants caterpillars like, and steer clear of pest-control products of all kinds. If aphids are a problem, as they sometimes are on the milkweed family plants that Monarch butterflies like, prune off and destroy infested parts of the plant.

Think about butterflies in winter. To make a great butterfly garden, plan ahead. Check the chart on this page or a butterfly book to find out which foods attract the butterflies you want to lure to your landscape. (See "Recommended Reading" on page 233 for books with information on butterfly gardening.)

Expect constant change. Provide the right foods and you'll be able to watch butterflies pass through their entire life cycle right in your own backyard. Some butterflies complete their life cycle in one season or less, while others lay eggs that lie dormant all winter and hatch in spring. Either way, the development process is the same.

First, adult butterflies lay their eggs on food, or host, plants. The caterpillars hatch, eat the food plants like crazy, shed their skins, and then eat, grow, and shed some more.

Finally, after lots of eating and growing, each caterpillar will form a chrysalis (a butterfly's version of a cocoon) in which to pupate. Inside the chrysalis, the caterpillar's body actually liquefies and re-forms as a butterfly. The butterfly will hatch, eat flower nectar, and search for a mate so it can start the process all over again.

Make a place in the sun. Choose a sunny spot and sun-loving plants for your garden, because butterflies need warm temperatures to move their wings. Butterflies are attracted to big patches of color, so order plants that will give you splashy displays that last from spring until fall. Single flowers are better than doubles since butterflies can reach the nectar more easily, but that still leaves you lots of choices.

Include bright annuals such as cosmos, French marigolds, and lantana (*Lantana camera*) in your garden. Add perennials such as New England aster (*Aster novae-angliae*), pineapple sage (*Salvia elegans*), and purple coneflower (*Echinacea purpurea*). And stretch the bloom season by including shrubs such as azaleas (*Rhododendron* spp.), butterfly bush (*Buddleia davidii*), and glossy abelia (*Abelia × grandiflora*).

Flowers aren't the only food. Butterfly caterpillars are picky eaters. Some, like Monarch butterfly caterpillars, will only eat plants in the milkweed family, while other butterfly caterpillars prefer herbs, trees, shrubs, or vines.

If you want to keep butterflies in your garden for more than a few minutes, plant the foods their caterpillars like. Adult butterflies typically lay their eggs on the caterpillars' food plants so the youngsters have a meal handy as soon as they hatch. You'll have to get used to seeing caterpillars munching on plants—but remember, that's why you planted them!

Plant a Buffet of Caterpillar Food

If you want to attract specific butterflies, plant the trees, shrubs, vines, or flowers that their caterpillars eat. Here's a sampling of butterflies and their caterpillars' favorite foods.

Butterfly	Caterpillar Food
American painted lady	Pearly everlasting (*Anaphalis margaritacea*), artemisias (*Artemisia* spp.)
Eastern black swallowtail	Carrots, dill, fennel, parsley
Gray hairstreak, marine blue, silver-spotted skipper	Beans
Great spangled fritillary	Violets (*Viola* spp.)
Gulf fritillary and variegated fritillary	Passionflowers (*Passiflora* spp.)
Monarch	Milkweeds, including butterfly weed (*Asclepias* spp.)
Red-spotted purple, spring azure, viceroy	Cherries, plums (*Prunus* spp.)
Spicebush swallowtail	Spicebush (*Lindera benzoin*)

99 Make Your Yard a Hummingbird Haven

I can't resist the magic of a hummingbird hovering over a brilliant red flower! I stand transfixed each time one of these tiny bundles of energy and iridescent feathers sips nectar from a bloom. This is definitely an experience worth repeating. You can know the wonder of hummingbirds in your garden next summer if you plan for them now. Just include some of the plants hummingbirds like best in your garden.

Red buckeye

Scarlet sage

You'll love the look of a hummingbird garden! It's not only filled with brilliantly colored flowers, but brilliantly colored birds too. Hummers' bills are long and narrow so they can reach deep into tubular flowers and lap up nectar with their tongues.

Trumpet honeysuckle

Zinnias

Pineapple sage

Look fast to see your visitors. Hummingbirds must surely be the most entertaining, certainly one of the most beautiful, and without question the fastest birds around. I've seen them suddenly take off, zip up and over the treetops, and be 50 yards away in just a couple of seconds.

Catch their eye with a splash of red and you're in for a treat. These swift birds can hover, fly forward, backward, and straight up and down—you'll see all four maneuvers as they zoom in for a sip of nectar.

Hummingbirds migrate over incredible distances stretching from Canada to Central America. Of the 21 species of hummingbirds that spend part of their lives in the United States, the ruby-throated hummingbird is the only one that nests east of the Mississippi River. It has a distinct ruby-red throat, a green metallic cap, and a long, needlelike bill.

In the West, look for black-chinned, broad-tailed, calliope, and rufus hummingbirds. And in California you may see Allen's, Anna's, and Costa's hummingbirds.

While away winter planning for hummers. I can't think of many more pleasant pastimes than paging through garden catalogs searching for hummingbird plants. Sure you can feed these birds sugar syrup in bright red containers (never add red food coloring, since it can harm the birds). But how much nicer for the birds, and more attractive for you, to put in plantings that attract hummingbirds and supply them with their natural food—flower nectar.

Lure birds in with a nectar feast. Which plants make the best "hummingbird feeders"? Brightly colored tubular flowers that contain lots of nectar. Hummingbirds' bills fit tubular flowers perfectly and make for easy eating. Red flowers are certainly hummingbird favorites, but they're not the only ones that will attract the little birds. Feel free to add bright pink, orange, purple, blue, and yellow tubular blooms to your garden too.

Convince hummers to stay. In addition to food, hummingbirds need the shelter of trees to nest. A wooded area near a stream or meadow is ideal, but you can substitute islands of trees, shrubs, and vines for the woods. And give the birds a mist fountain for water (mist sprayers are available at wild bird centers).

Favorite Hummer Plants

Annuals

Cleome (*Cleome hasslerana*)

Flowering tobaccos (*Nicotiana* spp.)

Petunias (*Petunia* x *hybrida*)

Scarlet runner bean (*Phaseolus coccineus*)

Scarlet sage (*Salvia splendens*)

Zinnias (*Zinnia* spp.)

Perennials

Hollyhock (*Alcea rosea*), Zones 2 to 9

Wild columbine (*Aquilegia canadensis*), Zones 3 to 8

Common torch lily (*Kniphofia uvaria*), Zones 5 to 9

Cardinal flower (*Lobelia cardinalis*), Zones 2 to 9

Lupines (*Lupinus* spp.), Zones 3 to 7

Bee balm (*Monarda didyma*), Zones 4 to 8

Penstemons (*Penstemon* spp.), Zones 4 to 9

Pineapple sage (*Salvia elegans*), Zones 8 to 10

Salvias (*Salvia* spp.), Zones 3 to 10

Speedwells (*Veronica* spp.), Zones 3 to 8

Trees, Shrubs, and Vines

Red buckeye (*Aesculus pavia*), Zones 5 to 8

Butterfly bush (*Buddleia davidii*), Zones 5 to 9

Trumpet vine (*Campsis radicans*), Zones 4 to 9

Flowering quince (*Chaenomeles speciosa*), Zones 5 to 10

Fuchsias (*Fuchsia* spp.), Zones 8 to 10

Rose-of-Sharon (*Hibiscus syriacus*), Zones 5 to 9

Cypress vine (*Ipomoea quamoclit*), Zones 8 to 10

Trumpet honeysuckle (*Lonicera sempervirens*), Zones 4 to 9

100 Make a Night Garden That's a Knockout

Most gardens are designed to be seen and admired during the day—which is when we are all usually too busy to enjoy them! But night gardens are made for the evening, when there's time to relax and enjoy blooms that glow in the moonlight and scent the air with perfume. Ahhh. Plan your night garden during winter and look forward to leisurely summer evenings to come.

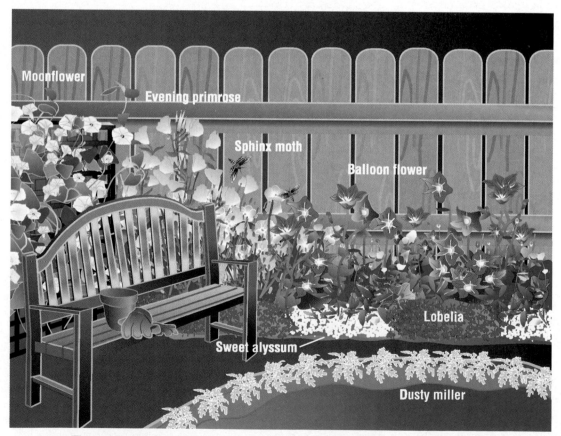

Moonflower
Evening primrose
Sphinx moth
Balloon flower
Lobelia
Sweet alyssum
Dusty miller

The soft half-light of the moon seems to make light-colored flowers and foliage glow, lending mystery and romance to a night garden. Mix flowering annuals, perennials, and vines to attract sphinx moths and other night-feeding moths.

Keep an eye on night colors. When the sun goes down, your perception of color changes. Colors such as red and orange that show up beautifully in the light of day tend to fade at twilight. You'll notice that in very dim light, red looks gray or black, but you can still pick out white and pale yellow, and blue and violet.

Light up the night with yellow and white. Pale yellow and white flowers will catch your eye at night—and the eyes of fascinating night-feeding moths. Evening primroses, with their broad yellow or white blooms, are a favorite of sphinx moths that look and sound like hummingbirds as they zoom about the flowers.

Create a fantasy in blue. Try lining an approach way with clumps of balloon flowers—their blue-violet coloring seems to glow in the dim twilight, lighting the path toward the night garden. Blue and violet water lilies are great choices for an evening water garden, too! (See the chart on this page for great nighttime flower choices.)

Make your garden glow with light-colored leaves. White, gray, silver, and yellow leaves really show up in the moonlight. Silvery-leaved ground covers like dusty miller are mainstays for adding pools of glowing foliage to the night garden. Surround tall night flowers with short, light-leaved foliage plants to really set them off.

Follow your nose. Because sight is limited in the night garden, fragrance becomes more important and perceptible. For a heavenly night fragrance, plant a large stand of flowering tobacco. Or grow a moonflower vine beside an arbor, fence, or trellis for glowing-white blooms and fragrance at sundown. If you'd like to use your arbor for day and night viewing, combine 'Heavenly Blue' morning glory vines with your moonflowers. The morning glories will open in the morning to give you a burst of blue. When they close in the evening, the moonflowers will open the show.

Plants That Are Right for the Night

Choose these flower and foliage plants to add color and fragrance to your night garden.

Name and Hardiness Zone Rating (for perennials)	Description
Moonflower (*Ipomoea alba*)	Huge, white fragrant blooms open at night on perennial vines that reach 8 feet long. Grow as an annual.
'Beacon Silver' spotted lamium (*Lamium maculatum* 'Beacon Silver') Zones 3 to 8	This perennial ground cover has silver-mottled or striped leaves and grows 12 to 18 inches tall.
Madonna lily (*Lilium candidum*) Zones 4 to 9	Classic, white trumpet-shaped lilies top 2- to 4-foot-tall perennial plants that grow from bulbs.
Sweet alyssum (*Lobularia maritima*)	Masses of small white blooms cover 4- to 10-inch-tall perennial plants. Grow as an annual.
Flowering tobaccos (*Nicotiana alata* and *N. sylvestris*)	Fragrant white trumpet-shaped blooms grow on 1½- to 4-foot-tall perennials that are grown as annuals.
Evening primroses (*Oenothera* spp.) Zones 4 to 8	Yellow or white saucer-shaped flowers open at night; perennial plants grow to 3 feet tall, depending on the species.
Balloon flower (*Platycodon grandiflorus*) Zones 3 to 8	Blue-violet flower buds look like inflated balloons on 2- to 3-foot-tall perennial plants. Buds open to star-petaled cups.
Dusty miller (*Senecio cineraria*)	Silvery-leaved foliage makes this 2½-foot-tall perennial plant glow in the dark. Grow as an annual.

Sources

The following companies carry plants and products mentioned in *Jeff Cox's 100 Greatest Garden Ideas.* Most listings are arranged under a general heading such as "**Vegetables and Grains**" or "**Ornamentals**." Several specialized plant topics like the "**Three Sisters Planting**" have their own headings. Some listings have specific plants or products included in parentheses behind the company name to make it easier to find the exact source you're looking for.

Cover Crops

Harmony Farm Supply and Nursery
P.O. Box 460
Graton, CA 95444
phone: 707-823-9125
fax: 707-823-1734
Website:
http://www.harmonyfarm.com

Johnny's Selected Seeds
Foss Hill Road
Albion, ME 04910-9731
phone: 207-437-4301
fax: 800-437-4290
207-437-2165 (outside USA)
e-mail:
homegarden@johnnyseeds.com
Website:
http://www.johnnyseeds.com

Seeds of Change
P.O. Box 15700
Santa Fe, NM 87506-5700
phone: 888-762-7333
fax: 888-329-4762

Southern Exposure Seed Exchange
P.O. Box 170
Earlysville, VA 22936
phone: 804-973-4703
fax: 804-973-8717

Territorial Seed Co.
20 Palmer Avenue
Cottage Grove, OR 97424
phone: 541-942-9547
fax: 541-942-9881

Fruits and Nuts

Bear Creek Nursery
(brambles, bush fruits, fruit trees, grapes, nuts; budwood, grafting supplies)
P.O. Box 411
Northport, WA 99157
fax: 509-732-4417
e-mail: Bear Creekin@plix.com

Brittingham Plant Farms, Inc.
(brambles, grapes, fallbearing red raspberries, strawberries)
P.O. Box 2538
Salisbury, MD 21802-2538
phone: 410-749-5153
fax: 800-749-5148

Edible Landscaping
(brambles, bush fruits, figs, fruit trees, nuts, fallbearing red raspberries, strawberries)
316 Spirit Ridge Lane
P.O. Box 77
Afton, VA 22920

Hidden Springs Nursery
(brambles, bush fruits, fruit trees)
170 Hidden Springs Lane
Cookeville, TN 38501
phone: 615-268-2592

Indiana Berry & Plant Co.
(brambles, bush fruits, fallbearing red raspberries, strawberries)
5218 West South
Huntingburg, IN 47542
phone: 800-295-2226 or 812-683-3055
fax: 812-683-2004

J. W. Jung Seed Co.
(brambles, bush fruits, fruit trees, grapes, strawberries)
335 South High Street
Randolph, WI 53957
phone: 800-247-5864

J. E. Miller Nurseries, Inc.
(brambles, bush fruits, fruit trees, grapes, nuts, fallbearing red raspberries, strawberries)
5060 West Lake Road
Canandaigua, NY 14424
phone: 800-836-9630
fax: 716-396-2154

Northwoods Nursery
(brambles, bush fruits, figs, fruit trees, grapes, strawberries)
27635 South Oglesby Road
Canby, OR 97013
phone: 503-266-5432
fax: 800-924-9030

Raintree Nursery
(brambles, bush fruits, figs, fruit trees, grapes, huckleberries, nuts, strawberries; grafting supplies)
391 Butts Road
Morton, WA 98536
phone: 360-496-6400
fax: 360-496-6465

Sonoma Antique Apple Nursery
(brambles, bush fruits, figs, fruit trees, grapes)
4395 Westside Road
Healdsburg, CA 95448
phone: 707-433-6420
fax: 707-433-6479
e-mail: tuyt20b@prodigy.com

Stark Bro's. Nursery and Orchard Co.
(brambles, bush fruits, figs, fruit trees, grapes, nuts, fallbearing red raspberries, strawberries)
P.O. Box 10
Louisana, MO 63353-0010
phone: 800-325-4180
fax: 573-754-5290

Garden Supplies

Amberg's Nursery, Inc.
(grafting supplies, pruning tools, trellis wire)
3164 Whitney Road
Stanley, NY 14561-9550
phone: 716-526-5405
fax: 716-526-6522

Benner's Gardens
(plastic mesh fence)
6974 Upper York Road
New Hope, PA 18938
phone: 800-753-4660
fax: 215-477-9429
e-mail: Benners@erols.com
Website:
http://trine.com/GardenNet/
deercontrol

Gardener's Supply Co.
(floating row covers, red plastic mulch, slug traps, weed barriers)
128 Intervale Road
Burlington, VT 05401-2850
phone: 800-863-1700
fax: 800-551-6712
e-mail: info@gardeners.com
Website: http://www.gardeners.com

Gardens Alive!
(bird and trellis netting, floating row covers, plastic mulch, respirators, slug traps, weed barriers)
5100 Schenly Place
Lawrenceburg, IN 47025
phone: 812-537-8650
fax: 812-537-5108

Harmony Farm Supply and Nursery
(composting worms, floating row covers, grafting and pruning tools, nursery jute, red plastic mulch, sprayers, weed barriers)
P.O. Box 460
Graton, CA 95444
phone: 707-823-9125
fax: 707-823-1734
Website:
http://www.harmonyfarm.com

A. M. Leonard, Inc.
(burlap and nursery jute, floating row covers, grafting and pruning tools, mattocks, respirators, sprayers, weed barriers)
241 Fox Drive
P.O. Box 816
Piqua, OH 45356
phone: 800-543-8955
fax: 800-433-0633

Ornamentals

Kurt Bluemel, Inc.
(ground covers, perennials, rock-garden plants, water-garden plants)
2740 Greene Lane
Baldwin, MD 21013-9523
phone: 410-557-7729

Bluestone Perennials
(ground covers, perennials, rock-garden plants, shrubs)
7211 Middle Ridge Road
Madison, OH 44057
phone: 800-852-5243

Busse Gardens
(ground covers, perennials, rock-garden plants)
5873 Oliver Avenue, SW
Cokato, MN 55321-4229
phone: 320-286-2654 or
800-544-3192
fax: 320-286-6601

Carroll Gardens, Inc.
(bulbs, ground covers, perennials, rock-garden plants, own-root roses, shrubs, trees, vines)
444 East Main Street
Westminster, MD 21157
phone: 800-638-6334

The Daffodil Mart
(bulbs)
7463 Heath Trail
Gloucester, VA 23061
phone: 800-255-2852
fax: 800-420-2852

Forest Farms
(ground covers, perennials, rock-garden plants, shrubs, trees, vines)
990 Tetherow Road
Williams, OR 97544-9599
phone: 541-846-7269
fax: 541-846-6963

Goodness Grows, Inc.
(perennials, roses, shrubs)
P.O. Box 311
Lexington, GA 30648
phone: 706-743-5055
fax: 706-743-5112

Greer Gardens
(perennials, shrubs, trees, vines)
1280 Goodpasture Island Road
Eugene, OR 97401-1794
phone: 800-548-0111
fax: 541-686-0910

Jackson & Perkins
(perennials, own-root roses)
P.O. Box 1028
Medford, OR 97501
phone: 800-292-4769
fax: 800-242-0329

Milaeger's Gardens
(perennials)
3848 Douglas Avenue
Racine, WI 53402-2498
phone: 800-669-1229

Plant Delights Nursery, Inc.
(ground covers, perennials)
9241 Sauls Road
Raleigh, NC 27569
phone: 919-936-4421
fax: 919-662-0370
e-mail: tony@plantdel.com
Website: http://www.plantdel.com

Roses of Yesterday and Today
(roses)
802 Browns Valley Road
Watsonville CA 95076-0398
phone: 408-724-2755 or
408-724-1408
fax: 800-980-7673

Tripple Brook Farm
(rock-garden plants)
37 Middle Road
Southampton, MA 01073
phone: 413-527-4626
fax: 413-527-9853

Van Bourgondien
(bulbs, perennials)
P.O. Box 1000
Babylon, NY 11702-9004
phone: 800-622-9997
fax: 800-622-9959

Andre Viette Farm and Nursery
(bulbs, daylilies, perennials, shrubs)
Rt. 1, Box 16
Fishersville, VA 22939
phone: 540-943-2315

Wayside Gardens
(ground covers, perennials, roses, shrubs, trees, vines)
1 Garden Lane
Hodges, SC 29695-0001
phone: 800-845-1124
fax: 800-817-1124

We-Du Nurseries
(perennials, shrubs, trees)
Rt. 5, Box 724
Marion, NC 28752
phone: 704-738-8300
fax: 704-738-8131

Weiss Bros. Perennial Nursery
(ground covers, perennials)
11690 Colfax Highway
Grass Valley, CA 95945
phone: 916-272-7657
fax: 916-272-3578

White Flower Farm
(ground covers, perennials, own-root roses, shrubs, trees, vines)
P.O. Box 50
Litchfield, CT 06759-0050
phone: 800-503-9624
fax: 860-496-1418

Three Sisters Planting

Abundant Life Seed Foundation
('Black Aztec' and 'Rainbow Inca' sweet corn)
P.O. Box 772
Port Townsend, WA 98368
phone: 360-385-5660
fax: 360-385-7455
Website: http://csf.Colorado.edu/perma/abundant

American Indian Program
('Iroquois White' flour corn)
300 Caldwell
Cornell University
Ithaca, NY 14853

Bountiful Gardens
('Rainbow Inca' sweet corn)
18001 Shafer Ranch Road
Willits, CA 95490-9626

W. Atlee Burpee & Co.
('Kentucky Wonder' pole beans)
300 Park Avenue
Warminster, PA 18991-0001
phone: 800-888-1447
fax: 800-487-5530

Gurney's Seed & Nursery Co.
('Connecticut Field' pumpkins, pole beans)
110 Capital Street
Yankton, SD 57079
phone: 605-665-1930
fax: 605-665-9718

Johnny's Selected Seeds
('Scarlet Wonder' pole beans)
Foss Hill Road
Albion, ME 04910-9731
phone: 207-437-4301
fax: 800-437-4290
207-437-2165 (outside USA)
e-mail:
homegarden@johnnyseeds.com
Website:
http://www.johnnyseeds.com

Seeds of Change
('Black Aztec' sweet corn)
P.O. Box 15700
Santa Fe, NM 87506-5700
phone: 888-762-7333
fax: 888-329-4762

Southern Exposure Seed Exchange
('Genuine Cornfield' pole beans, 'Texas Honey June' sweet corn)
P.O. Box 170
Earlysville, VA 22936
phone: 804-973-4703
fax: 804-973-8717

Vegetables and Grains

Abundant Life Seed Foundation
(vegetable amaranth, cold-tolerant oriental greens, determinate and indeterminate tomatoes)
P.O. Box 772
Port Townsend, WA 98368
phone: 360-385-5660
fax: 360-385-7455
Website: http://csf.Colorado.edu/perma/abundant

Beckers Seed Potatoes
(seed potatoes)
R. R. 1
Trout Creek, Ontario
Canada P0H 2L0

Bountiful Gardens
(vegetable amaranth, cauliflower, grains, cold-tolerant oriental greens, early tomatoes)
18001 Shafer Ranch Road
Willits, CA 95490-9626

W. Atlee Burpee & Co.
(cauliflower, lettuces, cold-tolerant oriental greens, early peas, bell peppers, sorrel, determinate and indeterminate tomatoes, early tomatoes, 'Super Sweet 100' tomatoes)
300 Park Avenue
Warminster, PA 18991-0001
phone: 800-888-1447
fax: 800-487-5530

The Cook's Garden
(male asparagus, cauliflower, gourmet baby vegetables, lettuces, cold-tolerant oriental greens, 'Super Sweet 100' tomatoes)
P.O. Box 535
Londonderry, VT 05148
phone: 800-457-9703
fax: 800-457-9705
Website:
http://www.cooksgarden.com

Garden City Seeds
(lettuces, orach, cold-tolerant oriental greens, early peas)
778 Highway 93 North
Hamilton, MT 59840
phone: 406-961-4837
fax: 406-961-4877

Johnny's Selected Seeds
(male asparagus, gourmet baby vegetables, cauliflower, gynoecious cucumbers, lettuces, cold-tolerant oriental greens, bell peppers, sorrel, soybeans, early tomatoes)
Foss Hill Road
Albion, ME 04910-9731
phone: 207-437-4301
fax: 800-437-4290
207-437-2165 (outside USA)
e-mail:
homegarden@johnnyseeds.com
Website:
http://www.johnnyseeds.com

Ronniger's Seed Potatoes
(seed potatoes, including fingerlings)
P.O. Box 1838
Orting, WA 98360

Seeds Blum
(vegetable amaranth, giant vegetables, grain, lettuces, cold-tolerant oriental greens)
HC 33 Idaho City Stage
Boise, ID 83706
phone: 800-528-3658
fax: 208-338-5658
e-mail:
103774.167@compuserve.com

Seeds of Change
(vegetable amaranth, lettuces, determinate and indeterminate tomatoes)
P.O. Box 15700
Santa Fe, NM 87506-5700
phone: 888-762-7333
fax: 888-329-4762

Shepherd's Garden Seeds
(gourmet baby vegetables, lettuces, cold-tolerant oriental greens, early peas, bell peppers, sorrel, early tomatoes, 'Sweet 100 Plus' tomatoes)
30 Irene Street
Torrington, CT 06790
phone: 860-482-3638
fax: 860-482-0532

Southern Exposure Seed Exchange
(lettuces, cold-tolerant oriental greens, bell peppers, determinate and indeterminate tomatoes, early tomatoes)
P.O. Box 170
Earlysville, VA 22936
phone: 804-973-4703
fax: 804-973-8717

Tomato Grower's Supply Company
(bell peppers, determinate and indeterminate tomatoes, early tomatoes)
P.O. Box 2237
Fort Myers, FL 33902
phone: 941-768-1119
fax: 941-768-3476

Totally Tomatoes
(bell peppers, determinate and indeterminate tomatoes, early tomatoes, 'Super Sweet 100 Hybrid VF' tomatoes)
P.O. Box 1626
Augusta, GA 30903
phone: 803-663-0016
fax: 888-477-7333

Vermont Bean Seed Co.
(lettuces, cold-tolerant oriental greens, early peas, sorrel, soybeans)
Garden Lane
Fair Haven, VT 05743
phone: 803-663-0217
fax: 888-500-7333

Water Gardening

Lilypons Water Gardens
P.O. Box 10
Buckeystown, MD 21717-0010
phone: 800-999-5459 or
301-874-5133
fax: 301-874-2959

Paradise Water Gardens
14 May Street
Whitman, MA 02382
phone: 617-447-4711 or
617-447-8995
fax: 800-966-4591

William Tricker, Inc.
7125 Tanglewood Drive
Independence, OH 44131
phone: 800-524-3492
fax: 216-542-3491

Van Ness Water Gardens
2460 North Euclid Avenue
Upland, CA 91784-1199
phone: 909-982-2425
fax: 909-949-7217

Wildflowers

Abundant Life Seed Foundation
(seeds)
P.O. Box 772
Port Townsend, WA 98368
phone: 360-385-5660
fax: 360-385-7455
Website: http://csf.Colorado.edu/
perma/abundant

Ion Exchange
(plants, seeds, seed mixes)
1878 Old Mission Drive
Harpers Ferry, IA 52416-7533
phone: 800-291-2143 or
319-535-7231
fax: 319-535-7362

Prairie Nursery
(plants, seeds, seed mixes)
P.O. Box 306
Westfield, WI 53964
phone: 608-296-3679
fax: 608-296-2741

Clyde Robin Seed Co.
(seeds, seed mixes)
P.O. Box 2366
Castro Valley, CA 94546
phone: 510-785-0425
fax: 510-785-6463

The Vermont Wildflower Farm
(plants, seeds, seed mixes)
Reservation Center
Wildflower Lane
P.O. Box 1400
Louisiana, MO 63353-8400
phone: 800-424-1165
fax: 573-754-5290

Wildginger Woodlands
(plants, seeds)
P.O. Box 1091
Webster, NY 14580

Wildseed Farms
(seeds, seed mixes)
1101 Campo Rosa Road
P.O. Box 308
Eagle Lake, TX 77434
phone: 800-848-0078
fax: 409-234-7407

Woodlanders
(bulbs, plants)
1128 Colleton Avenue
Aiken, SC 29801
phone and fax: 803-648-7522

Recommended Reading

General Gardening

Books

Benjamin, Joan, ed. *Great Garden Shortcuts.* Emmaus, PA: Rodale Press, 1996.

Bradley, Fern Marshall, and Barbara Ellis, eds. *Rodale's All-New Encyclopedia of Organic Gardening.* Emmaus, PA: Rodale Press, 1992.

Coleman, Elliot. *The New Organic Grower: A Master's Manual of Tools and Techniques for the Home and Market Gardener.* White River Junction, VT: Chelsea Green Publishing Co., 1995.

Miller, Crow. *Let's Get Growing.* Emmaus, PA: Rodale Press, 1995.

Magazines

Organic Gardening, Rodale Press, 33 E. Minor St., Emmaus, PA 18098.

Fine Gardening, The Taunton Press, Newtown, CT 06470.

Horticulture, Horticulture, 98 N. Washington St., Boston, MA 02114.

Butterfly Gardening

Roth, Sally. *Natural Landscaping: Working with Nature to Create a Backyard Paradise.* Emmaus, PA: Rodale Press, 1997.

Schneck, Marcus. *Butterflies, How to Identify and Attract Them to Your Garden.* Emmaus, PA: Rodale Press, 1990.

Composting and Worm Composting

Appelhof, Mary. *Worms Eat My Garbage.* Kalamazoo, MI: Flower Press, 1982.

Martin, Deborah L., and Grace Gershuny, eds. *The Rodale Book of Composting.* Rev. ed. Emmaus, PA: Rodale Press, 1992.

Dried Flowers

Platt, Ellen Spector. *The Ultimate Wreath Book.* Emmaus, PA: Rodale Press, 1995.

Raworth, Jenny, and Susan Berry. *Dried Flowers for All Seasons.* Pleasantville, NY/Montreal: The Reader's Digest Association, 1993.

Edible Landscaping

Creasy, Rosalind. *The Complete Book of Edible Landscaping.* San Francisco: Sierra Club Books, 1982.

Kourik, Robert. *Designing and Maintaining Your Edible Landscape Naturally.* Santa Rosa, CA: Metamorphic Press, 1986.

Reich, Lee. *Uncommon Fruits Worthy of Attention.* Reading, MA: Addison-Wesley Publishing Co., 1991.

Flower Gardening

The following books contain lists of recommended plants for sunny, shady, wet, and dry sites.

Benjamin, Joan, and Barbara W. Ellis. *Rodale's No-Fail Flower Garden: How to Plan, Plant, and Grow a Beautiful, Easy-Care Garden.* Emmaus, PA: Rodale Press, 1994.

Burrell, C. Colston. *A Gardener's Encyclopedia of Wild Flowers.* Emmaus, PA: Rodale Press, 1997.

Cox, Jeff. *Perennial All-Stars.* Emmaus, PA: Rodale Press, 1998.

Dewolf, Gordon, ed. *Taylor's Guide to Perennials.* Boston: Houghton Mifflin Company, 1986.

Hill, Lewis, and Nancy Hill. *Successful Perennial Gardening—A Practical Guide.* Pownal, VT: Storey Communications, 1988.

Phillips, Ellen, and C. Colston Burrell. *Rodale's Illustrated Encyclopedia of Perennials.* Emmaus, PA: Rodale Press, 1993.

Stell, Elizabeth, and C. Colston Burrell. *Rodale's Successful Organic Gardening: Landscaping with Perennials.* Emmaus, PA: Rodale Press, 1995.

Fruits and Nuts

Books

Holmes, Roger, ed. *Taylor's Guide to Fruits and Berries.* New York: Houghton Mifflin Company, 1996.

McClure, Susan, and Lee Reich. *Rodale's Successful Organic Gardening— Fruits and Berries.* Emmaus, PA: Rodale Press, 1996.

Nick, Jean M. A., and Fern Marshall Bradley, eds. *Growing Fruits & Vegetables Organically: The Complete Guide to a Great-Tasting, More Bountiful, Problem-Free Harvest.* Emmaus, PA: Rodale Press, 1994.

Otto, Stella. *The Backyard Berry Book.* Maple City, MI: Otto Graphics, 1995.

———. *The Backyard Orchardist.* Maple City, MI: Otto Graphics, 1993.

Page, Steve, and Joe Smiley. 3d. ed. *The Orchard Almanac: A Seasonal Guide to Healthy Fruit Trees.* Davis, CA: agAccess, 1995.

Whealy, Kent, ed. *Fruit, Berry and Nut Inventory.* 2d ed. Decorah, IA: Seed Saver Publications, 1993. (Available from Seed Savers Exchange, 3076 N. Winn Rd., Decorah, IA 52101. 319-382-5990)

Magazines

Pomona, North American Fruit Explorers (NAFEX), Rt. 1, Box 94, Chapin, IL 62628.
NAFEX is made up of fruit growers throughout the United States and Canada who are "devoted to the discovery, cultivation, and appreciation of superior varieties of fruits and nuts."

Insect and Disease Identification

Carr, Anna. *Rodale's Color Handbook of Garden Insects.* Emmaus, PA: Rodale Press, 1983.

Davidson, Ralph H., and William F. Lyon. *Insect Pests of Farm, Garden, and Orchard.* 8th ed. New York: John Wiley & Sons, 1987.

Ellis, Barbara W., and Fern Marshall Bradley, eds. *The Organic Gardener's Handbook of Natural Insect and Disease Control.* Emmaus, PA: Rodale Press, 1992.

Gilkeson, Linda, Pam Peirce, and Miranda Smith. *Rodale's Pest & Disease Problem Solver.* Emmaus, PA: Rodale Press, 1996.

Ornamentals and Landscape Design

Books

Armitage, Allan M. *Herbaceous Perennial Plants.* 2d ed. Champaign, IL: Stipes Publishing, 1997.

Clausen, Ruth Rodgers, and Nicolas H. Ekstrom. *Perennials for American Gardens.* New York: Random House, 1989.

Cox, Jeff. *Landscaping with Nature.* Emmaus, PA: Rodale Press, 1991.

Dirr, Michael A. *Manual of Woody Landscape Plants.* 4th ed. Champaign, IL: Stipes Publishing, 1990.

Druse, Ken. *The Natural Garden.* New York: Clarkson N. Potter, 1989.

Harper, Pamela J. *Color Echoes.* New York: Macmillan Publishing Co., 1994.

Hobhouse, Penelope. *Color in Your Garden.* Boston: Little, Brown, and Co., 1985.

McKeon, Judith C. *The Encyclopedia of Roses: An Organic Guide to Growing and Enjoying America's Favorite Flower.* Emmaus, PA: Rodale Press, 1995.

Roth, Sally. *Natural Landscaping: Working with Nature to Create a Backyard Paradise.* Emmaus, PA: Rodale Press, 1997.

Smith, Marny, and Nancy DuBrule. *A Country Garden for Your Backyard.* Emmaus, PA: Rodale Press, 1993.

Taylor's Guide Staff. *Taylor's Guide to Garden Design.* Boston: Houghton Mifflin Co., 1988.

Magazines

Fine Gardening, The Taunton Press, Newtown, CT 06470.

Garden Design, P.O. Box 5429, Harlan, IA 51593-2929.

Horticulture, Horticulture, 98 N. Washington St., Boston, MA 02114.

Soil

Gershuny, Grace. *Start with the Soil.* Emmaus, PA: Rodale Press, 1993.

Hynes, Erin. *Rodale's Successful Organic Gardening—Improving the Soil.* Emmaus, PA: Rodale Press, 1994.

Three Sisters Plantings

Cornell Cooperative Extension Information Bulletin 142LM15, *The Three Sisters: Exploring an Iroquois Garden.* The bulletin is available, for a fee, from Cornell University, Media Services Resource Center, 8 BTP, Ithaca, NY 14850.

Weaver, William Woys. *Heirloom Vegetable Gardening.* New York: Henry Holt and Company, 1997.

Vegetables

Entries marked with an asterisk (*) contain recommendations on how many vegetables to plant per person for your garden.

*Bradley, Fern Marshall, ed. *Rodale's Garden Answers.* Emmaus, PA: Rodale Press, 1995.

*Jeavons, John. *How to Grow More Vegetables, Fruit, Nuts, Grains, Berries, and Other Crops Than You Ever Thought Possible on Less Land Than You Can Imagine.* Berkeley, CA: Ten Speed Press, 1995.

Michilak, Patricia, and Cass Peterson. *Rodale's Successful Organic Gardening—Vegetables.* Emmaus, PA: Rodale Press, 1993.

*Nick, Jean M. A., and Fern Marshall Bradley, eds. *Growing Fruits & Vegetables Organically: The Complete Guide to a Great-Tasting, More Bountiful, Problem-Free Harvest.* Emmaus, PA: Rodale Press, 1994.

Stout, Ruth, and Richard Clemence. *The Ruth Stout No-Work Garden Book.* Emmaus, PA: Rodale Press, 1971. (No longer in print—check your library and used bookstores for copies.)

Whealy, Kent, and Joanne Thuente, eds. *Garden Seed Inventory.* 4th ed. Decorah, IA: Seed Saver Publications, 1995. (Available from Seed Savers Exchange, 3076 N. Winn Rd., Decorah, IA 52101. 319-382-5990.)
Seed Savers Exchange is a not-for-profit organization whose members save seeds from extinction. Members maintain a collection of heirloom seeds and distribute them to gardeners who want to help preserve old-time food-crop plants.

Water Gardening

Druse, Ken. *Burpee American Gardening Series—Water Gardening.* New York: Prentice Hall Gardening, 1993.

Heriteau, Jacqueline, and Charles B. Thomas. *Water Gardens.* Boston: Houghton Mifflin Co., 1994.

Index

USDA Plant Hardiness Zone Map

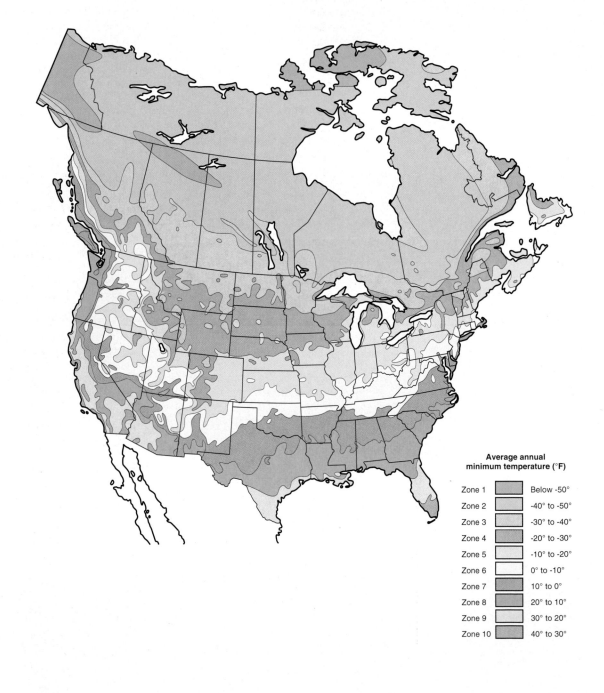

Average annual minimum temperature (°F)

Zone 1	Below -50°
Zone 2	-40° to -50°
Zone 3	-30° to -40°
Zone 4	-20° to -30°
Zone 5	-10° to -20°
Zone 6	0° to -10°
Zone 7	10° to 0°
Zone 8	20° to 10°
Zone 9	30° to 20°
Zone 10	40° to 30°